The Plant Doctor's PRESCRIPTIONS for a HEALTHY GARDEN

NOEL FALK

*Foreword by Bob Thomson,
host of "The Victory Garden" on PBS
and author of* The New Victory Garden

STACKPOLE
BOOKS

Copyright © 1991 by Stackpole Books

Published by
STACKPOLE BOOKS
Cameron and Kelker Streets
P.O. Box 1831
Harrisburg, PA 17105

Printed in the United States of America

10 9 8 7 6 5 4 3 2 1

First Edition

Cover design by Tracy Patterson
Illustrations by Cindie Brunner, except where noted
Interior design by Laura M. Pollack

Excerpt from *Silent Spring* by Rachel L. Carson. Copyright © 1962 by
Rachel L. Carson. Reprinted by permission of Houghton Mifflin Company.

Maps courtesy of the Agricultural Research Service,
U.S. Department of Agriculture

Library of Congress Cataloging-in-Publication Data

Falk, Noel.
    The plant doctor's prescriptions for a healthy garden / Noel Falk;
foreword by Bob Thomson. — 1st ed.
        p.   cm.
    Includes index.
    ISBN 0-8117-3049-2
    1. Gardening.   2. Garden pests—Control.   3. Plant diseases.
I. Title.   II. Title: Healthy garden.
SB453.F28   1991
635—dc20   90-45881
                                                                    CIP

The
Plant Doctor's
Prescriptions
for a
Healthy Garden

To
Kathleen, who brightens each day with her love and encouragement
Deana and Erin, my precious sprouts
Mom and Dad, for their prayerful support

Contents

Foreword

Introduction

1 Don't Call It Dirt 1

Soils • Organic matter • Acidity and alkalinity—pH
levels • Nutrients and fertilizers • Soil organisms

2 Just How Does Your Garden Grow? 8

Water • Light • Temperature • Space • Flower parts •
Pollination • Propagation

3 How to Make a Garden 15

Location and size • Preparing and caring for the soil •
Starting plants from seed • Laying out the garden •
Rotating crops • Companion planting • Succession
planting • Watering • Fertilizing • Mulching •
Controlling weeds • Common insect pests • Container
gardening

4 Minding Your Peas and Cukes 40

Cool-season crops • Hot-weather crops • Thinning
seedlings • Rhubarb • Asparagus • Spinach •
Cauliflower • Peas • Beans • Tomatoes • Peppers •
Eggplants • Root crops • Vining crops • Fall
planting • Common vegetable varieties

5 Growing Jams and Jellies (Small Fruits) 66

Strawberries • Raspberries • Blackberries • Blueberries
• Currants • Gooseberries • Grapes • Kiwis

6 Growing Peach Pie and Apple Crisp (Fruit Trees) 87

How to select a planting site • Fruit trees in small spaces • Soil and planting specifications • Pollinators • Colder climates • Pruning • Spraying • Deer repellents • Apples • Apricots • Cherries • Peaches • Nectarines • Pears • Plums

7 A Year's Worth of Color 110

Warm and cool colors • Starting from seed • Planting and care • Container planting • Annuals for cutting • Shady areas • Dry-weather annuals • Foliage plants • Ground covers • Backdrops for other flowers • Blue-flowering annuals • Vines • Annuals for drying • Geraniums and coleus • Indoor plants • Gladioluses • Dahlias • Caladiums • Cannas • Pests and diseases

8 Color That Comes Back 128

Continuous color • Fragrant perennials • Light • Shady areas • Ferns • Bulbs • Peonies and tree peonies • Day lilies • Blue-flowering perennials • Chrysanthemums • Attracting hummingbirds • Perennials for cutting • Perennials for drying • Container gardens • Robust perennials • Wildflowers • Flowers for "brown thumbs" • Pests and diseases • Poisonous perennials • Grasses

9 Woody Plants 150

Dwarf conifers • Arborvitae • Junipers • Broadleaf evergreens • Rhododendrons • Azaleas • Hollies • Pyracantha • Viburnums • Shrub dogwoods • Other spring-flowering shrubs • Roses • Hardy vines • Clematis

10 Branching Out 173

How to plant and care for trees • Pruning • Mulching • Herbicides • Fast growers • Streetside • Moist areas • Native flowering trees • Trees for fragrance • Specimen trees • Fall color • Attracting birds in winter • Live Christmas trees • Flowering dogwood • White birch • Spruces • Gypsy moth • Tent caterpillars • Galls

Index 199

Lists of Maps and Tables

Maps:

Frost Zones in the United States   x
Average Dates of Last Killing Frost in Spring 20
Average Dates of First Killing Frost in Fall 62

Tables:

Planting Timetable for Vegetables 41
Spacing Vegetables 42
Common Vegetables and Common Varieties 64
Perennial Flower Blooming Times 130
Bloom Times of Perennials for Partial Shade 133
When to Prune Flowering Shrubs 169

Foreword

Over the years I have always felt honored when an author has asked me to do a foreword to his or her new book, and I'm doubly honored when that person is an old friend of long standing, as Noel Falk is.

Several years ago, Noel called me from his home in Pennsylvania to ask if I would do a radio program with him. I had never met him, but I knew of him. Like me, Noel had begun a career as a radio personality and was developing talents whereby he could easily shift from one medium to another. We talked for about twenty minutes that first program and covered a lot of ground in a short span of time. We eventually met and, as the years rolled by, we did several more of those Pennsylvania-to-Massachusetts telephone hook-ups.

We have always been comfortable with each other and have, I believe, mutual trust and respect, even though we come from different backgrounds. (Noel has excellent academic credentials; I went into the grounds maintenance and nursery business right out of high school.) What Noel tells you about in his book would be the same message I would have written, and I am deeply honored to have a small part in his worthy endeavor.

Bob Thomson
"The Victory Garden"

USDA Plant Hardiness Zone Map

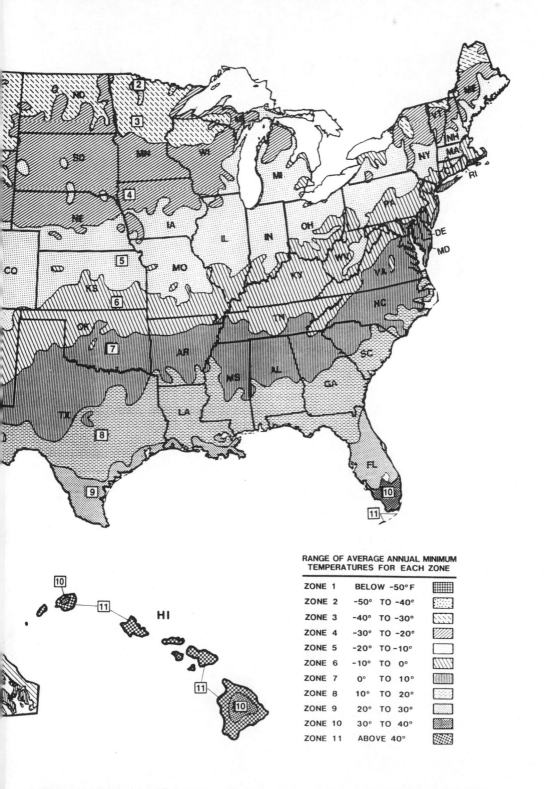

RANGE OF AVERAGE ANNUAL MINIMUM
TEMPERATURES FOR EACH ZONE

ZONE 1	BELOW -50°F	
ZONE 2	-50° TO -40°	
ZONE 3	-40° TO -30°	
ZONE 4	-30° TO -20°	
ZONE 5	-20° TO -10°	
ZONE 6	-10° TO 0°	
ZONE 7	0° TO 10°	
ZONE 8	10° TO 20°	
ZONE 9	20° TO 30°	
ZONE 10	30° TO 40°	
ZONE 11	ABOVE 40°	

Introduction

It seems almost everyone is a gardener. We may not all spend a lot of time hoeing vegetable gardens or weeding flower beds, but most of us have at least one plant that we care for in our homes.

My interest in gardening began when I was young. As a little tyke, I would pick handfuls of violets for my mother. They wilted quickly, but she always appreciated them and her appreciation encouraged me. I also remember the grape arbor below the porch. The arbor kept our play area cool during the summer, and I remember how much fun I had squashing the fallen grapes with my bike!

The large tree growing in the side yard by the creek fascinated me with its orange and green flowers. Dad told me it was a tulip tree, but I couldn't understand how some tulips could grow on the ground and others in trees. Another memory is of the sweet smell of the bush beside the sandbox. Many years after I played there, I learned that the bush was called a mock orange and, to this day, mock orange remains one of my favorite shrubs.

Peonies also come to mind when I think of the past. I remember them most clearly from the little church where Dad was pastor. The vases of peonies and other flowers that adorned the front of the church looked and smelled great. As I think back, I learned to identify quite a few perennials from those altar flowers.

I can't say that I was greatly interested in gardening back then. I didn't mind helping Dad plant the raspberries and irises, but pulling weeds seemed to be a waste of time because I knew they'd grow right back. Besides, I had learned from previous years' experience that vegetables and flowers would mature even in the presence of weeds. (Today I still can, and often do, grow a healthy crop of weeds in the vegetable garden.)

I had my first garden when I was eleven. I remember taking out four stakes and marking the corners of the would-be plot. Then I took the shovel and started to turn the soil, or "dirt" as I knew it then. That's when I learned not to bite off more than I could chew. I don't recall how successful that first venture was; it must not have been too bad because I've been gardening ever since.

My first paying job was in the field of horticulture; to be more specific, it actually was in a field of strawberries. Our neighbor had about a half-acre of plants, and he paid my sister and me to pick the berries. My second paying job was picking cherries in a friend's orchard. Now that was big money! I earned forty cents a bucket. My third job was doing the yard work and cleaning a horse stable for a neighbor who was a gentleman farmer. So, as you can see, I have a history.

Today, I still don't like to pull weeds, and I use a rototiller, rather than a shovel, to turn the soil. The vegetables I raise are a great pleasure to eat, but I don't garden to save money on the grocery bill. Flowers add beauty to my surroundings, but that's not why I plant them. I garden because it makes me feel good. It's a great way to relieve the tension of the day, and it gives me time to put things into perspective. The smell of the "dirt," the taste of the tomatoes, and the beauty of the flowers are all added benefits. And the fragrances of the mock orange and peonies remind me of a day when life was simpler and there seemed to be more time for fun.

I don't want to give the impression from what I've said that I take gardening lightly. My dad always made it clear that any job worth doing was worth doing right. That's true, too, for gardening. Time and work constraints can interfere with your plans and the garden might eventually become a real mess. But you should enter each season with the attitude that this will be the best garden you've ever grown. All things should be done properly. When planting trees and shrubs, never take shortcuts in preparing the site. Never plant hundred-dollar trees in fifty-cent holes!

The key to successful gardening lies not only in the soil in which a plant grows, but also in taking the time to plan before the first spadeful of soil is turned or the first seed is sown. Many of us are impulsive when it comes to gardening. Spring arrives, so we buy vegetable seeds and sow them. We see a rhododendron we like, so we buy it. We find plants "on sale," so we take some home. Many of us give little, if any, thought to which plants are best suited to our flower beds or to the size of the vegetable garden.

When planning for any plant or garden, there are two important factors to keep in mind. The first is the growth habit of a plant—that is, how big, how fast, and in what shape it grows. The second critical element is the environment of the planting area. Such factors as soil type, amount of light, room available for plant growth, and soil drainage must always be considered.

January is the best time to begin planning your spring garden. On those cold, windy, wintry evenings when the ground is frozen and last summer's warmth is only a faded memory, you can start looking through the seed catalogs to find ideas and the flowers and vegetables that interest you most. You must not only check the growing conditions of each plant but also compare price and quantity of seed per package. If you want to do some landscaping, you should review books on landscape plants to find those ornamentals that are the most appealing and the most suitable.

Being a successful gardener also includes knowing when to do those chores that need to be done. The garden or landscape is not finished when the seeds are sown and the trees are put in. Plants need to be watered, fertilized, pruned, and mulched. If they are to thrive, you must know when to carry out these activities, and you must set aside the time to accomplish them.

Serious gardeners keep records; such information as how well vegetables grew during the past season can be helpful when planning next year's garden. Making notes of the varieties you used will help you choose varieties in subsequent years. Keeping track of any adverse weather conditions is also essential because, of course, weather affects how well plants grow. It takes time and work to keep records but the benefits of doing so are well worth the effort.

As gardeners, we should always be aware that there is only so much soil to till and so much water available. What we do can affect the environment in general and short-term gains may not be worth their long-term consequences. I know that chemicals are occasionally needed to control certain pests, but those chemicals should be selected wisely and applied properly. Whenever possible, we should substitute natural products and other less-dangerous methods of control.

After reading this, being serious about gardening probably seems like a lot of work. Do I always do everything I'm suggesting? No, not always. But I do try to do my best when I garden, and I like to think that each year I improve in some area of gardening. For me what's important is that I try and that I have fun. So, do take it seriously but enjoy yourself!

1

Don't Call It Dirt

When most of us started gardening, we didn't think too much about what plants needed so they could grow. We just stuck them in the ground, or sowed the seeds and left them to do their thing. We also didn't think much about what we put the plants or the seeds in. All we knew was that plants grow in dirt. The more we learn about gardening, though, the more we realize that not all dirt is the same. To be accurate, in fact, what plants grow in isn't even dirt—it's soil. To be better gardeners, we must understand more about soil and its effect on plant growth.

Soil is the medium that links plants with the living world. It provides the minerals and water necessary for plant development, it supplies oxygen to the roots, and it anchors the plant to a specific location. There are some exceptions to these conditions. Some plants, for example, can be grown in water; this process is known as hydroponic gardening. Other plants, for example, bromeliads and Spanish moss, actually grow on other plants—such as trees—without soil. And in some cases, plants can grow in soilless mixtures of perlite, vermiculite, or sand. Soil, however, is the growth medium that most of us usually use.

What is soil?

Soil is a mixture of inorganic minerals, organic matter, water, air, and living organisms. The minerals, derived from the location's bedrock, determine the texture of the soil: that is, whether it is fine, like clay, or coarse, like sand. Organic matter, called humus, is the result of the decay of plant materials, animal wastes, and soil organisms. It is usually what gives soil its dark color. Pore spaces between the materials and organic matter enable the soil to hold air or water. The size of the soil particles will influence what, and how much, can be held. The amounts of each of these soil components will depend on place and time. Amendments such as compost, peat moss, and manure can greatly improve the quality of poor soil.

Also found in soil is a host of little critters and microorganisms. Bacteria, nematodes, larvae, adult insects, slugs, and worms all call soil home. Many, though not all, of these creatures are beneficial to the gardener.

What is the difference between heavy and light soils?

Heavy soils contain an abundance of tiny mineral particles such as clay and silt. Light soils, though, consist of large mineral particles—sand—and we refer to them as sandy soils. Neither of these extremes, however, is the best for gardening. Most soils, or what we call loam, are a mix of clay, silt, and sand. The loam is named after the particle size that is most abundant. Thus, soil that has more sand than clay or silt is called sandy loam.

The space between the soil particles, known as pore space, can hold either air or water. When heavy soil receives precipitation, the pore spaces fill quickly with moisture and the soil becomes very sticky. It does not dry out readily, and if it is worked while in this condition, it will puddle or become cloudy. Wet, heavy soil has very little air. If plants are set in it, they often will drown because their roots are deprived of oxygen.

Light soils contain much larger pore spaces because of the larger sizes of the soil particles. The spaces are so large that water percolates down through the soil layers instead of lodging in the spaces. These light soils are great for root growth but water must be added constantly to keep plants alive.

How much organic matter does soil contain?

About five percent of the average garden topsoil is organic material or humus. Some soils, however, contain much larger amounts. For example, more than half of the content of peat soils, commonly used in horticulture, is organic matter. This material in the soil helps maintain good "tilth"—the soil remains easy to till or cultivate.

Organic matter also is the main source of nutrients that are so important to plant life. It holds quantities of nitrogen, phosphorus, and sulfur, as well as lesser amounts of many other nutrients that usually are released by microorganisms during decomposition. In healthy soil, organic materials assure a steady supply of necessary nutrients to plants.

Adding organic matter to light soil can increase its capacity to hold water. Humus worked into heavy soil loosens it up and thus reduces its tendency to puddle.

What are some sources of organic material?

Compost, plant matter that has been decomposed by microorganisms, is the most common source of organic material. Grass clippings, weeds, kitchen scraps, and leaves can be added to a compost pile. For best results, finely shred them before adding them to the pile; smaller bits will decompose more quickly than large pieces. Once decomposed, the compost can be added to the garden. In spring, spread a one-inch layer over the soil, then work it in with a rototiller.

"Green manure" can also enhance soil. You can create it by turning under green crops in the spring. The decomposition of the turned-under young green plants enriches the soil with nitrogen and organic material. In the fall, after vegetable plants have been removed, such crops as winter rye, winter wheat, common vetch, and crimson clover can be grown in the garden. Seed for these crops is available at farm supply stores.

Farms can supply us with a ready and renewable source of organic material: manure. This "by-product" of cows, horses, chickens, pigs, and sheep is rich in plant residue. The nutrient content of these manures varies. Poultry manure, for example, is high in nitrogen; that of sheep is high in potassium.

Never use fresh manure around herbaceous plants because its high quantities of nitrogen can burn them. To avoid damaging or killing your plants, work manure into your garden soil in the fall.

What are sweet and sour soils?

Sweet and *sour* are not terms we usually associate with soil. A sweet soil, though, is one that is alkaline; a sour soil is one that is acidic. These qualities have to do with the pH of the soil.

What is pH and how does it affect plants?

Chemists have developed a method of measuring the acidity and alkalinity of soils, and the results of that test are expressed in the pH scale. The "p" stands for power and the "H" stands for hydrogen ion. The scale ranges from 0 to 14 with a neutral point at 7. Soils with a pH lower than 7 are acidic; those with a pH higher than 7 are alkaline.

As we know, plants need many nutrients to grow and most of these are present in the soil. It is soil pH, however, that influences which elements will be available to the plants and which will be changed to an insoluble form and thus made unavailable. When the soil pH is about 6.5, all necessary nutrients are soluble and can be taken up by the plants. When the pH is raised or lowered, though, certain elements, phosphorus, for example, cannot be taken up by the roots. At the same time, when the pH is too low, nutrients such as zinc and copper become so soluble that they become toxic to plants. Most vegetable- and flower-garden soils should be maintained at a pH of 6.5 to 6.8. Of course, some plants, such as blueberries, do better in soils with a lower pH, and others, such as clematis, need a higher pH.

If you can determine the soil pH and adjust it accordingly, you can help plants take advantage of natural soil nutrients. Recent studies also have shown that by adjusting the soil pH, several soilborne vegetable diseases can be controlled.

How do you measure soil pH?

Several soil test kits are on the market, but most are not accurate. The best way to determine pH level is to call your county agricultural extension office and ask for the name of a university lab that will analyze your soil samples. When you gather the sample, collect soil from eight or ten spots in the garden, mixing all of it together to make a composite sample. The soil should come from several inches below the surface in the area of root growth. Do not use surface soil.

Have the pH test done in very early spring or early fall. This schedule will allow sufficient time to correct any problem before the next growing season. How often you check your soil pH depends on what you find when you first test it. If the pH is at one extreme or the other, you should test it the next year to see whether your corrective measures were successful. If the pH was brought into acceptable levels, then you do not need to test it again for another three years.

How do you change soil pH?

When the pH is too low, you can make the soil less acidic by adding lime, which contains calcium. The calcium increases the soil's alkalinity. Lime is available commercially as either ground or hydrated limestone. Although the hydrated form performs more quickly than the ground form, it also can leach away faster. Ground limestone is a better choice because it is effective over a longer period of time.

Limestone also is available in a calcite or dolomite form. I recommend the dolomite form; it will contribute not only calcium but also several additional nutrients essential for plant development. Wood ash and bone meal are two other sources of calcium that can be used to adjust pH. The amount of calcium needed to correct a low pH will depend not only on the pH of the soil, but also on the type of soil. Soils high in organic matter need more lime to change the pH than do soils low in organic matter.

A soil with a pH reading that is too high can be lowered by applying gypsum, aluminum sulfate, and organic matter, such as manure or compost. The amount of each of these needed to lower the pH will vary. Be sure to read and follow label directions and to use organic sources whenever possible.

Which nutrients do plants need to grow properly?

Plants need seventeen nutritional elements. Three of these—oxygen, carbon, and hydrogen—come from air and water. The remaining fourteen come primarily from the soil and are taken up by plant roots. Of these, plants need large quantities of nitrogen, phosphorus, potassium, calcium, sulfur, and magnesium, which therefore are termed macronutrients. Plants need only small amounts of the rest: iron, manganese, boron, molybdenum, copper, chlorine, zinc, and cobalt, which are called micronutrients. It is important to remember that if any nutrient is missing, plant growth will be impaired.

Of all the soilborne nutrients, nitrogen, phosphorus, and potassium are used up fastest by plants and usually need to be replaced on occasion. Do this by applying organic materials or fertilizer.

Can I use commercial fertilizer?
What do the numbers on the bag mean?

Gardeners usually apply commercial fertilizer to the soil to add nutrients. Most fertilizers contain the three nutritional elements—nitrogen (N), phosphorus, (P), and potassium (K)—and, thus, are considered complete. The numbers on a fertilizer bag represent the percentage of the available N–P–K in that fertilizer. The nutrients are always listed in the same order. A 5–10–5 code means the fertilizer contains five percent available nitrogen, ten percent available phosphorus, and five percent available potassium. The rest of the material in the bag is filler or inert ingredients and has no nutrient value. In a 5–10–5 fertilizer, for example, eighty percent of the material is filler.

The nutrients in commercial fertilizers can be either organic or inorganic. Organic fertilizers tend to act more slowly than do inorganic forms because the organic elements must be broken down by microorganisms in the soil before those elements can be absorbed by plants. The nutrients of organic fertilizers are released gradually, however, and they will be available over an extended period of time for plants to use. Inorganic forms are immediately available to plants, but they also are subject to leaching. This means that they can easily be carried by groundwater and could pollute streams or underground water supplies.

Some natural fertilizers do not contain all three primary plant nutrients. For instance, bone meal consists primarily of phosphorus with a little nitrogen; blood meal is rich in nitrogen; seaweed and granite sand contain large amounts of potassium; fish meal and fish emulsion have all three nutrients but are highest in nitrogen.

How do nitrogen, phosphorus, and
potassium affect plant growth?

Nitrogen is the nutrient needed in largest quantities by plants during all stages of growth. It is an essential component of chlorophyll and all proteins. Plants respond to the presence of nitrogen by producing dark green leaves and much vegetative growth. When plants are deficient in nitrogen, they fail to grow rapidly and their foliage turns yellow.

Plants need phosphorus to mature properly—to build a healthy root system, develop flowers, form seeds, and produce fruit. A phosphorus deficiency can be recognized by a purple hue in leaf veins and stems. Weak stems and delayed maturity are other indications that a plant needs phosphorus.

Why plants need potassium is not understood. The nutrient is thought to be involved in many chemical functions that take place during normal plant growth. I like to say that it improves the vigor of plants, which includes their winter hardiness. Soil low in potassium will produce plants that are generally weak and that lack well-formed root systems.

How do we know which critters in the soil are good and which are bad?

Determining which organisms are beneficial to plants and which will retard growth is not a simple task. Certain species of bacteria can cause plant disease and others are very important to decomposition. Nitrogen-fixing bacteria are responsible for converting nitrogen in the air into a form that plants can use. Some nematodes infect plant roots, but others are carnivores that feed on fellow nematodes. Earthworms help aerate the soil, but most beetle larvae, such as wireworms, maggots, and grubs, are extremely harmful to plants.

Before fumigating the soil or applying a chemical to control these critters, you must be certain of the effect the product will have on the organisms, on the plants, and on the environment in general. If fumigating or applying chemicals will kill beneficial insects along with those that are harmful, I would recommend against it. Remember, chemicals can leach and get into water supplies, and they also may have harmful long-term effects.

There are many forms of biological control that are available to gardeners. These controls might be a bit more selective in what they will affect, and they are much safer for the environment. For example, did you know that you now can buy bacteria and nematodes that can be applied to your lawn and garden to kill larvae such as grubs and cutworms?

2

Just How Does Your Garden Grow?

Those of us who have been gardening for a few decades know that during some years plants flourish and during others they flounder. Often the results depend not so much on what we do wrong as on environmental conditions beyond our control. All plants need water, light, nutrients, space, and proper temperatures to develop and thrive. Every species requires a favorable amount of each of these factors if it is to carry on the metabolic processes necessary for life.

How much water do plants need?

Water is not only an environmental factor required by all living things, but it is also their primary composite. A watermelon, for example, is about ninety-five percent water, a potato eighty percent. The amount of moisture each species needs varies. A tomato plant takes up almost fifty gallons of water in a growing season. An apple tree uses about five hundred gallons to produce a bushel of apples. Even many dry seeds are up to fifteen percent moisture. Some plants live in arid environments and survive on little water; others, aquatic plants, for example, thrive only when rooted in water. Requirements also vary with the season. During winter in most parts of the country, plants use much less water than they do during the summer.

How do plants use light?

Light is essential for photosynthesis. Plants produce food through this process, but we are also thankful for the waste product they release—oxygen. To grow normally, plants must receive the proper kind, or quality, of light in the right amount, or intensity, and for appropriate length of time, or photoperiod. The quality of light is a bit difficult to understand because we don't "see" in the same way plants do. Visible light can be broken down into various color bands. We all have seen this when we've looked at a diamond or when light strikes broken glass at just the right angle. Plants mainly use the red and blue segments of visible light. Actually, plants are green because they reflect most of the green and yellow wavelengths of light.

A second aspect of light is its intensity. Shade-loving plants, such as azaleas, do their best when light intensities are low. On the other hand, most vegetables must be grown in full sunlight to produce flowers and fruit. When light intensity is too great, however, it will scorch foliage and, occasionally, even the bark of trees.

Various plant species require different photoperiods, or numbers of daylight hours. Some plants, such as chrysanthemums, are considered "short-day" plants because they only flower when daylight is less than twelve hours long. Summer-flowering annuals are "long-day" meaning they require at least twelve hours of light to flower. For some plants, such as the tomato, which are known as "day-neutral," the length of the photoperiod is not important.

How critical is temperature to plant development?

All plants have their ranges of optimal temperatures, because temperature affects different plants in different ways. Its effects also vary with the developmental stages of a plant. Older, established plants tolerate extremes better than do young seedlings; older growth is less influenced by temperatures than is new growth, and roots and flower buds are less tolerant of low temperatures than are other parts of a plant.

Most growth ceases in a plant when the temperature drops below forty-two degrees. Most garden plants respond best to temperatures between sixty and ninety degrees. Some plants need cool evening temperatures if they are to flower. Many fruits need a period of chilling (when temperatures are below forty-five degrees) to break dormancy. Hardy plants are those that tolerate the lowest temperatures in their area. Cool-season crops grow best in spring and fall; warm-season crops develop best during the heat of summer. Spinach, radishes, peas, rutabagas, and onions are cool-season crops. Corn, lima beans, cucumbers, eggplants, tomatoes, and peppers need warmer weather to develop properly.

Can plants grow in small spaces?

As with other environmental factors, the amount of space plants require varies greatly. Proper spacing in the vegetable garden is important if you want a high yield. Trees and shrubs will have a better growth habit or form if they are given adequate space.

Some plants compete more successfully than do others when space is limited. Dandelions, for example, may flourish to the detriment of everything else. And what are they competing for? Water, light, and nutrients. Learn how much space a plant needs before you buy it.

How do plants form seeds?

Seeds are the result of the pollination and fertilization of a flower. Some flowers produce a single seed, others produce many. Flower stems have an enlarged portion, known as the receptacle, which holds the floral parts together. The flower consists of sepals, petals, stamens, and a pistil. The sepals are modified leaves that protect the flower when it is a bud. The petals are usually brightly colored to attract insects or birds. The male parts, or stamens, produce the pollen, which contains sperm cells. The female part, or pistil, contains the ovary, where the egg cells are formed. The top of the pistil, the stigma, is sticky and holds the pollen. If a flower is properly pollinated and fertilized, the ovary enlarges and seed develops.

Do all flowers have the same reproductive parts?

Some flowers lack one or more of the floral parts. What is most important to understand is that some plants will produce either male or female flowers, so the flowers will have either the pistil or the stamen, not both. Some plants, such as cucumbers, produce male and female flowers on the same plant. In other species, there

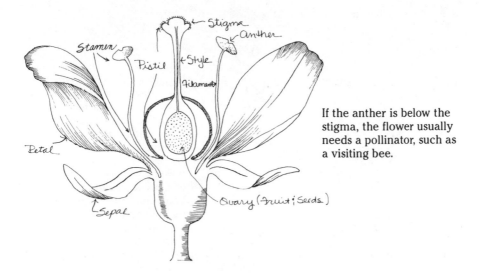

Labels on the diagram: Stamen, Pistil, Stigma, Anther, Style, Filament, Petal, Sepal, Ovary (fruit; seeds)

If the anther is below the stigma, the flower usually needs a pollinator, such as a visiting bee.

are distinct male and female plants. The American holly is an example of a plant that is male or female. If the flowers on the female plant are pollinated, it will produce the red berries, which contain the seed. When male flowers are not close by, however, the female will not produce any berries.

Why do some seeds have two parts and others only one?

A seed is quite an interesting structure. Basically, it is a very young plant, or embryo, with either one or two seed leaves, known as cotyledons, wrapped with a seed coat. If placed in the right environment, the seed coat will burst, the seed will germinate, and a new plant will grow.

The cotyledons are the source of energy for the developing seedling before it can produce its own food. Plants that produce seeds with two cotyledons, beans and peanuts, for example, are called dicots. They are among the most common vegetables and flowers. They can be recognized by their leaves, which have branching veins. Almost all deciduous trees are dicots.

Plants, such as corn, that produce seeds with only one cotyledon are called monocots. Leaves of monocots have parallel veins; they do not branch. All of the grains are monocots. So are grasses, tulips, onions, and irises.

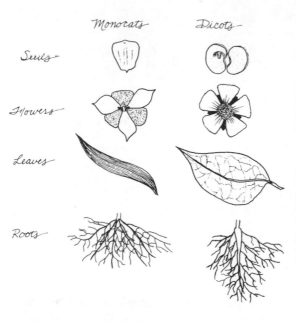

In monocots, such as corn, seeds have only one part; flower parts occur in sets of three; leaves have parallel veins; and roots are fibrous. In dicots, such as beans, seeds have two halves; flower parts occur in fours or fives; leaves have branching veins; and, often, the root system includes a tap root. *Illustrations by author*

What is pollination?

Pollination is the transfer of pollen from the stamen to the sticky top of the pistil known as the stigma. This process occurs naturally in several ways but is most commonly accomplished by insects and the wind. Self-pollination, which involves the transfer of pollen to flowers of the same plant, is common among such garden vegetables as beans and peas. Cross-pollination occurs when the pollen produced by one plant is transferred to the flower of another plant, which occurs in a corn patch. A few plants, such as some cabbages, are self-sterile, which means that the pollen will be ineffective if it falls on the stigma of any of the plant's own flowers. Cross-pollination is essential.

In what other ways are new plants propagated?

The use of seed to produce more plants is a form of sexual propagation. Asexual, or vegetative, propagation involves the use of plant parts, such as leaves, stems, roots, and buds, to start new plants. About half of all cultivated plants are produced by some form of vegetative propagation.

One method of vegetative propagation that many of us have tried is the use of a swollen, fleshy, underground stem known as a

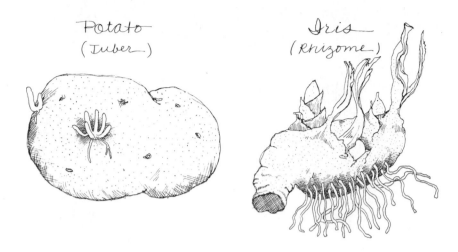

Potato
(Tuber)

Iris
(Rhizome)

tuber. The potato is a tuber that has many buds or eyes. By cutting the potato into pieces that each contain at least one eye, we can grow many plants.

Irises produce modified stems, called rhizomes, just below soil level. At various locations along these stems are nodes that can give rise to leaves. When the clumps of rhizomes are separated and replanted, new plants will grow. Kentucky bluegrass, canna lily, and lily-of-the-valley are other examples of plants that produce rhizomes.

Runners are modified horizontal stems that are above soil level. Strawberry crowns are noted for their production of runners. Plants usually develop about twelve inches away from the parent along the runners. These young plants grow roots and are easily separated from the crown after the roots form and take hold.

Onions and tulips develop from bulbs, which are short stems with fleshy leaves around them. Bulbs often develop small bulbs, or bulblets, from which new plants are grown. Garlic produces many bulblets known as cloves.

Roots can be used at times to produce plants. Sweet potato stems and dahlias grow from tuberous roots. When some perennials—for example, rhubarb, day lilies, and chrysanthemums—die back, their crowns and roots can be divided.

Leaves and stems are other sources for propagating plants. Placed in the proper growth medium, they will develop roots and

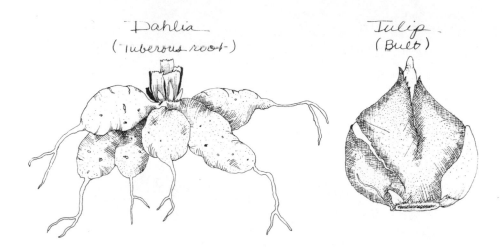

Dahlia
(Tuberous root)

Tulip
(Bulb)

then stems and leaves. The medium must be free of disease so that the cuttings, the plant parts used, do not become contaminated. Geraniums, tomatoes, rhododendrons, roses, yews, poplars, and pines can be started from cuttings.

Azaleas and many brambles can be propagated by layering. In this procedure, a stem is pinned to the ground so that roots can grow where it comes into contact with the soil. In a process of natural layering, the stem tips of the raspberry, one type of bramble, often droop to the ground and develop roots at the point of contact.

Grafting is an ancient art of propagation, and it is the way most trees are now grown commercially. Two parts from different plants are joined together so that they fuse and continue to grow. The upper part of the graft, which can be a bud or a stem, is called the scion. It is attached to a root stock. Success in grafting is greatest if the two parts are from the same species, but compatibility can happen even between species of the same genus. For example, apple branches can be grafted to pear-root stock.

3

How to Make a Garden

I've explained that the environment plays an important role in plant development, and I've discussed a bit of the biology of plants and their propagation. Now let's get to work in the vegetable garden. This might sound easy, but notice I said "work." For the first-time gardener, or for the person trying to position the garden in a new landscape, the task is not simple.

How do I choose a location for the vegetable garden?

As a general rule, the garden should be part of an overall landscape plan. It should fit in with the other outdoor living needs of the family.

The best soil for growing vegetables is probably under the turf in the front yard. Yet that most likely is not the best site for the garden—not if we have kids and we want to remain friends with the neighbors.

There often is little choice of garden sites, especially if the lot is small. With the growing popularity of townhouse living, the available land diminishes and the problem only increases.

Most vegetable gardens are started in soil that is less than desirable. Depending on the soil type, however, you can add ingredients over the years that will increase its porosity and fertility and make it very productive. So don't rule out a location on the basis of the soil. The most important factor to consider when you choose a garden spot is sunlight. Vegetables need at least six hours of direct sunlight and do their best when they're grown in full sunlight from morning to night. You probably can't move a building that is restricting sunlight, but you can compensate for many of the limitations imposed by a property.

For example, you can remove a tree to make room for a garden. Of course, consider what kind of tree is in the way. If it's a silver maple or other weak-wooded tree, don't think twice; get it out of there. Such trees are predisposed to problems. If it's an oak, though, try to work around it.

You also have to consider the topography, or the lay of the land. Level ground usually is a better choice than is a slope, provided the level area drains well. The slope can erode if its angle is too steep, but a slope with a slight angle is preferable to a soggy level area.

Don't let garden shape influence the site you select. Gardens do not have to be square or rectangular. In fact, a garden with fluid lines is more attractive and often blends better into the overall landscape design.

How large should I make the garden?

Available space often determines the size of a garden. If the garden must be small, consider growing vegetables that don't need much space: beans, beets, carrots, onions, peppers, radishes, spinach, tomatoes, and turnips.

If space is not a limitation, however, a variety of other circumstances will determine size. Ask yourself why you want a garden. If a family is trying to grow enough vegetables to meet its needs for a year, then the garden will need to be large. Of course, the size of the family will also have a bearing on the size of the garden.

Most of us, though, do not try to grow all of our vegetables, so the variety of vegetables raised will have a greater influence on size. Cucumbers, squash, and melons require lots of space. So does corn. If these are the plants you want to grow, you'll need a large garden.

One last consideration, and the most important one, is the amount of time you have available to work in the garden. It is frustrating to watch a garden fill with weeds and not have time to pull them. Plan a garden that you can care for properly, so that at the end of the gardening season you can feel a sense of accomplishment and satisfaction.

Do I till the sod under or remove it when I make a garden?

The sod can be turned under, but I do not recommend this. The grass and weeds that the turf comprises can continue to grow if they are not buried deep, and you'll end up with a garden full of weeds later in the summer. In addition, if roots or underground stems remain in the ground, weeds and grass can grow back. It is much better to remove the sod before you till the soil. This way, you eliminate not only the plants but also the seeds that could be present.

One last method of preparing a garden plot is to use a herbicide on the vegetation. Be sure to select one that is systemic: it gets into the system of the plant and kills the roots. Not only must the tops of the weeds and grasses be killed, but also the underground portions of the plants as well. Once the plants have died, the organic remains can be raked off or turned under to add nutrients to the soil. It is important to use a herbicide that breaks down and does not harm the environment. There are herbicides on the market that allow you to plant seven days after use. It is imperative that you follow label directions, no matter which herbicide you use.

When and how often does a garden need to be tilled?

There are several reasons for tilling garden soil and they are all very important. Tillage improves the physical condition of the soil. It opens compacted soil, creating an environment that is more conducive for seed germination and root growth. Accumulated organic residues from the previous year's garden should be turned under. This will enhance the tilth of the soil, add organic material, and rid the soil surface of possible plant diseases. Tilling also reduces the number of weeds present that could compete with vegetables. Lastly, it makes us feel better to see a clean soil surface before we plant the garden.

Tilling involves more than the annual turning of the soil by spading, plowing or rototilling. It includes any method that manipulates the soil. Raking, cultivating, and hoeing are other forms of tillage.

The time of annual tilling varies with the soil type. Heavy soils are best turned in the fall of the year so that freezing and thawing over the winter can produce a healthy spring seed bed. Fall tilling also allows you to plant early spring crops, such as onions, peas, and radishes. If you don't want to or can't till the entire garden in the fall, work on a small section so it will be ready for early spring crops.

Don't turn the soil when it is too wet. You'll end up with a lot of clods and a very poor soil for seeding. To tell if the soil is right for tilling, pick up a handful and squeeze it. If it forms a lump, it's too wet.

Sandy soils are best tilled in the spring, and they should be planted in the fall with cover crops such as winter rye. A cover crop helps prevent soil erosion and will provide organic matter in the spring. Add manure to sandy or heavy soils only in the fall, and do not add more than a layer of one or two inches at a time.

Is cultivation always good for the garden?

The answer is no! But there are several good reasons to cultivate if it is done properly and at the right time. Cultivation, or rototilling to a depth of about two inches, helps control weeds, aerates the soil, and improves the moisture-holding capacity of the soil. Most of us cultivate to stay ahead of the weeds. Weeds can harbor insect and disease pests, and they compete with the vegetables for nutrients, water, sunlight, and space. Harvests will be reduced if weed populations grow unchecked. The best time to control weeds is when they are small and before their root systems are well established.

After a rain, weeds seem to spring up almost overnight. You should cultivate as soon as the soil surface dries. Deep cultivation brings moist soil to the surface where the moisture will evaporate and be lost to the garden, so cultivate only one or two inches deep and don't cultivate too close to the vegetables' roots. If you damage them, you'll end up with other problems.

Do not cultivate when temperatures are high and rainfall is low; this only opens the soil, which increases evaporation rates and further stresses the plants.

When weeds get too large for surface cultivation, you will have to pull them. Great fun, huh! Better to rid the garden of weeds when they are small so that you have very few to pull later.

What is *Wall o' Water*? How does it benefit the gardener?

Wall o' Water is a product introduced a few years ago to help stretch the gardening season. It is a piece of plastic about thirty-six

Wall o' Water

Sunlight heats the Wall o' Water, which in turn heats the soil under it and lets you plant earlier in the spring.

inches wide by forty-eight inches long that is folded in half with the ends sealed together. About every three inches, the two layers are narrowly sealed, creating a series of closed tubes. The tubes are filled three-fourths full with water. The water in the tubes absorbs the heat from the sun during the day and releases it slowly at night, warming the soil inside.

Advertisements for Wall o' Water claim that it keeps plants safe to sixteen degrees. Plants thus can have an early start well before the last spring frost, and you can start harvesting fruit earlier.

In March, set the Wall o' Water as a tepee in the garden where a plant, such as a tomato, is to be placed. In two weeks, the tomato can be planted in the center. The heat trapped in the water will protect the tender plant from frosty night temperatures. Wall o' Water also can be used for crops other than tomatoes—cabbage, cauliflower, broccoli, and lettuce, for example.

Can I start my vegetables indoors from seed?

Actually, I'd say that's the best way! Not only will you save a few dollars, but it can be a lot of fun. It also is a way to have some varieties of vegetables that you cannot purchase locally. Cabbage, cauliflower, broccoli, tomato, pepper, and eggplant are only some of the vegetables that you can start from seed. Most seed packages list instructions on how and when to start the seed. The *when* is essential so that the seedlings are ready to set out at the appropri-

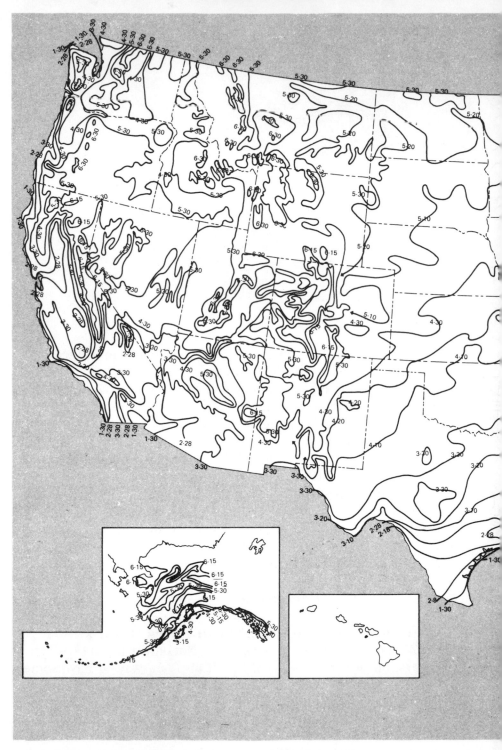

Average Dates of Last Killing Frost in Spring

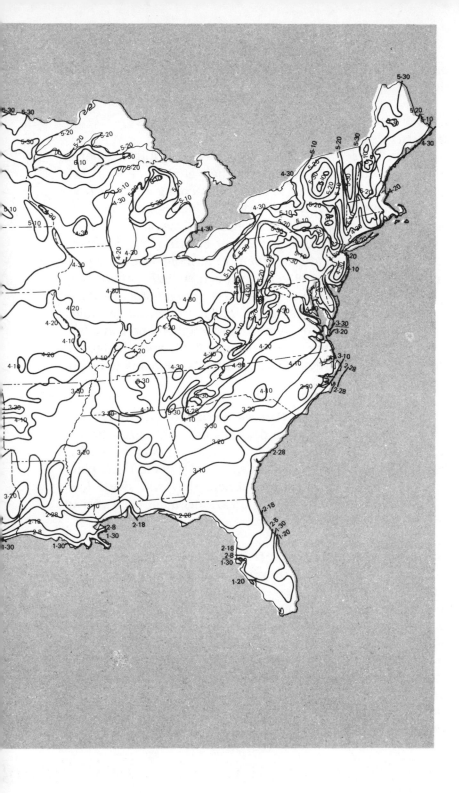

ate time. Refer to the map that shows the last average spring frost dates to determine when you should start the seed.

How do I prepare vegetable transplants for the garden?

Transplants, or seedlings, that have been grown in the house are tender and sensitive to changes in their environment. If they were planted outside and the temperatures changed much from those in the house, they would probably die. So you need to "harden off" the plants, which is a process of helping the transplants gradually get used to their outdoor environment. Set them outside during the day and bring them in at night when the temperature falls. If they did not receive much sunlight where they were growing indoors, you won't want to overdo it outdoors. Place them where they will get morning sun and afternoon shade. Doing this for a week or so until the plant tissues toughen and can adapt to greater temperature variation, stronger light, and changes in moisture levels. Once hardened off, transplants are ready to be put in the garden.

How should I arrange the vegetable garden?

How you arrange the garden depends on space, size, and the vegetables you plant. There are many varieties of each vegetable, and they can differ in the amount of space they need. Don't plant tall vegetable plants, such as corn, where they will shade low-growing crops. Experiment with garden arrangement each year to find what will work best for you.

If I always plant the vegetable garden in the same place, do I need to rotate the crops?

Some crops feed heavily on certain nutrients. Corn, for example, uses a lot of nitrogen. When planted in one area for an extended period of time, such crops can deplete the soil of these nutrients. So rotate your vegetable crops every few years. Crop rotation, together with the use of natural fertilizers will balance the soil nutrients. If the garden is large, sow a strip of it with a cover crop, such as soybeans or red clover, as part of the system of rotation. Over several years, the entire garden will benefit from the increase in nitrogen, and from the addition of organic matter when the cover crop is turned under in the fall.

Rotating crops, such as tomatoes and cabbage, also reduces the incidence of insect pests and disease. Pest populations can increase when a crop is always planted in one spot. Moving that particular crop to the other end of the garden can lessen pest numbers in successive years.

What is companion planting?

Companion planting is growing two varieties of plants together to enhance the growth of one or both. It also can mean planting two varieties of plants together to better use available garden space without hindering the growth of productivity of either variety.

Many people also use companion planting to repel pests from the garden. This method has proven successful in some cases; in others it leaves much to be desired. Marigolds and nasturtiums are reported by some gardeners to repel Japanese beetles and Colorado potato beetles. Bulb plants—onions, garlic, and chives, for example—are said to ward off many beetles. Sage, rosemary, and thyme appear to be effective in ridding the garden of certain insects.

Various vegetable combinations work well together if you want to use space efficiently. You can grow a short-season crop and a late-maturing one. Onions, which mature in late summer, grow well beside lettuce, spinach, and cabbage, which mature in spring. You can grow corn near many early-season crops. It is also possible to raise vegetables between rows of asparagus. Experiment with some combinations.

Is succession planting beneficial in the vegetable garden?

Succession planting means planting new vegetables following the harvest of a short-season crop, and it can help you get the most out of the garden plot. It definitely is a way to extend the gardening season. Early crops, such as radishes, peas, spinach, and lettuce, can be followed by green and lima beans and tomatoes. Then after you harvest the green beans, you can remove and plant fall crops of cabbage and spinach.

What's the best way to water the garden?

When rain does not supply enough moisture for the vegetables, they can wilt. Temporary wilting usually does not hurt most plants, but it can led to problems in some. Water-stressed tomatoes, for example, will produce fruit with blossom-end rot. Too much water, however, can also lead to problems. Vegetables such as cabbage, carrots, radishes, and tomatoes can split if they get too much water.

A watering can and a garden hose are usually the most convenient ways to add water to the garden. With either method keep the water off the foliage. Too much water on the leaves can promote diseases. Apply water to the ground around the plant. Soaker hoses, sprinklers, and drop irrigation systems are other methods that can be employed.

It is best to water during the early morning, so that the water will sink into the soil rather than be immediately evaporated by the sun. In addition, if water does get on the leaves, it will have time to evaporate, preventing disease problems.

The amount of water you add will depend on the vegetables you are growing, the garden soil, and the weather conditions. In general, water so that moisture penetrates at least twelve to eighteen inches of soil. Much of the water held in the top few inches will be lost to evaporation. Shallow watering encourages shallow root growth, which makes the plant more susceptible to stress as the sun dries the soil. Deep watering, on the other hand, ensures adequate water for growth and prompts the roots to grow deeper.

How often should I water?

How often you water depends, of course, on the maturity of the plants and the environmental conditions. Plants or transplants that have just been placed in the garden need water almost every day. Once they are established and there is sufficient rainfall, you should water less frequently.

As we all know, weather conditions can vary greatly throughout the growing season. During some years it seems as though the rain never stops; at other times it never comes, so the frequency and amount of rain also will determine how often we water. The rule of thumb is that vegetables should receive at least one inch of rain or its equivalent each week during the growing season.

Can "gray water" be safely used on plants that we eat?

Most gray water—the waste water that comes from washing clothes, dishes, or ourselves—can be used safely in the garden. The exception is the soapy water from washing clothes. Soapy water can contain high levels of boron and phosphates so it is best avoided. Rinse water, however, is safe to use on garden plants, but because some chemicals can remain in it, the water should not touch the foliage or fruit.

Don't use gray water on a regular basis in the garden. Constant use can build up toxic chemicals, such as boron and phosphates. You can use gray water in a drought but supplement it with clean water.

What does it mean to *side dress* vegetables?

Side dressing is the application of a fertilizer along each side of a row crop during the growing season. This replenishes nutrients in the soil that either have been used by the plants or leached away. Crops such as corn, tomatoes, cucumbers, and squash benefit from this treatment. Side dressing is also done frequently during the growing season to grow extremely large pumpkins.

Applying fertilizer directly to the row is preferable to broadcasting fertilizer, which scatters it over the entire garden. The fertilizer is then worked into the soil. What I do not like about broadcasting is that weeds as well as vegetables benefit from the nutrients you apply.

Can I use fish emulsion as a foliar fertilizer?

Yes, fish emulsion is commonly applied as a foliar spray. That is, it is sprayed on the foliage where the plant can absorb it. It is a fast-acting source of nitrogen, phosphorous, and potassium. When used in a concentration that is too strong, it can burn the leaves; so be sure to read and follow label directions.

Fish emulsion is an organic fertilizer made from fish parts. What parts? I'm not sure, but as we all know, "parts is parts!" I use fish emulsion a lot when I set vegetable transplants in the garden. For this purpose, I mix it with water and apply it to the soil around the plants. A few weeks later I follow up with another application. The American Indians used fish as a fertilizer long before we were gardening here.

What kinds of mulches can I use in the vegetable garden?

Properly used, mulch provides many benefits. It reduces weed populations, lowers temperature variation in the soil, conserves soil moisture, reduces erosion, improves crop yields, keeps fruits clean, prevents cultivation injury, and just plain makes the garden look better.

Many materials can be used as mulch on the garden. Compost, leaves, and straw are a few of the natural materials that you can apply. Newspapers, paper bags, and black plastic are some suitable artificial products. In recent years, I have used a black woven fabric. This fabric permits rain but not weeds to penetrate. It works best when covered with a thin layer of straw.

There are some negative side effects to mulch. Unfortunately, mulch sometimes harbors insect pests and diseases. Mulches such as grass clippings and maple leaves can compact and prevent moisture penetration and, if used too close to plants, can smother their roots.

Can I use preemergent weed controls on my vegetable garden?

Chemical preemergent weed controls kill weed seedlings as they germinate. Some of these herbicides are selective and will not harm the developing vegetable seedlings. Others, however, are nonselective and could kill everything. To be effective, the chemicals must remain very near the soil surface. Heavy rains can cause them to leach out, though, so that their application is ineffective. I think it wise and prudent not to use preemergent chemicals in the garden. There are many other methods of controlling weeds, although they might involve a bit more effort. As good stewards of our environment, we must start using fewer chemicals even if it means a little more weed-pulling.

What are some common vegetable garden insect pests?

Common insect larvae found in the garden include the cutworm, cabbage looper, tomato hornworm, corn borer, and wireworm. Adult insects that are troublesome include the Colorado potato, cucumber, and bean beetles, aphid, squash bug, and whitefly.

Insects have different life stages and the methods of control we use vary with these stages. Most insects undergo a process known as complete metamorphosis. Let's consider the butterfly or the housefly. Both lay eggs, which hatch into larvae. The larvae of butterflies and moths are called caterpillars, fly larvae are maggots,

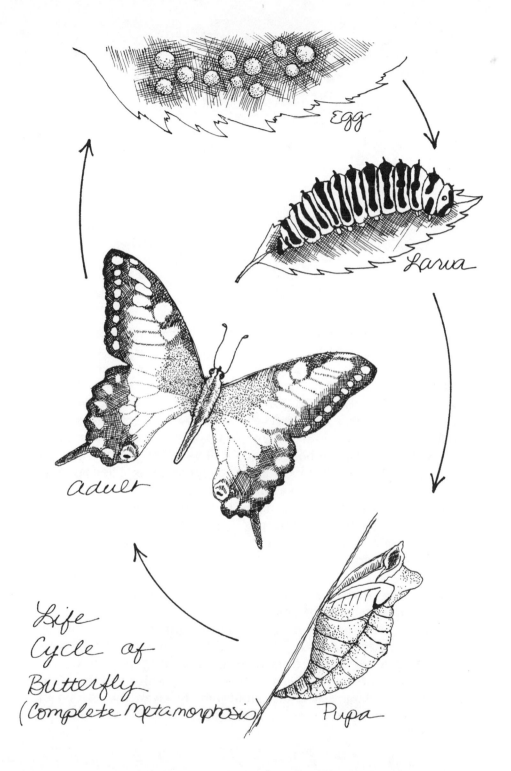

Egg

Larva

Adult

Pupa

Life
Cycle of
Butterfly
(Complete Metamorphosis)

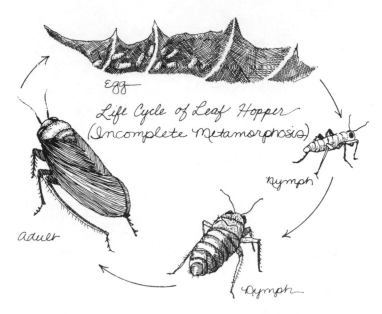

Life Cycle of Leaf Hopper (Incomplete Metamorphosis)

Egg

adult

nymph

nymph

and beetle larvae are grubs. Other larvae include wireworms, miners, and borers. Most larvae chew holes in plant parts as they feed. After much eating and much growth, the larvae enter a pupal stage. Sometimes they develop chrysalises or cocoons. Some species form only ridged coverings. During this period of what looks like inactivity, the insects change into their adult forms. Most adult garden insects either chew plants or suck juices from them.

Other insects, leaf hoppers and grasshoppers, for example, go through a change called incomplete metamorphosis. They lay eggs that gradually develop into adults. During the several stages before adulthood, they are called nymphs. Grasshopper nymphs look like little grasshoppers without wings. This is not as radical a change as complete metamorphosis. Nymphs usually chew the plant's vegetation or suck its sap.

What are some nonchemical methods of controlling insects?

There are three general nonchemical methods that you can use to control insects: cultural, physical, and natural. One of the easiest ways to prevent insects from entering your garden is to keep it clean. The presence of weeds will draw pests, which will then feed on your vegetables. It is also important to clean the garden of weeds and debris in the fall so that insects will not have a place to overwinter.

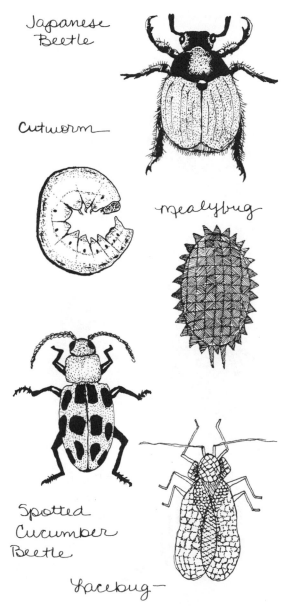

Japanese
Beetle

Cutworm

mealybug

Spotted
Cucumber
Beetle

Lacebug —

Common Garden Pests

Japanese Beetle: 1/2 inch
Cutworm: 1 to 1 1/2 inches
Mealybug: Up to 1/5 inch
Spotted Cucumber Beetle:
   1/2 inch
Lacebug: Less than 1/4 inch
*Cutworm illustrated by
author*

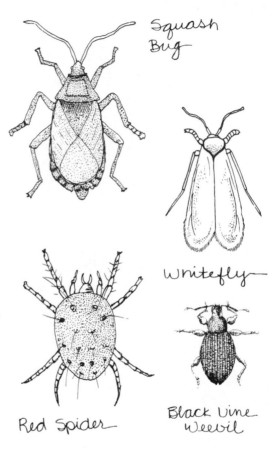

Squash Bug

Whitefly

Red Spider

Black Vine Weevil

Common Garden Pests

Squash Bug: $1/4$ to 1 inch
Whitefly: $1/10$ inch
Red Spider: Smaller than a
pinhead
Black Vine Weevil: $3/8$ inch
Colorado Potato Beetle:
Adult—$3/8$ inch

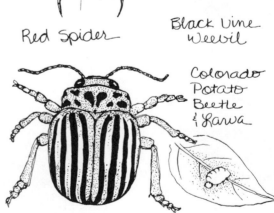

Colorado Potato Beetle & Larva

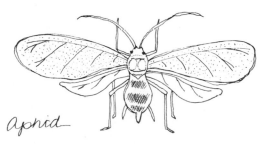

Aphid

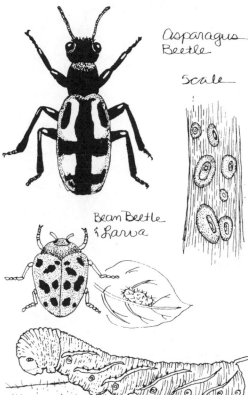

Asparagus Beetle

Scale

Bean Beetle & Larva

Tomato Hornworm

Common Garden Pests

Aphid: About $\frac{1}{10}$ inch
Asparagus Beetle: $\frac{1}{4}$ inch
Scale: $\frac{1}{5}$ inch
Bean Beetle: Adult—$\frac{1}{3}$
  inch
Tomato Cutworm: 3 to 4
  inches

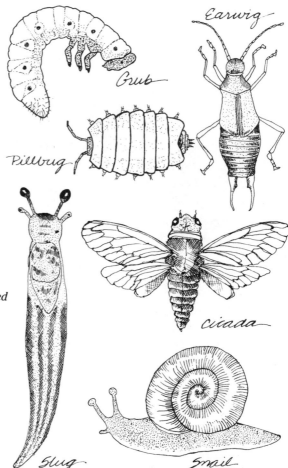

Common Garden Pests

Grub: $3/4$ to $1^1/2$ inches
Pillbug: $1/4$ to $3/4$ inch
Earwig: $1/2$ to 1 inch
Slug: Up to 4 inches
Cicada: 1 to $1^1/2$ inches
Snail: Up to 4 inches
Grub and pillbug illustrated by author

Physical control methods are simple and effective. One of the best ways to control many larvae and adult beetles is to remove them from plants by hand and destroy them. This way you can be certain they will not do any further damage. Another physical control for such pests as cutworms is to bury a bottomless can an inch or so in the ground encircling the young plants. This will prevent the larvae from reaching the plant. The use of sticky, yellow strips of plastic is a common method of controlling whitefly. Place the strips in the garden soil near susceptible plants, such as tomatoes.

There are now numerous methods of natural and biological control. Natural sprays of many types have been developed. Oil, garlic, red pepper, and grapefruit sprays are some homemade varieties.

Insecticidal soap is a natural product that is commercially available. This contact spray contains the potassium salts of fatty acids, similar to what is in many soaps. It is very effective on smaller insects and is not harmful to us, beneficial insects, or our pets. Rotenone and pyrethrum are two insecticides that are derived from plants. Both of them can be very effective on pests, but they will kill the beneficial insects, too. Rotenone also has been found to be toxic to fish and can do serious damage if run-off or leaching from the site occurs. You must take care when you use these products.

Some insects are beneficial because they feed on other insects. Many can be found in and around our gardens, and some can be ordered from garden catalogs. Praying mantises, lacewings, ladybugs, and parasitic wasps are some of the most common "good" insects, and some nematodes feed on cutworms, wireworms, and other soilborne larvae.

Let's not forget that even birds, bats, toads, spiders, and snakes eat insects, so don't harm them when you find them in your garden.

One last critter that needs to be mentioned is the slug. These guys enjoy a number of vegetables including tomatoes.

Slugs, and their cousins, snails, can be controlled with baits or by setting out jar lids containing beer. The lids must be placed in the soil so that their lips are at ground level. The slugs are attracted by the smell of the beer, fall in and drown. Another slug-control tactic is to sprinkle them with salt, which dehydrates them so that they die.

These insects and arachnids are on your side: they prey on insect pests.

Lacewing: $1/2$ inch
Ladybug: Up to $1/2$ inch
Garden Spider: $1/4$ to several inches
Praying Mantis: 3 to 4 inches

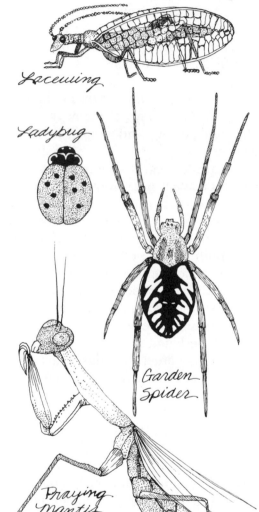

Lacewing

Ladybug

Garden Spider

Praying Mantis

Honeybee

Bumblebee

wasp

Bees pollinate crops, and many wasps parasitize insect larvae that feed on garden plants.

Honeybee: 3/4 inch
Bumblebee: 1 inch
Wasp: 1/2 to 1 1/2 inches

Are there safe chemicals that I can use in my garden?

There are many chemical insecticides or toxins, but in most cases you should use them only as a last resort. Some are systemic; that is the chemical gets into the system of the plant on which it is sprayed. Never use systemic chemicals on vegetable plants because the chemical will enter the fruit of the plant. Nonsystemics, which are more commonly used, must either be sprayed on the plant to coat its surface or sprayed on the insect. Those that are applied to the plant must be ingested by the insect to be effective. Contact poisons, such as Sevin and malathion, invade the body surface of the insect and eventually kill it.

Sevin and malathion are two of the safest chemical insecticides to use in the garden. But be sure to read and follow label directions. Labels are legal documents. If you use the product in a manner other than the way the label specifies and you cause damage, you could be held liable.

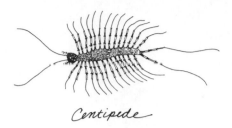

Centipede

The centipede, ¼ inch to 6 inches long, has one pair of legs per segment and feeds on insects. The millipede, ¼ inch to 4 inches long, has two pairs of legs per segment and feeds mainly on plants and decaying matter. *Illustrations by author*

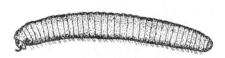

Millipede

Are there any alternatives for controlling diseases other than chemicals?

Chemicals, including fungicides, are used most often to treat plant diseases. Fungicides are systemics, so they cannot be used safely on plants in the vegetable garden. Safer makes a natural fungicide. It is new on the market, however, and I don't know how well it works.

For many diseases—various blights and wilts, for example—there are no chemical controls, and once they appear in the garden, all you can do is remove the infected leaves or plants.

Prevention is the best means of controlling diseases. Buy only plants that are disease-resistant, a characteristic that usually is noted on the labels of seed packages or nursery plants. Keep your plants healthy. Disease organisms can be present in the soil, but plants do not necessarily succumb to them until stressed by weather or other conditions.

What animal pests like the vegetable garden?

Groundhogs, deer, rabbits, raccoons, chipmunks, and voles are a few of the notable mammals that make an appearance in the garden. (Voles differ from moles, which usually do not bother the garden.) Birds often damage fruits and there are some that enter

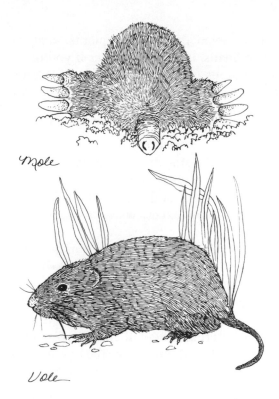

Mole

Vole

Moles eat grubs, but voles eat the roots and bark of plants. Voles often run in mole burrows.

the garden and devour your seeds immediately after you have so painstakingly sown them.

The best control for these visitors is a physical barrier, such as fencing and mesh coverings.

Do vegetables grow well in containers?

Yes, plant propagators have developed varieties that are well-suited to container gardening. I've successfully grown the 'Florida Petite', a cherry tomato in four-and-a-half-inch pots. The plants were extremely compact and produced about a dozen tomatoes each. Most vegetable plants sold for container gardening are only half the size of the standard varieties or even smaller. Most also mature about two weeks earlier than the standard varieties.

The size and shape of the container will determine the type and variety of vegetables you can raise in it. For example, you probably would not want to try to grow most varieties of carrots in a shallow container. There are some short-rooted types, though, such as 'Short 'n Sweet', that do well in shallow containers. Window boxes work satisfactorily for onions, beans, peas, lettuce, herbs, and many root crops. You can even grow vining plants, such as cucumbers, melons, and pole beans, in window boxes if you use a trellis. Tubs are ideal for tomatoes, peppers, and eggplants, and some varieties are suited to window boxes as well. I once even saw a sweet potato growing in a hanging basket.

What do container plants need?

The container should be both pleasing and functional. It should be large enough for the vegetables to grow and be able to support the weight of the plant as well as soil and water. The container must have holes in the bottom to allow excess water to drain away. Otherwise, root rot can set in.

You can buy a soil mix or make your own. If you make your own, I recommend one part each of soil, sand, and peat moss. You can add some composted manure to enrich the soil, but when doing this, cut back on the amount of peat moss. Before mixing, the garden soil should be sterilized to kill weed seed, insects, and disease-causing organisms. To sterilize, heat it in an oven at a temperature of one hundred eighty degrees for thirty minutes. Sand and peat are generally free of pests, and most composted manure has already been sterilized.

Light is critical to successful container gardening, just as it is to any other kind of gardening. Container gardens should receive at least six hours of sunlight daily. If you are growing vegetables indoors, put your containers in a southern exposure if possible. In an other exposure, you'll need supplemental light. The source of the added light should be a special lamp made for growing plants. Two such lamps are Grow-Lux and Agro-Lite. Although some bulbs are incandescent, many are fluorescent. Most vegetables are long-day plants, so they should receive from fourteen to sixteen hours of fluorescent light daily. Place the lamp four to six inches away from the plant.

Think about temperature, too. Each plant variety has an optimum temperature range. Most plants will do well in daytime temperatures of seventy to eighty-five degrees. For some plants, such as tomatoes, to flower, night temperatures must be ten to fifteen degrees lower than daytime temperatures.

Most containers lose water rapidly in the summer sun because of evaporation. At the same time the plants are losing water as a result of transpiration. This means that you must water regularly and frequently. Check the soil for moisture before watering. Too much water will drown roots, but too little water will cause them to wilt, wither, and die. Place a toothpick or matchstick in the soil near the root zone of the plant (the soil at the container's edge is always drier). If the soil is moist, it will cling to the stick, an indication that the plant doesn't need water. If the stick comes out clean, add water. Pour it around the plant, not just on one side. Fill the container to the top so that excess salts from the water or from fertilizers wash out the bottom. Water container plants in the morning; watering at night encourages disease if water gets on the foliage.

Container plants also need to be fertilized regularly because they are growing in a limited amount of soil and their nutrients are being leached from the soil by watering. Use a liquid fertilizer, which you can apply as you water. Be sure the soil is moist before applying a fertilizer so that you don't burn the roots.

Trial and error is often the best way to learn what your plants need. If the vegetables are growing tall but not producing fruit, try a fertilizer higher in phosphorus and potassium. Cutting back on the nitrogen should slow the plant growth. Regardless of which fertilizer you use, always follow the label directions.

If the plants produce fruit, their flowers must be pollinated. If there are no insects around to do the job, you'll have to do it. Self-pollinators need only a gentle shake when the flowers are open. If you are growing plants such as cucumbers indoors, you will have to transfer pollen from the male flowers to the pistil of the female flowers. A small paintbrush will do the trick.

4

Minding Your Peas and Cukes

The soil is ready. What vegetables should we plant, though, and how should we plant them? There are so many to choose from. Just defining a vegetable is hard, because there is no good horticultural definition of vegetable or fruit. For example, is a tomato a fruit or a vegetable? Botanically, it is a fruit because it contains the seed. For horticultural and legal purposes in the United States, however, it is considered a vegetable. (This was decided by the Supreme Court in 1893 in response to a question regarding import duties.)

Vegetables are considered to be any plant, or part thereof, that is eaten during the main course of the meal. Fruits are plant parts eaten as dessert. So what is rhubarb? If eaten as a relish, it's a vegetable. When used in a pie, it's a fruit. For our purposes it's a vegetable. And cantaloupe and watermelon? Yes, they're sweet and, except for some pickle recipes, we usually think of them as fruit. But they are garden companions, unlike most of the fruits we know, so we'll include them here.

What are cool-season crops?

Cool-season crops are those that are planted in early spring and need cool temperatures to mature properly. Some of them can be planted four to six weeks before the last average spring frost. They include broccoli, brussels sprouts, cabbage, kale, lettuce, leeks, onions, peas, radishes, spinach, and turnips. There are some

PLANTING TIMETABLE FOR VEGETABLES

Cold-hardy plants for early-spring planting		Cold-tender or heat-hardy plants for late-spring or early-summer planting			Hardy plants for late-summer or fall planting except in the North (plant 6 to 8 weeks before first fall freeze)
Very hardy (plant 4 to 6 weeks before frost-free date)	Hardy (plant 2 to 4 weeks before frost-free date)	Not cold-hardy (plant on frost-free date)	Requiring hot weather (plant 1 week or more after frost-free date)	Medium heat-tolerant (good for summer planting)	
Broccoli	Beets	Beans, snap	Beans, lima	Beans, all	Beets
Cabbage	Carrots	Okra	Eggplants	Chard	Collard
Lettuce	Chard	New Zealand spinach	Peppers	Soybeans	Kale
Onions	Mustard	Soybeans	Sweet potatoes	New Zealand spinach	Lettuce
Peas	Parsnips	Squash	Cucumbers	Squash	Mustard
Potatoes	Radishes	Sweet corn	Melons	Sweet corn	Spinach
Spinach		Tomatoes			Turnips
Turnips					

others, not quite as hardy, that can be planted two to four weeks before the last frost. Beets, carrots, cauliflower, parsnips, potatoes, and rutabagas are a few of these semihardy varieties.

Which vegetables grow best in hot weather?

Quite a few vegetables are tender and need warm temperatures to mature. Cucumbers, lima beans, peppers, squash, sweet corn, sweet potatoes, and tomatoes, as well as cantaloupes and watermelons, love hot summer weather. It is important that they receive adequate amounts of water, though, if they are to do their best.

Sometimes I sow too many seeds in the garden and the seedlings germinate very close together. Should I thin them out?

When you sow seed, spacing it according to the directions on the back of the package can be difficult. Sometimes it is advisable to plant the seed closer than suggested, or to double-seed, to be sure the rows are full. But if you double-seed and all the seed germinates, you'll have to thin the rows. Otherwise, each plant will not produce well or the crowding will lower the quality of the fruit. Remember, too, that crowding can make the plants more susceptible to disease and environmental stress.

On the other hand, I regularly grow some varieties much closer than recommended and end up with a bumper crop. I usually sow pea and bean seed by scattering the seeds in wide rows.

SPACING VEGETABLES

Vegetables	Spacing In Rows (Inches)	Spacing Between Rows (Inches)
Asparagus	12–18	48
Bean, bush lima	3–4	24–36
Bean, pole lima	10–12	36–48
Bean, bush snap	2–4	18–24
Bean, pole snap	4–6	24–36
Beet	2	15–18
Broccoli	12–24	18–36
Brussels sprout	12–24	18–36
Cabbage	12–24	18–36
Cantaloupe	12	48–72
Carrot	2	15–24
Cauliflower	12–24	18–36
Celery	6	24–36
Corn	6–12	24–36
Cucumber	8–12	48
Eggplant	12–24	24–36
Honeydew	12	48–72
Kohlrabi	4–6	15–24
Lettuce, head	10–15	18–24
Lettuce, leaf	3–6	12–18
Okra	12–24	18–24
Onion	1–4	15–24

Parsnip	2–4	18–30
Pea	1–2	18–30
Pepper	12–24	24–36
Potato	8–12	30–36
Pumpkin	36–48	48–72
Radish	1	12–18
Rhubarb	24–36	36–48
Rutabaga	4–8	18–30
Spinach	2–4	12–24
Squash, summer	24–48	36–60
Squash, winter	36–48	48–72
Sweet potato	12–18	36–48
Swiss chard	12–15	24–36
Tomato	24–48	36–48
Turnip	2–4	18–30
Watermelon	36–48	48–72

When and how do I plant perennial rhubarb?

Early spring is the best time to plant rhubarb. It needs a well-drained soil that is rich in organic material. The pH should be about 6.5. The usual method is to divide the crowns of established plants so that the "starter plants" each have a section of the root and a large bud. Set them about three feet apart with the bud about three inches below the soil level. Spread bone meal in the bottom of the planting holes. Don't harvest the rhubarb petioles, or leaf stems, for the first two years. After that, you can harvest them for about two weeks each spring.

Rhubarb plants remain healthy for four to eight years. Then the leaves and petioles begin to decrease in size. Rejuvenation will occur if the plants are divided and placed in a new location. Rhubarb uses a lot of nitrogen for leaf growth, so fertilize it regularly. Otherwise, the plants will "bolt" early, that is, flower and go to seed, and the leaves will remain small. If this happens, fertilize right away and cut off the flower stalk so that the plant's energy goes back into producing foliage.

One of the nicest things about rhubarb is that it attracts few pests. The rhubarb curculio, a red beetle three-fourths of an inch long, is found in the East. The adults puncture the petioles of the rhubarb while they feed. Sometimes the females will lay eggs in the punctures. The rhubarb curculio is also fond of curly dock, and if you keep this weed under control, the beetle should not be a problem.

How should I plant asparagus and maintain the bed?

Asparagus is generally planted in the spring of the year from one-, two-, or three-year-old roots purchased from a nursery. It also can be started from seed, but you will have to wait an extra year or two before you can harvest it.

To plant asparagus, dig a trench about twelve inches deep and wide enough to spread out the roots. Add about two inches of compost or dried cow manure to the trench and cover it with an inch or two of garden soil. Then mix some bone meal into the soil and set the roots in every eighteen to twenty-four inches. Cover them with two inches of soil and water them. As the asparagus begins to grow, fill in the trench with the remaining soil and cover it with mulch to help suppress weed growth.

Do not harvest spears the first year. You can cut them sparingly the second year, and by the third year you can harvest them for about eight weeks.

Fertilize each year after harvest is finished. It also is important to keep weeds out of the asparagus bed. If they get ahead of you, cut the bed down in the fall after frost kills the foliage. Fall also is a good time to add two inches of cow manure to the bed. Then in the spring, as soon as you can get into the garden, till the soil to a depth of two inches. This will remove any perennial weeds that are present and will mix in the manure. Rake out the debris and cover the rows with more mulch. Some gardeners use salt on their asparagus beds to help control weeds.

What other pests should I look for in the asparagus bed?

Keeping the asparagus bed free of weeds is critical to reducing the chance of asparagus rust. This fungus causes a discoloration of the spears and needlelike leaves. The foliage first takes on a rust color but later turns black. Using disease-resistant varieties and keeping the beds clean will reduce the likelihood of the rust.

The asparagus beetle is a problem in many areas of the country. The adults, which are dark with yellowish spots, overwinter in garden debris and emerge just as the asparagus begins to grow in the spring. They feed on the developing spears, which deforms or marks the asparagus. You can control these pests by hand or with Sevin or insecticidal soap.

I've heard that white asparagus is tasty. How is it grown?

White asparagus is the same plant as green asparagus. It's white because of the absence of light. In early spring, stakes are placed in the ground in the row of asparagus. The stakes should stand about fifteen inches above soil level. Then a sheet of black plastic is draped over the stakes. As the asparagus emerges from the ground, it will be white because it is growing in the dark and lacks chlorophyll. The plastic also will prevent damage from late frosts. If it is put on early, harvesting should begin earlier than that of uncovered asparagus because the plastic will heat the soil, encouraging earlier growth.

My spinach seems fine until the weather warms up. Then it goes to seed. How can I prevent this?

Usually spinach "bolts," or produces seed, as the days get longer and hotter. It is a cool-season crop that should be planted in early spring. However, there are several slow-bolting or long-standing types.

The average spinach plant produces about two dozen leaves during its short growing season. The fall crop can be planted about forty days before the first average fall frost.

Spinach is easy to raise, and I think it tastes better fresh than do most leafy vegetables.

What pests attack spinach?

As spinach matures early in the season, keep your eyes open for tiny spinach flea beetles. These guys will riddle the leaves, but they are easily controlled with insecticidal soap.

There is also the spinach leaf miner, whose larvae tunnel

through the leaves, making them unsuitable for eating. When you find these burrowers, pinch them off and remove the affected leaves.

Why don't the heads on my cauliflower plants grow very big?

All of us who have planted cauliflower have had this problem. The biggest culprit is the weather. Cool evening temperatures—in the upper forties—can stress the plant and the head that forms will remain small.

The best advice I can give is to wait to plant until the chance of frost has passed in your area. Don't start the seed too early indoors. Eight weeks before the last frost date is the right time. Don't wait too long to plant either, because the heads, or curds as the professionals call them, must be harvested before the hot weather arrives. Holding the transplants too long before planting can also cause small curd development, as can high temperatures, insect damage, drought, and a lack of nitrogen.

I know there is such a thing as purple cauliflower, but why does my white cauliflower sometimes get a purple color?

White cauliflower curds will sometimes take on a purple or green color when they are exposed to sunlight. Today there are many self-blanching varieties on the market, and they will remain white. To ensure that the heads stay white, gather the leaves of the plant together and fasten them around the head with a piece of cloth or twine.

The change in color of the curds from white to purple could indicate that the heads will not be good for eating. When there is too much color, the flavor could be bitter. When there is only a slight color change, the heads are still tasty. The less light the curds receive, the better the flavor will be.

Are there any diseases that affect cauliflower?

Many diseases can be present in cauliflower and other members of the cabbage family: cabbage, broccoli, brussels sprout, and turnip. Using disease-resistant varieties is important. So is practicing good gardening techniques, such as rotating crops and keeping the garden free of weeds. Many common garden weeds are closely related to the cabbage family and can transmit disease.

Club root is a disease that many of us have heard about. The root of the cauliflower (or other cabbage-family member) becomes deformed and develops galls. The leaves begin to yellow and the plant dies. The presence of this disease is related to the soil pII. A pH lower than 7.1 favors it.

Other diseases that affect members of the cabbage family are white, head, and black rots, black leg, and downy mildew, most of which are difficult, if not impossible, to cure. To prevent the spread of a disease, get rid of an infected plant when you first notice the problem.

What is the difference between green, snow, and sugar snap peas?

Green peas are also known as English peas. They are grown for the seeds, or peas, rather than the pods. They should be harvested when the peas are large and tender and the pods have a velvety green color. Snow peas and sugar snap peas are varieties that have edible pods. The snow peas are picked when the pods are about three inches long and before the peas develop. (If left to develop, though, the peas can be shelled and used as green peas.) Sugar snap peas are grown like the other types but are harvested when the peas inside are full and tender and the pods are velvety and light green. Both the peas and the pods of this variety are edible. They can be eaten raw, used fresh in salads, cooked, or, if harvested young, stir-fried.

Almost all peas are vining plants and need some type of support, but some types of snap peas are more bushlike and still produce prolifically.

Are there any diseases or pests common to garden peas?

Several insects enjoy peas almost as much as I do. But there are far more diseases than insects to contend with, and some of them can destroy the entire crop. One of the most common is root rot. This disease is caused by a number of fungi, and more than one can affect a plant at a time. Pea plants that have root rot become discolored and die. If the roots are soft and have a reddish or brown cast, root rot is the culprit.

Peas are prone to root rot because their shallow roots are easily damaged with the hoe or cultivator when the soil around the plants is worked.

Fusarium wilt is another disease that is fairly common in the garden and that affects peas. The yellowing of bottom leaves and the curling of the leaf margins are signs of the disease. The roots look quite healthy, but the plant still withers and dies. Fusarium wilt can stay in the soil for years, so select pea varieties that are resistant to disease.

One other group of diseases is blights. Spotted foliage and pods are their signatures. Cool, wet springs seem to increase the likelihood of these diseases. Blights can be passed on to the seeds, so never plant pea seeds from affected plants.

It is recommended that beans be planted two to four inches apart, but can't they be closer?

Yes, beans really can be planted closer together. I usually scatter the seed in furrows four to six inches wide. Before I cover the row, I add some organic fertilizer. Scattering the seed goes against what we read in most books, but it works for me. The plants seem to be just as productive, when compared with plants spaced normally, and the harvest is greater per foot of row because there are many more plants. I also plant peas this way and have the same success.

I don't recommend doing this when planting pole beans or tall, vining varieties of peas. When planting beans and peas that need support, I plant rows six inches apart and place a wire fence between the rows so that the plants will grow on both sides of the fence.

What are the little yellow insects that I find on my bean plants?

These are the larvae of the Mexican bean beetle. These fuzzy critters, along with the adults, can devastate a bean patch in short order. They not only skeletonize the leaves, but they also feed on the pods and the stems.

The adult beetles are copper-colored with black spots. The females lay yellow masses of eggs on the underside of the foliage in June. Each female lays about five hundred eggs in groups of fifty or so at a time. The best control is to remove the adults by hand along with any leaves that have eggs on them. Sevin and insecticidal soap can be effective, too, and there are parasitic flies and wasps that can be used to control the beetle.

What does *VFN* mean? I often see it with the names of tomato varieties.

Actually, there are now one to four letters following variety names: V, F, N, or T. These letters indicate that the varieties are resistant to various tomato pests. The *V* means the variety is resistant to verticillium wilt, the *F,* to fusarium wilt; the *N,* to nematodes, and the *T,* to tobacco mosaic virus. Of these, the verticillium and fusarium wilts are the most common problems. I suggest that you always select varieties that are resistant to these diseases.

Can tomatoes be started in the garden from seed?

Most gardeners set out tomato transplants in the spring after the danger of frost has passed. However, many other gardeners start their own tomato seed indoors about four to six weeks before the last average frost date. Growing your own transplants is a way of getting varieties not commonly available. It also saves you money.

I know of gardeners who grow tomatoes by sowing the seed directly into the garden soil. Those who raise tomatoes this way believe that the plants are more vigorous and catch up to transplants in only a couple of weeks. To get a jump on the season, you can use the Wall o' Water.

When you set out transplants, place them in the ground so that most of the length of the stem is covered with soil. Roots will develop along the buried stem. Water the new transplants with a liquid fertilizer that is rich in phosphorus.

Do tomatoes need to be staked?

How is this for an answer: It depends. It depends on the growth pattern of the variety you're planting. The tomato is a plant that can have either determinate or indeterminate growth. Those plants that are determinate, such as 'Marglobe', 'Tiny Tim', and 'Roma', will grow shoots with leaves but will eventually form flower buds at the ends of the shoots. These shoots or stems will not get any longer. The plants will stay somewhat compact and will not be very tall. Tomatoes that are determinate can be grown on stakes, but I believe they do better when grown in tomato cages. If the growth habit is compact, they need no support. In any case, what is important is that the developing fruit not be allowed to rest on the soil. This will prevent disease and pest problems and will keep the fruit clean.

Plants with indeterminate growth will continue to grow shoots and will produce flowers along the stems. These plants tend to get very large and do their best when growth is controlled. 'Burpee's VF Hybrid', 'Better Boy', 'Big Boy', and 'Early Girl' have indeterminate growth. When you plant an indeterminate tomato, set a stake about eight feet tall in the ground near it. Limit the number of stems to two, and tie them to the stake every eight to ten inches as they grow. Pieces of cloth cut into strips make ideal ties. Remove suckers that form along the stems.

What is blossom-end rot and how can I prevent it?

If you've grown tomatoes for long, you've probably had a problem with blossom-end rot. This common disease causes the end of the tomato opposite the stem to turn brown and rot. It is promoted by a lack of available calcium in the soil and by a lack of water. Adding limestone to the soil will correct the calcium problem. Regularly watering throughout the summer will reduce the possibility of water stress. Mulching over the soil around the plants will lessen the evaporation of moisture from the soil and also alleviate heat stress.

Are there any other diseases or pests that affect tomato plants?

Numerous diseases and a few insects can harm tomato plants and fruit. Flea beetles, aphids, whiteflies, and spider mites can all cause problems, but I have never had any of them do serious damage to my tomatoes. All of them can be controlled by spraying insecticidal soap or using Sevin. There is a safer way to get rid of whiteflies, which are attracted to the color yellow. Place yellow cardboard or plastic strips coated with a sticky substance in the garden to lure and trap them.

One of the largest garden insects is the tomato hornworm. This caterpillar is three to four inches long and feeds on the foliage and fruit of the plants. As you can imagine from their size, they eat a lot. The adults, which are moths, do very little damage other than to lay more eggs. The best control method is to pick the caterpillars off the plants by hand. The bacterium *Bacillus thuringiensis* can be used to control this and other caterpillars.

Verticillium and fusarium wilts are two more common diseases of the tomato. Verticillium wilt causes the oldest foliage to yellow and drop off. The stem tips usually do not lose their leaves, but they can droop and their leaves might curl. The plant might last through the season, but it will not produce very much or very good fruit.

Fusarium wilt generally is not a problem unless the temperature of the soil reaches eighty degrees. Early symptoms are much like those of verticillium wilt, but the foliage yellows to the stem tips. The stems then wilt and die. To prevent problems with wilt, select cultivars that are disease-resistant.

The environment sometimes can affect the fruit. If the weather is damp and cool when the plants are in flower, the bloom can stick to the developing fruit, and the fruit will be misshapen as it grows. When there is a great deal of rain during the summer, growth cracks may form on the fruit. In both cases, the fruit is good to eat; it just doesn't look as nice. Young fruit that is exposed to the sun sometimes forms sunscald, which is first noticed as a light patch on the skin of the fruit. Later, it will become a sunken area on the surface of the green tomato. Fruits with sunscald should be removed before they mature; they are not worth eating and only invite disease.

How can I grow better peppers?

I believe that the reason we have problems with peppers is that we show them too much love. How do we do that to vegetable plants? We give them too much nitrogen. Excess nitrogen will cause the lush growth of vegetation and, unfortunately, bud drop. So for peppers, use a fertilizer that is higher in phosphorus and potassium. Some folks who grow good peppers swear that using Epsom salts is the secret to their success. Epsom salts is magnesium sulfate and, when used as a foliar application, it seems to produce healthier plants and larger fruit.

Blossom-end rot is a common disease of peppers as well as tomatoes. If the problem develops, it can be corrected just as it is with tomatoes: add limestone to the soil and water more frequently.

I've had difficulty growing eggplants. Any ideas about what the problem might be?

The eggplant is a close relative to both the potato and the tomato. It is native to India, and there are now Japanese eggplant varieties available as well. These are slender, only about two inches in diameter, and about ten inches long. Generally, they mature earlier than the more common varieties.

In many areas, eggplants are put in the garden as transplants, because they cannot be set out before the chance of frost has passed. They can take up to three months to mature when started from seed. Plant them in a good garden soil and add fertilizer high in phosphorus. Continue to fertilize them monthly, using a 5–10–10 or 5–10–5 garden fertilizer. Some good natural fertilizers are available, too. A lack of nitrogen causes the plants to become pale, lose their vigor, and produce undersized fruit.

Be careful when cultivating and weeding around eggplants. These plants have shallow root systems, and disturbing the soil close to the roots, especially in the summer, could hurt the plants.

You need to watch for several pests that like eggplants. One of the most notorious is the tiny flea beetle. The adult beetle, which is black, chews tiny holes in the leaves of eggplants and potatoes. Sevin and insecticidal soap are effective controls. Sometimes aphids and Colorado potato beetles will munch on the eggplant foliage. Use insecticidal soap to control them.

Verticillium wilt can be a problem, too. This fungus is most troublesome when the weather is cool. It is the same disease that affects tomatoes. To help prevent it, use disease-resistant varieties and rotate eggplant crops in the garden.

You might be interested to know that eggplants grow well in containers if they are watered and fertilized regularly.

I love carrots but have trouble growing them. What would you recommend?

One of the biggest problems of carrot cultivation is poor soil. By "poor," I mean heavy soil, which is not good for root crops. A raised bed filled with a good loam or a slightly sandy soil is an excellent solution. The bed does not have to be any more than a foot deep, as the longest carrots do not grow much longer than ten inches.

Carrots are biennial plants. That is, they do not go to seed until the second year in the ground, but the roots should be dug at the end of the first summer because you probably don't want seed.

Carrots can have difficulty germinating if conditions are not right. Never cover the seed with more than half an inch of sand, peat, or perlite. Never use heavy soil. Keep the seed bed moist and allow two weeks for germination.

As with all vegetables, there are many varieties from which to select. Two varieties with the longest roots are 'Gold Pak' and 'Imperator'. These will grow to about ten inches long. 'Danvers Half Long' and 'Spartan Bonus' grow to about eight inches long. 'Nantes Half Long', 'Royal Chantenay', and 'Goldinhart' are six- to seven-inch-long varieties. Short varieties, those less than six inches long, include 'Short 'n Sweet' and 'Little Finger'. The carrots with the shortest roots are best for heavy soil.

There are few pests to worry about with carrots. The carrot rust fly is one that is sometimes seen in the Northeast. The larvae of the fly feed on the developing carrot root. You can usually avoid the problem, though, by harvesting the carrots in early July and rotating your crops.

How are beets planted?

Beets are planted the same way carrots are, and as with carrots, one of the biggest problems is getting them to germinate. Cover the seed with sand, peat, or perlite, not with heavy soil. If germination is good, thin the beets so that they stand two to four inches apart. If you really like beets, plant them at two-week intervals so that you can enjoy them longer.

Few pests bother beets. Leaf miner and curly-top virus can render the tops unsuitable for eating. If you plant and harvest your beets early, though, you should have little trouble with the pests. If you ever find small, black spots in the beet root, the problem is a boron deficiency in the soil. Water the plants with a solution of about two tablespoons of borax per gallon of water.

Where can I find yellow turnip?

Yellow turnip is more commonly known as rutabaga. The true turnip and rutabaga, or Swedish turnip, are closely related, but they are not the same plant. The rutabaga is the result of a cross between turnip and cabbage. Rutabaga is a cool-season crop, but in many places it is grown as a fall crop because the root takes so long to mature. Plant rutabagas after harvesting peas and early pota-toes. They can take frosts and continue to grow after the tender crops have been harvested.

The roots of turnips often grow rapidly and become hollow or pithy. The rutabaga root is solid and yellow, and has a longer shelf life than the turnip. As far as I'm concerned, its flavor is far superior to that of the turnip.

When growing rutabagas, be on the lookout for the cabbage maggot. Young plants are more susceptible to this pest than are established ones. The main symptom is brown streaks in the foliage, which indicate that the maggots are tunnelling.

The maggots overwinter as a pupae and emerge in April as adults. The adults, a little smaller than houseflies, begin laying eggs at the base of transplants of cabbage, cauliflower, and broccoli. In a couple of days, the eggs hatch. The larvae feed on the plant roots for about thirty days, then pupate. About three weeks later the adults emerge to begin the process again. Up to four generations can develop each year. These later generations feed on rutabagas, turnips, beets, brussels sprouts, and celery.

Maggot fly is difficult to control. Chemicals can be used in the soil, but that often is not desirable. Covering crops with netting can prevent the adult females from landing to lay eggs, but this is a chore. Another idea is to introduce beneficial nematodes that will attack the maggots to the soil.

How should onions be harvested and stored?

Onions can be grown from seed, transplants, or sets. It is gener-ally thought that the bulbs grow largest from sets started in early spring. Onions can be harvested early as spring onions or left in the ground and pulled towards the end of summer. Break off flower stalks as they develop.

The most common method of harvesting is to pull onions from the ground when the tops of three-fourths of the crop are bent over. I recommend that, when most of the tops have fallen, you knock over by hand those that are still standing. This encourages the proper sealing of the bulb, which results in better preservation. The bulbs should be left in the ground for a couple of days after the tops have been knocked over. Then pull them out and allow them to dry in the sun for a day or two. Next, place them in a garage or shed where they will receive good air circulation and can dry further.

After about seven days, the dry tops should be cut off about an inch above the bulb and the bulbs placed in onion bags or old panty hose to hang in a cool, dry area for the winter. I am convinced that, for keeping quality, the best variety of onion to use is the 'Stuttgarter'.

Are there many pests to look for on onions?

Few insects other than the root maggot will bother onions, but there are several diseases that can affect them. Several fungi attack them in field crops, but most of these are rarely encountered in a garden.

Botrytis neck rot often appears on onions in storage. The neck of the onion shrivels, and the bulb becomes soft and discolored and begins to smell. The disease is present in the soil as the onions grow. Neck rot is usually only a problem when the bulb is damaged and the onions are not properly cured. Doubled-necked onions, which do not keep well, are prone to the disease. Check stored onions occasionally and remove any soft onions to prevent the spread of the disease.

When is the best time to plant garlic?

Although garlic can be planted in early spring, I find that I get larger bulbs when I plant it in October. I purchase a bulb of garlic from the store and break it into individual cloves, or bulblets. After tilling a row of soil, I press the individual cloves into the ground about four inches apart with their pointed tips about one inch below the surface of the soil.

As the bulbs grow the following year, they form flower stalks from the centers of the bulbs. I break off these stalks to conserve energy for the bulbs and encourage them to grow larger. By the end of August they can be pulled from the ground.

There is another type of garlic called 'Elephant' garlic. More closely related to the leek, this garlic is milder and has fewer, but much larger, cloves. 'Elephant' garlic produces a stalk that forms a large, round cluster of purple flowers.

Is horseradish a hardy perennial?
How should I plant it?

The roots of horseradish are indeed hardy. They are best planted in the early spring and will be ready for harvest in October and November. Although they grow in various soils, they do best in a rich, moist, sandy loam. Even though the roots are hardy, it is best to harvest them annually. If roots remain in the ground for more than a year, they become woody. Cut off the small lateral roots, and save those that contain stem buds for spring planting. In the spring, set the young roots in the ground about twelve inches apart and two inches below the surface.

It is easy to overfeed horseradish. Too much nitrogen will produce plants with many leaves but a small root.

Is it all right to plant potatoes that were purchased at a supermarket?

You can use supermarket potatoes as seed potatoes, but I do not advise it because all you know about them is that they are potatoes. Seed potatoes that are for garden use have been certified to be a particular variety and are as free of disease as possible. They cost a bit more than the others, but you're more sure of a good crop.

There is another important consideration when you plant potatoes. They like an acid soil, one with a pH of about 5.8. If you add lime to the garden in early spring, remember not to lime the area where you want to plant potatoes.

When planting, be certain that each piece of tuber has at least two eyes. Cover the pieces with only two to three inches of soil. I have heard of some cases in which the potatoes are just pushed into the soil and then covered with four to six inches of leaves. This might be worth a try.

For a pleasant change, try some yellow-fleshed varieties, such as 'Yukon Gold' or 'Augsburg Gold'.

What is the worst pest of the potato?

Potatoes can suffer from many diseases and pests. So select varieties that are as disease-resistant as possible. Some varieties are also resistant to insects. In all my years of gardening, the pest I have encountered most often is the Colorado potato beetle. I have also found it feeding on eggplants and tomatoes, which are related to the potato.

The adults overwinter in dead plants or weeds and come out in early May. The adult beetles are less than half an inch long and are yellow-orange with black stripes. After they mate, the females lay clusters of eggs on the underside of leaves. These hatch into orange, humped larvae with black spots. As they emerge, they join the adults in eating the foliage of the potato plants. They are voracious eaters and devour a plant almost overnight.

The best method of control is to pick off the adults as you find them. If you see egg masses on the foliage, remove the infected leaves. Dusting the plants with an insecticide, such as Sevin, also can be effective, but it will not affect the larvae eating from the underside of the leaves.

Why do some of my potatoes have holes in them when I harvest them?

The holes in the potatoes are probably caused by the larvae of the click beetle. We call the larvae wireworms. The wireworm also feeds on beans, corn, onions, carrots, beets, and strawberries. The larvae can grow to be one and a half inches long. They are yellowish to dark brown and have definite segments. Some require up to five years to complete the process of metamorphosis.

Tubers are a special delight for the wireworm, but affected potatoes are still good to eat. I recommend that they be set aside when you dig up the crop and used first. Some chemicals can be used to kill the larvae, or you can introduce nematodes to do them in.

Can potatoes be planted in the fall?

I have never planted potatoes in the fall but I know a man who has with success. He digs the furrows, cuts the seed potato into pieces, and lays the pieces in the rows. Then he covers the rows with three feet of leaves for the winter. The leaves compact and decompose and in the spring the potato stems emerge. His potatoes are some of the largest I've ever seen. The shape of the potatoes is perfect, since they did not have to conform to any soil barriers, such as rocks. By the way, the gentleman lives in central Pennsylvania, not in the South.

Why don't early flowers on cucumbers form fruits?

Many of the popular varieties of cucumber are gynoecious, which means that the cucumber produces both male and female flowers on the same plant. Often the first flowers are male and thus will not yield fruit. After about a week, female flowers form and, if pollinated, produce cucumbers.

Why do cucumbers sometimes taste bitter?

The exact cause of bitterness is not understood. Some varieties seem to be more prone to bitterness than others. This could mean that it has a genetic basis. The age of the plant might be a factor, because bitterness often occurs near the end of the growing season. Environmental conditions may also play a role. When cucumbers are grown in normal summer temperatures with proper amounts of fertilizer and water, they seldom taste bitter.

The fruits should be harvested before they begin to turn yellow. Once they have started turning yellow, they are overly mature, will not keep well, and do not taste very good.

My cucumber and squash plants sometimes start to die in the garden before harvest. Why?

There is a group of diseases that are common not only to cucumbers but also to squash, pumpkins, cantaloupes, and watermelons. Prevention is worth a pound of cure. When buying seed, look for those varieties that are resistant to disease, and when watering the plants, keep moisture off the foliage. Immediately remove any plant that is diseased.

Many diseases that affect members of the cucumber family overwinter in affected plant debris or in the seed. So even a rotting squash should be taken out of the garden. Do not compost any diseased plant material.

Mildew, both downy and powdery varieties, is often a problem. Powdery mildew appears as white spots on the underside of older leaves. Soon the entire leaf becomes white and drops off. The fruit is then exposed to the sun and usually does not ripen properly. Powdery mildew is more prevalent when summers are hot.

Downy mildew causes small yellow spots to appear on the leaves. Over time, they enlarge and eventually the affected leaves die. The disease progresses from the bottom of the plant to its top. Target spot and leaf spot are two other diseases that cause foliage to develop spots. Leaf spot is recognized by the presence of brown spots with white centers, often with a yellow halo around the spots.

Scab affects cucumbers and cantaloupes. The fruit develops brown, corky spots usually less than half an inch in diameter. The disease can also attack young stems and petioles, girdling them and causing them to die. Warm, humid conditions help scab flourish. Cottony leak, belly rot, and wet rot are three other diseases that can affect the fruit.

Bacterial wilt and fusarium wilt cause foliage to yellow and wilt during the heat of the day. The plants look like they need water, and often the leaves look fine when checked the next morning. The wilt will recur for several days and eventually the plants will die.

Members of the cucumber family are susceptible to several diseases. You should select disease-resistant varieties, because there is no cure once the plants have been infected.

Are insects a problem for cucumbers?

The striped and spotted cucumber beetles are the most bothersome pests. Both are about half an inch long. The striped critter is yellow with three black stripes down the back of its wings. The spotted beetle is yellowish with eleven black spots on its back. The adults overwinter in plant material and in the spring start feeding on the foliage of many types of plants. After mating, the female lays her eggs in the soil. Upon hatching, the larvae begin feeding on the roots and stems of the plants. As if the larvae didn't cause enough damage with their eating, they can carry several diseases, including wilt, which they pass on to the plant. Control the pest by removing the adults by hand or by using insecticidal soap or another appropriate product.

What can I do to control squash vine borer in my garden?

The vine borer is probably the most difficult squash pest to control. In late June, this caterpillar bores into the stems of squash, eating as it goes. Soon the vine wilts and dies. In the past, gardeners controlled the pest by spraying the base of the vines with rotenone each week for a month. Now, the chemical most recommended is Sevin. It, too, should be sprayed once a week for four weeks.

There are control techniques to use in place of spraying. You can buy beneficial nematodes and introduce them into the soil. They reproduce rapidly and infect and kill the larvae of many insects, and they are not harmful to earthworms.

Friends of mine have tried a couple of other control methods with some success. The first is to place a ring of aluminum foil around the base of each squash plant. The foil reflects the bright sky and confuses the female moths, which are looking for a place to deposit eggs. The second method is even simpler: place mothballs around the base of the squash vines to repel the insects.

If you don't use anything to discourage or repel the borer, check the vines daily beginning in late June. If you discover a hole, cut out the borer. Then cover the cut with a couple of inches of soil. Roots will form on the buried stem.

Is the squash bug the same as the squash vine borer?

No, the names refer to two kinds of insect. The squash bug is a true bug and goes through incomplete metamorphosis, so there is no larval stage in its life cycle. The adult spends the winter under debris in the garden, in or under buildings, or almost any place where it can find protection. After the squash is planted and starts to grow, the adult lays orange- to brown-colored eggs on the underside of the leaves. The eggs hatch into colorful nymphs with red legs and head and a green body. Within a few hours the red color darkens. After the first several molts, the nymph becomes gray. In about five weeks it becomes an inch-long adult.

Both the nymphs and the adults feed by sucking the juices out of the leaves and stems and then the fruits. If there aren't too many bugs, the damage will be tolerable. If population levels are too high, however, you should spray with insecticidal soap, or better yet, remove the bugs by hand and destroy them.

The 'Butternut' and 'Royal Acorn' squashes are resistant to squash bugs.

If space is limited, should I plant summer or winter squash?

I think you should make room for both. It really is just a matter of taste, though. I happen to like both. Summer squash, such as zucchini, tastes delicious steamed, stuffed, used in casseroles, or fried. A new yellow summer squash on the market called 'Sun Drops' is very productive. The fruits are oval and grow to about four inches long.

Acorn squash is a winter squash that is easy to prepare and tastes great. Cut it in half, clean out the seeds, and bake it with some butter and brown sugar or maple syrup. Some of the winter squashes are also used to make "pumpkin" pies.

Are there such things as seedless watermelons?

Yes, seedless watermelons do exist. The biology and genetics of their development are a bit complicated, and the melons still have some small, white, soft seeds, which are edible. Although the plants produce sweet fruit, I do not believe they have the flavor of some of the more common seeded varieties. Besides, half the fun of eating watermelon is spitting the seeds!

What are some vegetables that can be planted for fall harvest? When should they be planted?

In the spring it is important not to plant many vegetables while there is still a chance for frost. Likewise, fall crops must be set in the garden so they have sufficient time to grow and develop before the first frost of fall arrives. There is no one date that is accurate for planting because we simply cannot know when the frost will first arrive. But there are some guidelines that can be helpful.

Transplants of cabbage, cauliflower, and broccoli should be planted six to eight weeks before the first expected fall frost. Remember, these plants can take light frosts. Beans, lettuce, peas, and carrots need to be planted from seed seven to ten weeks before the first frost.

All of these crops should be planted just as you would plant them in the spring. When making selections, it is essential that you pay attention to the maturation date on the seed package. Some varieties are ready for harvest before others. The maturation date is used to calculate planting time. If, for instance, the green beans require sixty days to mature and the first expected frost date is October 25, the seeds need to be planted by August 25. It is better to plant a bit early than a little too late, so you might want to get the seed in by August 15. That gives you a ten-day cushion.

What are some of the tried and tested varieties of vegetables?

It should be understood that most gardeners find varieties that work well for them. The vegetables might grow better, taste better, get larger, or whatever. Look at the list of common vegetables and common varieties that many people do well with.

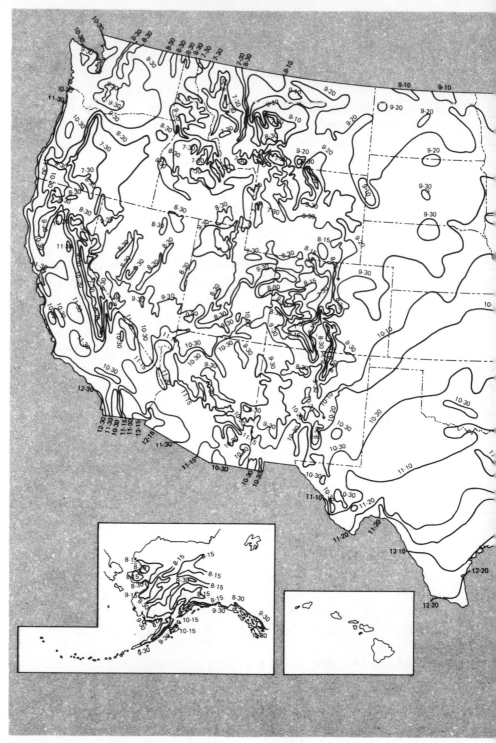

Average Dates of First Killing Frost in Fall

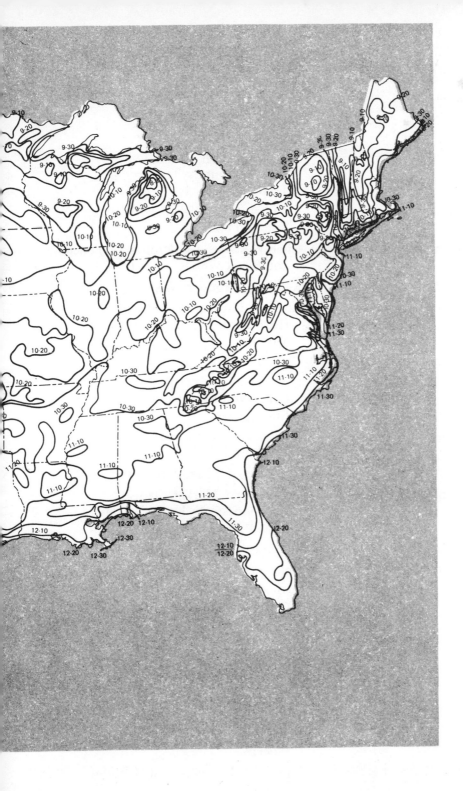

COMMON VEGETABLES AND COMMON VARIETIES

Vegetable	Varieties
Asparagus	Martha Washington, Mary Washington
Bean, bush snap	Blue Lake Bush, Greencrop, Royal Burgundy, Tendercrop, Tendergreen
Bean, pole snap	Blue Lake Pole, Kentucky Wonder, Romano Pole
Bean, bush wax	Cherokee Wax, Goldcrop Wax, Pencil Pod Black Wax
Bean, pole wax	Kentucky Wonder Wax
Bean, bush lima	Burpee's Improved, Fordhook 242, Henderson Bush Lima, Jackson Wonder
Bean, pole lima	Christmas, King of the Garden
Beet	Cylindra, Detroit Dark Red, Early Wonder, Burpee's Golden, Ruby Queen
Broccoli	Calabrese, Italian Green Sprouting, Waltham 29
Brussels sprout	Catskill, Long Island Improved
Cabbage	Copenhagen Market, Danish Ballhead, Early Jersey Wakefield, Golden Acre, Stonehead Hybrid
Cabbage, red	Mammoth Red Rock, Red Acre
Cantaloupe	Delicious 51, Hearts of Gold, Iroquois
Carrot	Danvers Half Long, Imperator, Red Cored Chantenay, Scarlet Nantes
Cauliflower	Early Snowball, Self-blanche
Celery	Golden Self-blanching, Utah 52-70
Corn	Golden Bantam, How Sweet It Is, Iochief, Silver Queen
Cucumber	Straight Eight
Eggplant	Black Beauty
Honeydew	Crenshaw
Kohlrabi	Early Purple Vienna, Early White Vienna

Lettuce, head	Bibb, Buttercrunch, Great Lakes, Iceberg
Lettuce, leaf	Black-Seeded Simpson, Grand Rapids, Oak Leaf, Salad Bowl
Okra	Clemson Spineless
Onion, red	Red Hamburger
Onion, yellow	Stuttgarter, Yellow Sweet Spanish
Onion, white	White Sweet Spanish
Parsnip	Hollow Crown
Pea, green	Green Arrow, Little Marvel, Wando
Pea, edible pod	Sugar Snap
Pea, snow	Oregon Sugar Pod II
Pepper, hot	Hungarian Wax, Jalapeno M
Pepper, sweet bell	California Wonder
Pepper, sweet non-bell	Sweet Banana
Potato	Kennebec, Red Pontiac
Pumpkin	Jack-O'-Lantern
Radish	Champion, Cherry Belle, Sparkler, White Icicle
Rhubarb	Victoria
Rutabaga	Purple-Top Yellow
Spinach	Bloomsdale Long Standing
Squash, summer	Burpee's Fordhook Zucchini, Early Prolific Straightneck, Early Yellow Summer Crookneck
Squash, winter and other	Buttercup, Table Queen Acorn, Waltham Butternut
Sweet potato	Centennial
Swiss chard	Fordhook Giant, Rhubarb Chard
Tomato, cherry	Gardener's Delight, Red Cherry
Tomato, standard	Beefsteak, Better Boy, Big Girl, Burpee's VF Hybrid, Celebrity, Early Girl, and many other favorites
Turnip	Purple-Top White Globe
Watermelon	Charleston Gray, Crimson Sweet, Sugar Baby

5

Growing Jams and Jellies (Small Fruits)

Most of us garden because we enjoy doing it. To spend time outside tilling the soil and pulling weeds is often more fun than it is work. Although there are rewards in just seeing things grow and develop, it's only when we taste the vegetables or spread the jam on the morning toast that we really know what gardening is all about. And the small fruit that goes into that special jam is well within our grasp, both figuratively and physically.

Small-fruit gardening involves growing shrubs, vines, brambles, and herbaceous perennials that produce edible fruit. Blueberries, gooseberries, and currants are found on rather compact shrubs, and grapes and the hardy kiwis on vining plants. Brambles such as blackberries and raspberries can be grown easily in the backyard, but they also are found in the wild. Last but not least are strawberries, which are found on crowns that come back year after year.

Many people think that limited space prohibits growing many of these fruits in the landscape. However, as you will see, some of these plants actually can be used as landscape plants. They have attractive summer foliage, produce flowers, bear bright and edible fruit and, in some cases, display colorful fall foliage. Of all the small fruits, though, it is the strawberry that is found in most gardens, even when space is limited. When you buy strawberry plants, don't think of the work involved in planting and caring for them. Think of fresh strawberry pie, strawberries topping your ice cream, fresh strawberries on your morning cereal, and strawberry shortcake. You see, these are the essence of gardening!

What type of soil do strawberries need?

Strawberries do their best when the soil pH is between 5.8 and 6.8. They grow in a variety of soils except where drainage is poor. It is best to plant strawberries where potatoes, peppers, eggplants, and tomatoes have not been grown previously because these plants can harbor diseases that will harm strawberries.

What is the best time of the year to plant strawberries? How should they be planted?

Set out strawberry plants as early in the spring as possible. Light frosts will not harm them. When planted early, they can establish themselves so that they may even produce flowers the first year. Remove these flowers, though, so that the plant's energy is used for growth. Be sure to water the plants regularly if rains do not provide sufficient moisture.

The location you select for the strawberry patch should receive full sunlight; strawberries do not produce well in shady areas. It is best to prepare the site in the fall. Remove as many weeds as possible and then rototill the soil to a depth of about eight inches. You may have to apply an herbicide to kill the weeds before tilling. You should take a soil sample and have it analyzed so that you know what, if anything, needs to be done to ready the soil for spring planting.

In the spring, till the soil again and work in an appropriate fertilizer based on the results of the analysis. Set the strawberry crowns in the ground so that they are at soil level. They can be spaced from six to twenty-four inches apart in rows; however, I believe that ten to twelve inches is adequate. Rows should be about three feet apart. Don't spread the roots out near the surface because strawberries tend to be shallow rooted. Instead, open the root system, but keep the roots deep. Cover them with soil, then water them, using a liquid fertilizer. In late spring, side-dress the plants with 10–10–10 fertilizer and keep the bed watered.

It is important to keep weeds out of the strawberries. It is also essential, when working in the garden during the summer, not to cultivate too closely to the plants and not to cover the crowns with

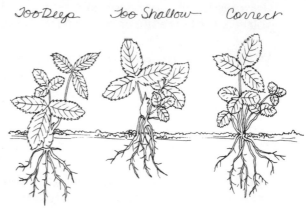

Too Deep   Too Shallow   Correct

Set the crown of the strawberry plant at ground level. Burying it with either soil or mulch will smother the plant. Setting it too high will expose the roots, which tend to grow shallow.

soil. Water the plants well in late summer because this is when the cells that will form next season's flowers are developing, and the development of these cells can affect the size of the fruit.

Should strawberries be mulched?

You do not need to mulch around the plants during the growing season except to keep the berries off the ground. In the winter, the plants should be mulched for protection. After the soil has frozen, apply straw, pine needles, or salt hay, and cover the plants with only enough mulch that the tops of the plants are visible. Burying the crowns in mulch will smother the plants.

In the spring, as the plants begin to grow, remove the mulch cover. Use mulch between the rows to retard weed growth and conserve moisture. As the plants begin to flower, place it under the plants to keep the flowers and fruit off the ground.

Should all new runners be left on the mother plant?

About six weeks after planting, strawberry plants begin to form runners. Each mother plant can produce three or more runners, although no more than five daughter plants should be allowed to develop from an original plant. When a runner reaches a length of about nine inches, a daughter plant will form. The runner continues to grow and more daughter plants form. Remove all but the first daughter plant on each runner.

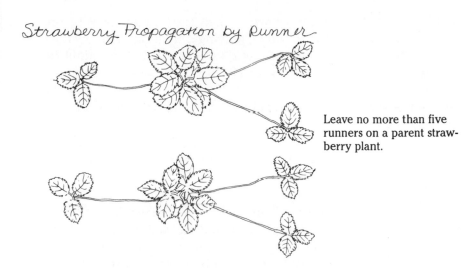

Strawberry Propagation by Runner

Leave no more than five runners on a parent strawberry plant.

As the daughter plants grow, arrange them around the mother plant, keeping them nine inches away from the parent and at least nine inches from one another. Place a small rock on each runner to keep it in place, but remove the rock when the new plant takes root.

Many people feel it is a waste to destroy any new plants that are produced by a mother plant, but the first plant produced by a runner is more vigorous than the rest and will be better established than those produced later in the summer.

How do I maintain a strawberry bed, and how long will it last?

As on most topics of horticulture, there are many opinions about how long a strawberry bed lasts. I have friends who have maintained the same bed for ten years. They claim that it is still very productive but that many of the berries it produces now are not as large as were earlier berries. I think the average life of a good strawberry patch is three to four years. An extreme in strawberry gardening would be to maintain two beds, one that will produce this year's fruit and another planted to produce next season's fruit. This method involves planting a bed each year.

It you don't want to replant every year or so, you can renovate the beds to extend their productive life. As soon as harvest is complete, mow the beds with a lawn mower. The blade setting should be such that it removes most of the leaves, but high enough that it does not injure the crowns. Then turn under most of the daughter plants with the rototiller, leaving only a six-inch row containing the mother plants and any daughter plants that might be growing there. Next, fertilize with 10–10–10 at a rate of one and a half pounds per hundred square feet. Finally, thoroughly water the bed and be certain it receives enough water during the rest of the growing season.

What are some good varieties of strawberries to grow?

I find that one of the best varieties is 'Earliglow'. Not only is it one of the first to flower each spring, but its berries have a great flavor, the plants are disease-resistant, and the fruit freezes well and makes great jelly. 'Honeoye' produces lots of very large berries. 'Sparkle' is another variety that should be considered for the garden; it produces later in the season. Using 'Sparkle' with one of the other varieties will extend the picking season, which means you get to enjoy fresh strawberries longer.

When and how should the strawberries be harvested?

Berries usually can be harvested about one month after the blossoms appear. Never pick a berry that is not entirely red; any green or white on the berry means it is not ripe. Check the plants every two days. When picking, do not squeeze the berry and pull it off the plant. Rather, hold the berry and pinch off its stem.

Don't be surprised if the berries harvested later in the season are smaller than those harvested earlier. Size diminishes as the season progresses. Harvest for each variety should last for two to three weeks.

How can I keep birds away from my berries?

If you have ever grown strawberries, you know that there are many critters that try to get the berries before you do. Birds are the most notorious pests, and of the birds, mockingbirds and starlings are the worst. They love to eat bright red berries. To prevent this, place netting over the berries when they start to ripen. This will stop most bird damage, but some persistent birds have been known to get under the netting to obtain a prize berry.

One method used to frighten birds from a patch is to set out an inflatable owl or snake. Real owls and snakes prey on small birds, and most of the little feathered guys will stay clear of them and anything that looks like them.

Do strawberry plants attract many pests?

When grown properly, strawberries have few pests compared with other plants. However, the slug is often encountered in the berry season. Slugs, which come out at night, love to eat sections out of the strawberries as the fruit ripens. But sprinkling the slugs with salt will end the pest and the problem.

Various root weevils can be a nuisance. The larval form of the strawberry root, black vine, rough strawberry root, and clay-colored root weevils all feed on—what else—roots. If any of these is a problem, you should select a site for the bed where strawberries have not been grown before.

Whiteflies, aphids, and spider mites can damage strawberries, too. Insecticidal soap is very effective on these pests and is safe to use. Malathion can control Japanese beetles and spittle bugs, which might not be affected by insecticidal soap.

Gray mold botrytis, which attacks the fruit, is the cause of greatest concern. It usually infects berries that come into contact with the soil. Soft tan circles on the fruit, which gradually enlarge, indicate the presence of the disease. The best way to prevent the problem is to keep the berries off the ground by mulching around the plants. Once gray mold attacks the berries, it is difficult to cure for the season.

Various wilt diseases can devastate strawberry beds, so be sure to select disease-free cultivars. The resistance characteristic is usually mentioned on the tag that comes with the plants. Because some of the wilts also attack tomatoes, peppers, and other vegetables, it is best to plant strawberries where these other plants have not previously been grown.

Are raspberries easy to grow? How much space do they need?

Raspberries are one of the easiest fruits to grow in the garden and also one of the hardiest. They grow best in the northeastern part of the United States and in Canada's Atlantic provinces. If you've tried to buy the berries at a roadside farm stand, you know they are expensive. So if you like raspberry jam as much as I do, or if you like the berries on cereal or ice cream, plant some berry brambles.

When planting raspberries in rows, space them three feet apart in rows that are six feet apart. If you intend to grow a dozen plants or so, you will need about one hundred fifty square feet. But if space is limited, do not overlook the possibility of setting a couple of plants in the back corner of your property. You will not have enough fruit to freeze, but you will have some fresh berries each summer.

What is the best kind of raspberry to grow?

There are two ways to characterize raspberries. The first is by the color of the berry, which can be red, yellow, black, or purple. The yellow raspberry actually is a variety of the red, and the purple is a hybrid of the black and red. There also is a salmon-colored berry, which is a form of the black raspberry.

The second way raspberries are characterized is by the number of crops produced in a year. Most varieties have single-season crops of berries that mature in early summer. The others are called ever-bearing and produce two crops: one in early summer and the other in the fall.

The most common raspberry is the single-crop red raspberry. This variety accounts for more than seventy-five percent of the raspberries grown in the United States. It seems to be the hardiest variety and the only one that will grow in most of Canada.

What is the difference between red and black raspberries?

Actually, there are several differences other than color. Red raspberries are propagated from root suckers, whereas black raspberries are propagated by tip layering. The berries of the red grow from the main stem, which does not possess laterals; the berries of the black form on side branches or laterals. In addition, the ever-bearing red raspberry produces berries in the fall on the ends of canes that came up that spring. During the following summer, berries will develop on the lower portions of these canes.

There is one other important difference: black raspberries are much more susceptible to disease than are red ones. If you want to grow black raspberries, use only plants propagated by tissue culture. These will be free of disease and should be productive for years.

What type of soil do raspberries need?
When and how should they be planted?

Raspberries enjoy a well-worked, organic soil that is slightly acidic. Excessive soil moisture can be a problem. Select a site in a sunny location. In the summer or fall before you want to plant the raspberries, kill the weeds in the area and work up the soil. Work in some 10–10–10 fertilizer, about two cups per one hundred square feet. You also might cover the area with an inch of manure and work it into the soil. As with strawberries, it is wise not to plant raspberries where tomatoes, potatoes, eggplants, and peppers have been grown.

Plant bare-root raspberry stock in the early spring. Planting bare root saves money, and the likelihood of success with this method is as great as it is with planting raspberries that were grown in containers. Set the plants in the ground at the same depth they had been growing. Once you have planted them, cut the canes back. On red raspberries, leave an eight-inch "handle." On black raspberries, the handles can be a source of infection, so cut them back to ground level.

Do raspberries need mulch?

Raspberries do not have to be mulched but, generally speaking, mulching helps. Young plants need to be kept free of weeds. Mulching will prevent weed growth, conserve soil moisture, prevent the heaving of the plants in the winter, and keep the soil cooler in the summer. Proper applications of mulch also have been found to encourage more-vigorous cane growth.

Should raspberries be pruned?

Raspberries need to be pruned twice each year. Red raspberries should be pruned in late winter before growth starts. The plants are dormant at that time in the growth cycle, so the process is called dormant pruning. Prune, or "head back," the cane tips slightly, removing only the portions that might have been killed by the cold of winter. Pruning back too severely might eliminate the most productive portions of the canes. When dormant pruning, be sure to cut out any weak or spindly canes, too. These will never set many berries.

Remember that red raspberries have biennial canes. They flower and set fruit in the second year of growth, then die. You should prune out the second-year canes right after the fruit is harvested.

Black raspberries also have biennial canes and need to be pruned after harvest. A difference between red and black raspberries is that the black need summer pruning. The berries of the black are produced on lateral branches off the main canes, so in the summer, when the canes are about two feet tall, cut three to four inches off the developing canes. This will encourage the growth of strong lateral branches.

During late winter, prune the laterals to a length of about twelve inches to encourage the growth of more and larger fruit. While dormant pruning, cut out any weak, diseased, or broken canes.

What are some of the hardy raspberry varieties?

'Latham' is probably the most popular red raspberry. It produces large fruits of good quality. If the area in which you live is extremely cold in winter, I would suggest planting 'Boyne'. Some say this variety is a bit sweeter than the 'Latham', and of course, it is hardier.

If you want to plant an ever-bearing variety, try 'Heritage'. This variety is extremely winter-hardy and produces medium-sized fruits. The summer crop matures in the latter part of June, and the fall crop should be ready for harvest by August or September.

'Cumberland' and 'Bristol' are two of the most widely available black raspberries. Both produce large, firm berries, and they are adaptable to many growing conditions.

What pests attack raspberries?

The raspberry fruitworm is probably one of the most common pests. The adult fruitworm, a beetle, overwinters in the soil, then in the spring begins feeding on the developing leaves, buds, and stems. The adults mate and lay their eggs on the plants. The larvae then feed on the developing fruit, causing it to drop. To control raspberry fruitworm, spray with Sevin three times at intervals of seven to ten days in the spring as foliage and buds begin to grow.

The rednecked cane borer and the tree cricket also can cause damage from time to time. Consult your local agricultural extension office for recommended methods to control these critters in your area.

There are several diseases that damage raspberries. Mosaic virus is one of the worst. You can dramatically reduce the likelihood of this and other diseases by selecting disease-resistant varieties. In addition, get rid of wild raspberry populations that might be in the area; they can harbor disease.

How do I grow and prune blackberries?

Plant blackberries just as you would black raspberries, and prune them just as you would black raspberries, with one exception: during summer pruning, leave about three feet of cane when you prune the terminals rather than cut three to four inches off when they reach two feet, as you would with raspberries. Blackberries also produce fruit on second-year growth so cut off the canes after they have finished producing their summer crop.

Can blackberries be used as landscape plants?

Blackberries can be grown in the landscape if you have sufficient space. They should be planted and cared for much like the black raspberry. Blackberries develop suckers from the roots, so you'll have to prune to prevent their taking over the yard. If you can spare an area of about four-by-four feet, you should be able to produce enough berries to enjoy some fresh ones and even to make jam. Plant one bramble in each corner of the plot.

Most of us are familiar with wild blackberry varieties. Horticultural breeding has produced new varieties that yield larger berries with smaller seeds. Actually, there are several forms of blackberries. The most common ones have stiff, erect canes. There is, however, a trailing form of blackberry that is referred to as the dewberry. Two other types of trailing blackberries, known as the loganberry and the boysenberry, are on the West Coast. The trailing forms generally do not grow well in the North; cold temperatures seem to be the limiting factor.

Can wild blackberries be transplanted from the fence row to the garden?

Technically, the answer is yes. Wild blackberries can be transplanted from the fence row to the garden, and if it is done properly, they will grow successfully and produce fruit. But the experts say it is best not to do this. Wild blackberries and other wild brambles can harbor a number of pests so bringing wild plants to the garden could cause the spread of disease and insects. It is usually recommended that when planting brambles in the garden, any wild forms in the area be destroyed to prevent contamination.

The diseases and insects that affect blackberries are the same as those that attack raspberries.

What kinds of blueberry can be grown successfully in the garden?

There are several species of blueberries and the requirements necessary for growth depend on the species. The lowbush blueberry is a common wild fruit found in Maine. It also grows wild over thousands of acres in eastern Canada. These blueberries are harvested by hand and produce yields of close to a thousand pounds per acre. It is interesting to note that periodic burning is necessary to keep wild populations productive. Unfortunately, there are no cultivars of this blueberry available for home gardens.

Highbush blueberry is the variety most gardeners grow. There are cultivars that will grow in Zones 5 to 9. Gardeners in the South can plant a species known as the rabbit-eye blueberry. Several cultivars are available and they will grow in a wider range of conditions than will the lowbush or highbush types.

Can highbush blueberries be grown in any soil?

Soil probably is the most important consideration when you plant blueberries. Blueberry plants produce very fine, fibrous roots. Clay soils are too heavy for proper root development because they usually do not drain well. Newly planted blueberries will begin to grow in clay soils but often will die within months. Sandy soils, although open, often do not have sufficient organic material. They also do not hold water and tend to dry too rapidly for blueberries.

The best soil is a sandy loam with an abundance of organic material. If your soil is not satisfactory, you can grow blueberries in raised beds with an appropriate soil mix. Blueberries are shallow-rooted plants, so the beds do not have to be deep. Frequent waterings will ensure that the plants do not dry out.

Soil pH is another important concern. Blueberries are acid-loving plants and need a soil pH of 4.5 to 5.2.

How should I prepare an area for planting blueberries?

It is best to prepare a site for blueberries the summer before you plant them. The first step is to select a site that drains well. Either pull the weeds or apply a systemic herbicide to ensure that their roots as well as their tops are killed. (Be sure to read and follow label directions.) Then work several inches of sand and peat moss into the soil with a rototiller. If you have compost, use it instead of the peat moss. Work the soil to a depth of about one foot. Have the soil tested in the fall to be certain it is at the proper pH. If the test shows that the pH is too high, add ammonium sulfate to the soil to lower the pH to the appropriate level.

When and how should blueberries be planted?

As with most small fruits, spring is the ideal time to establish blueberries. Plants two to three years old usually are available and are the best size for planting. Set them in the prepared beds four to six feet apart in rows six feet apart. If you buy bare-root blueberries, prune their tops by about one-fourth and remove damaged roots and any small branches growing from the bases of the plants. If flowers form in spring after planting, remove them. I know it hurts to do that, but at this stage the plants' energy should be used for growing the roots and shoots rather than flowers.

Two things become important as the blueberries start to grow. If the soil in which they are growing is right for them, it is open and does not hold moisture well, so you must water or irrigate the plants frequently. But heavy watering brings about the second factor—weeds—and blueberries trying to establish themselves do not compete well with weeds. Pulling by hand and tilling are the two best methods of weed control. If you use a rototiller, be sure not to till too deep or get too close to the plants. They can suffer if their young roots are disturbed.

Use several inches of organic mulch around the blueberry plants. The mulch will help suppress weed growth, keep the soil temperature cooler, and reduce the rate of evaporation from the soil.

Are blueberries self-pollinating?

Blueberries are self-pollinating. Experience has shown that planting at least two cultivars for cross-pollination does improve the quallty and quantity of fruit. Try planting 'Blueray' and 'Bluecrop'.

Do blueberries need regular pruning?

Like most plants, blueberries respond to pruning, and the lack of it results in weak plants with spindly stems. These stems may produce many flowers, but the berries will be small.

Blueberries should be pruned in early spring while the plants are dormant. Remove a couple of canes that are more than four years old each winter or early spring. Prune back the tips of the other branches so that about six buds remain. If tips are not pruned back "hard" enough, more fruit will develop but it will be much smaller. Proper pruning will also cause the fruit to ripen earlier. When pruning established plants, it is important to remove stems from the center of the plant, which will open the plant to the sun and reduce the possibility of disease. At the same time, it will increase yields.

Like raspberries, blueberries produce fruit on the growth of the previous season. After harvest, prune lightly to get rid of old and dead wood.

How should blueberries be fertilized?

Test the soil around blueberries every two years. The results will indicate if the soil pH is within acceptable levels and if all necessary soil elements are present. The important thing to remember when fertilizing blueberries is that they are not heavy feeders as are many other fruits. Heavy fertilization could promote considerable vegetative growth and little fruit production. When fertilizers are needed, they should be applied in spring before the buds open.

Blueberries need nitrogen more than any other nutrient, and it is best applied in the form of ammonium nitrogen, which helps acidify the soil. If the soil has a pH below 5, you can use urea. Depending on the soil, you also might need to add phosphorus and potassium. One other element that is important for proper growth is magnesium. Leaves develop reddish veins if the soil lacks enough of this nutrient.

Is it true that currants and gooseberries should not be grown in the landscape?

There is some validity to the statement that currants should not be grown in the landscape. A disease called white-pine blister rust uses certain species of currant and gooseberry plants as a host during its life cycle. Spores of the disease are released in the spring and affect various pines, including the eastern white pine. Over a period of three to six years the pine can die as a result of the infection.

Black currants are most prone to this disease, which weakens the plant and affects production. In many areas, quarantine laws prohibit planting black currants. Most commercially propagated varieties of gooseberries and of red and white currants, however, are resistant to the disease.

Do currants and gooseberries need special growing conditions?

Currants and gooseberries do not require any special care in planting. They can be grown in any garden soil, even a clay loam, provided it does not remain waterlogged for extended periods. At the other extreme, they are sensitive to a lack of water and can drop their foliage if summers are dry.

When selecting a site for currants and gooseberries, choose a place where they will receive some filtered sunlight in the afternoon. This will reduce the drying effect of the sun. But do not plant them too close to large trees or shrubs, which will compete for available water and nutrients.

How and when should currants and gooseberries be planted?

Currants and gooseberries often can be purchased bare root. Most plants are one or two years old and the key is to select those that are well rooted. When planting in rows, space the plants about four feet apart in rows about eight feet apart. Currants and gooseberries tend to drop their foliage early in the fall and produce it early in the spring, so they frequently are planted in the fall. If fall planting is not possible, set them in the ground as early as possible in the spring.

Currants and gooseberries are beautiful plants. Spring flowers, summer fruit, and fall foliage color make them ideal for use in the landscape. Don't confine them to the garden in the backyard.

What care do currants and gooseberries need after they are established?

Currants and gooseberries are heavy feeders and require spring and fall applications of 10–10–10 fertilizer. Mulch around the plants to provide them with moist, cool soil and to discourage weeds.

All varieties of these plants should be pruned in late winter. To keep bushes healthy and productive, remove three- to four-year-old woody stems in late winter. If some branches are getting too long, head them back. The fruit on both currants and gooseberries grows on one-year-old wood and on some older spurs.

What kinds of grapes can I grow? How about those good 'Thompson Seedless' grapes?

I'm afraid it's not possible to grow 'Thompson Seedless' grapes everywhere. California is the major grower of these grapes and produces more than fifty percent of the world's raisins with them. Approximately one-third of California's half a million acres of vineyards is engaged in the production of 'Thompson Seedless'.

There are three classes of grapes, and location determines which ones can be grown. For those of us in northern sections of the United States, the American type is the most common. The 'Concord' is a popular cultivar grown by many gardeners, and the 'Fox' grape is an American variety native to the Northeast.

Another class of grapes is the European type. California grape producers grow many European cultivars because the environmental conditions of California are similar to the areas in Europe from which these cultivars originated. There also are areas in the Northeast where European grapes can be grown, but Massachusetts is the northernmost state. The 'Thompson Seedless', 'Emperor', and 'Tokay' are several of the most popular table grapes in this class.

The third class is the Muscadine. Grapes of this class grow best in the Southeast. Apparently, temperature limits their spread northward. They cannot tolerate temperatures that drop much below ten degrees.

When selecting a site for grapes, what factors should I consider?

Grapes in the Northeast are well adapted to a wide variety of soils as well as pH values, but drainage is the main consideration. A clay loam rich in organic material is probably ideal. Choose a site that allows the grapes to receive full sun and good air circulation. These two considerations will help prevent rot diseases on fruit and mildew on the foliage.

How should grapes be planted?

Plant grapes in the spring and prepare the soil the previous fall. If you are going to plant grape in rows, rototill the length of the row to a width of three feet to remove any weeds and to loosen the soil for easy digging. If the soil is low in organic material, work in peat moss, compost, or manure to a depth of about ten inches. The type of soil will determine the amount you use. At least two inches would be helpful.

In the spring select one-year-old healthy vines that are well rooted. When planting bare-root grapes, make sure you keep the roots moist. Dig the planting holes at eight-foot intervals in rows eight feet apart. Prune broken roots and any that are excessively long. Then spread the roots out in the hole and cover them with soil. When the hole is filled with soil, water the roots and apply a liquid fertilizer. If the soil in the planting hole settles, add more soil. Next, cut the vine back to two buds.

Green manures are often planted between the rows of grapes in the spring. Green manures are crops, such as winter rye, that are grown solely to be worked into the soil. While growing they will hold the soil in place around vines that are grown on sloping terrain, which is a common setting for vineyards. In the fall, they are turned under to improve the quality and fertility of the soil, and the area is replanted the next spring.

What is the best type of trellis to use for grapevines?

Many gardeners install a trellis of posts and wire before they plant grapes. If time does not permit this, put the trellis in before the plants start to grow the second year. I recommend wooden posts rather than metal ones. Although metal posts are easier to get in the ground, they are more prone to bending during the summer when the fruit load is heavy and strong winds are blowing. When possible, use posts of locust, which will last much longer than those made from other woods. Oak will do if locust is not available. Soak the wooden posts, regardless of the type of wood, in a wood preservative to extend their usefulness.

End posts should be six to eight inches square and about ten feet long. The inner posts of the trellis need to be only about four inches thick and eight feet long and set about sixteen feet apart. Set the end posts at an angle, and guy and anchor them.

Use heavy-gauge No. 9 or 10 wire on the wooden framework. Drill small holes through the posts to pass the wire through. If you want a two-wire trellis, place the top wire five and a half to six feet from the ground and the bottom wire three feet from the ground. Tighten the wires each spring and loosen them each fall to prevent the loosening of the end posts over the winter.

How should grapevines be trained and pruned?

The training of grapevines begins soon after the planting. Place a short, sturdy stake in the ground next to the plant for it to use during the second growing season. During the first season allow the plant to grow several shoots. In the following dormant period, select the healthiest shoot and use it as the trunk for the vine. Then prune off the other shoots. Tie the trunk to the stake so that it will grow straight. As spring and summer progress, the vine will continue to grow. When the vine grows a little above the top wire, prune off the growing tip. This will cause lateral buds to open and the vine will send out shoots. Allow only two shoots to grow on each wire, and allow them to follow the wires along the trellis. Remember, the faster the branches can be developed, the earlier grape production can begin. Grapes will grow only from stems that develop from buds on one-year-old canes.

Subsequent annual pruning should be carried out in late winter before the sap starts to flow, although bleeding of the sap at pruning will not harm the vine. The goal of pruning is to remove enough shoots and canes that the plant produces only the quantity of fruit it can support.

The second year's dormant pruning begins with the removal of all stems growing from the trunk other than the four horizontal branches. The four branches should then be fastened to the wire and the stake removed. Prune to the branch any weak or broken shoots. Continue pruning so that there is an eight- to ten-inch space between shoots. Then cut these shoots back so that only two buds remain on each shoot. These remaining pruned shoots are called spurs. The terminals, which are the ends of the branches growing along the wires, will have to be pruned when they reach the posts or neighboring plants.

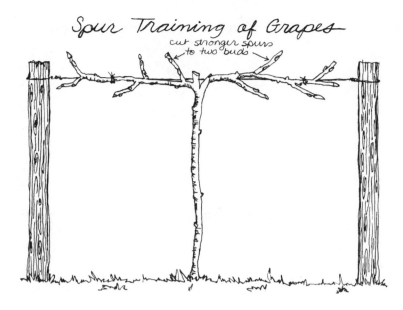

Spur Training of Grapes
cut stronger spurs to two buds

This type of pruning will result in the formation of two shoots from each spur, which will produce clusters of grapes. Then annually, during successive dormant seasons, prune off the poorer shoot and prune the other back to two buds. This method of pruning is a type of spur pruning.

Another method is called cane pruning. Allow two shoots to develop at each arm of the trellis. In the following dormant season, tie one shoot to the trellis and cut it to eight to ten buds. Prune back the other to two buds, forming a spur. The one tied to the trellis will produce the fruit of the year. The spur will develop several shoots.

During the next dormant season, cut off the shoot that was tied to the trellis. Select one of the shoots that developed from the spur and tie it to the trellis. Prune it back to eight to ten buds and then prune the second major shoot back to two buds. Remove any other shoots that might have formed. Continue to prune this way during each successive dormant season.

How and when should grapes be fertilized?

The answer to this question varies with location and soil. Always have the soil analyzed to establish the pH and fertility. When fertilizers are needed, apply them in the spring about a month before the buds open. Grapes respond quickly to applications of nitrogen; too much will cause excess foliage and weak shoots. It is best to check with the experts in your area when

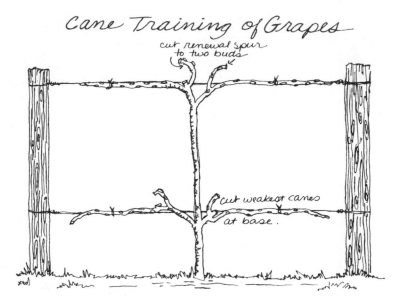

Cane Training of Grapes

cut renewal spur to two buds

cut weakest canes at base.

deciding what type of fertilizer to use and how much to apply.

If the analysis of the soil reveals that the pH is too high and that the soil needs nitrogen, then fertilize with ammonium sulfate because it releases nitrogen quickly. Be sure to follow label directions so the plants are not burned by the fertilizer.

What are some common diseases and insects that affect grapes?

A disease that many of us have encountered when growing grapes is black rot. This usually affects grapes just as they are starting to enlarge and when you are dreaming of all the grape juice you can drink. It first appears as a small, dark spot, often on the bottom of the fruit. In a few days the spot will enlarge and the entire berry will become dark brown and soft. After another week the berry shrivels, becomes hard and black, and drops to the ground or just hangs there, reminding you of the disaster.

Removing fallen grapes and leaves helps control the problem. Dormant spraying in late winter is also important in preventing the disease, as is regular spraying during the growing season. A spray of bordeaux mixture is a favorite form of disease control for many grape growers.

Mildew is another common problem. In late summer, yellow or white spots appear on the leaves, which usually become enveloped by the disease and often fall off. The grapes themselves can become inedible because of the mildew. Proper air circulation around the plant will help prevent the disease.

Japanese beetles are one of the better-known insects that feed on grape leaves. They appear in summer and skeletonize the leaves, which then drop. If defoliation is severe, the grape harvest will be reduced. If you find this pest, you can use Sevin to control it.

There are other insects that enjoy the fruit and foliage of grapes, so prevention of these pests is essential. Dormant spraying helps control insects as well as disease. Horticultural oil sprays will smother any overwintering adults or eggs.

Can I grow kiwi fruit in my garden?

The kiwi is quickly becoming a favorite fruit of many people. Most kiwis purchased in the grocery store are grown in California or are imported. There are several kinds of the vining kiwi plant, which is native to Japan, China, and India. The fruits are rich in phosphorus and calcium, yet low in sodium. A kiwi contains about twenty percent more vitamins than does an orange.

The fuzzy kiwi familiar to most of us can only be grown in warm climates, but at least two others are said to grow well in areas that have cold winters. The hardy kiwi *Actinidia arguta annasnaga* is said to grow where temperatures reach twenty degrees below zero. This kiwi needs to be planted in a sunny area that is protected from wind. It needs good drainage but otherwise is not particular about the soil. Male and female flowers are produced on separate plants, so at least one male plant is needed to supply pollen for the female plants that produce the fruit. One male can provide enough pollen for five female plants.

Another hardy, fuzzless kiwi is the 'Isaai', which is hardy into Zone 4. This plant is said to be a self-fruiting kiwi that produces fruit the year after planting.

Only time will tell how successful these varieties will grow in areas that have cold winters.

How should kiwis be planted?

Kiwis should be planted in spring after the soil has warmed. When planting them in a row, space them about ten feet apart. Kiwis grow much as grapes do and thus need some type of support. Arbors and trellises, even walls, can be used. In northern areas it is advisable to wrap the trunks of kiwis for the first three years to protect them from winter injury. Some people not only wrap the trunk but also mulch the plants to a depth of one foot.

When are kiwis ready for harvest in the East?

In the East, the fuzzless kiwis usually are harvested from late August to October, depending on the variety grown. It is best to let the fruit mature on the vine so it develops a sweet flavor. Some people believe that the smooth kiwis have a better flavor than the fuzzy variety available in stores.

6

Growing Peach Pie and Apple Crisp (Fruit Trees)

Most of us, from the time we could swallow something other than milk, were fed strained fruit. Applesauce was probably the first tree "fruit" we ever tasted. And it's a wonder we still enjoy apples after that introduction. Pears, peaches, and plums, all strained of course, were added to our diets soon after the apples.

As we grew up, our tastes changed and peach pie and apple crisp were a lot more appealing than that strained stuff. Actually, our enjoyment of fruit from trees has probably increased. Today, most of us have several fruit trees in our yards. Apples, peaches, cherries, plums, apricots, nectarines, and pears are some of the common tree fruits grown. Although we find that most of these trees grow well, it is not always so easy to grow quality fruit.

Fruit trees are not very productive when they're left to fend for themselves. A whole host of pests will attack not only the fruit but also the trees. Not only do those pests need to be controlled, but every winter there's all that pruning to be done, too.

I'm not trying to discourage you from planting fruit trees, but if you expect to get a good crop of fruit you must give the trees a lot of care. (Unfortunately, the pies and tarts don't grow on trees.) The work involved in keeping fruit trees healthy, productive, and pest-free is all worth it when you finally get to eat a slice of cherry crumb pie.

What special considerations should be kept in mind when selecting a site for fruit trees?

Actually, there are a couple of factors to remember. To do their best, all fruit trees need a lot of sunlight, so do not place them where they will be shaded. Do not set fruit trees in a valley or in low areas where the soil is often moist; fruit trees do not like "wet feet." In addition, low areas often are colder than surrounding hills or ridges. Trees in these areas could suffer winter dieback, or late spring frosts could injure or kill flower buds. It is best to plant fruit trees on hills or other elevated areas. This will help prevent the problems already mentioned as well as promote good air circulation, which can limit disease problems.

My yard is small, but I would like to grow some fruit trees. Is it possible?

There are several ways to grow fruit trees in areas that are not very large. Most standard trees reach a height of thirty to fifty feet and have a spread of thirty to forty feet. These trees would be much too large to use in a small backyard. There are, however, dwarf varieties. Some are genetic dwarfs, and others were dwarfed by human ingenuity.

Genetic dwarfs usually result from natural mutations that occur in the seed produced by the tree. This change in the seed's genetic material can result in a tree that is much smaller than the parent tree. In some fruits, such as apples, normal stem growth is restricted naturally, resulting in the growth of spurs. Spurs are stems that remain very short and compressed. The spurs produce the flowers and then, if all goes well, the fruit. The growth of short stems limits the size the tree can grow.

Even genetic dwarfs can get rather tall, growing to about three-fourths the size of a standard tree. The growth of genetic dwarfs can be controlled, though. One way to restrict growth is to grow the tree in a container. By limiting root development, the top of the tree stays more compact. Root pruning is another method of controlling top growth, as is regular top pruning.

The best method of keeping many types of fruit trees small is to graft on dwarfing rootstock. Much research in the dwarfing of apple trees has resulted in the development of numerous rootstocks that will dwarf apple trees by ten to sixty percent of standard size. There are dwarf stocks available for most other fruits, although the diversity is not nearly as great as with the apple. Most fruit trees sold in

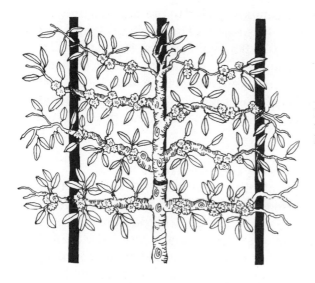

Espalier fruit trees along a
wall or fence if space is
limited.

nurseries and garden centers are grafts grown on dwarfing stock.
They are usually sold as dwarfs or semi-dwarfs. The dwarfs grow to
twelve to fifteen feet, the semi-dwarfs to eighteen to twenty-five
feet.

A second, attractive way of growing fruit in confined areas is
espalier (pronounced "is-pal-yer") training. This system involves
growing the fruit tree on a vertical plane, such as along a wall or a
fence, or on a trellis similar to that used in training grapes. Cordons,
or side arms, are allowed to grow about eighteen inches apart
along the fence or trellis and are then fastened to the supports.
Terminal growth, the growing tips of cordons and trunk, is removed
to control the size of the tree. Sometimes the cordons are shaped to
create various patterns. Espalier training results in attractive trees
that grow in abundance of fruit in confined areas.

Can fruit trees be grown in almost any soil?

Some soils are far better for fruit trees than are others. Most
fruits do not grow well in heavy soils, such as clay, which hold a lot
of water. Only pears are productive in this soil condition. Apples
can grow in clay soil, provided it is not wet for long periods. Most
other fruit trees prefer a well-drained loam.

The other soil extreme is light, sandy soil. Most fruit trees grow
well in this medium if supplied with enough nutrients and water.
Sandy soils do not hold water well and nutrients tend to quickly
leach away, but this situation can be corrected by working in or-

ganic matter. Peat moss and compost added to the soil help prevent rapid drainage of water as well as leaching of nutrients. It also can help keep the soil at a pH of 6 to 6.5, which is best for many fruits.

Where soils are heavy, raised beds can be created for growing fruit trees. These beds must be considerably larger than those used in the vegetable garden. For the average fruit tree, the bed should be about thirty inches deep, five feet square, and filled with a loam soil.

When should fruit trees be planted?

Spring is the best time to plant most fruit trees. The earlier they can be planted in the spring, the more time the roots have to become established. Root systems that are well developed should have little problem supplying water for the plant during the normal climatic conditions of summer. If trees are planted in late spring or summer, they need to be watered regularly. Any newly planted tree should be watered if rainfall is below normal.

Most nurseries sell fruit trees either in containers or bare root. In a few cases it is even possible to buy field-grown trees that are balled and burlapped. Trees in containers were probably potted in late winter by the nursery or the grower. The root systems are not yet well developed, but because the trees are in containers, you will not disturb their roots and can plant them when you are ready. Bare-root fruit trees, however, must be treated differently because there is no soil to protect the roots. As is the situation with most bare-root plants, they must be planted before the buds start to open in spring or after the leaves drop in the fall. It is also important to keep their roots moist before planting so that the root hairs do not dry out.

Bare-root trees are much less expensive than those in containers or those that are balled and burlapped. The money you save on them, though, makes up for the extra care they need to get started.

How should fruit trees be planted?

There is no secret to planting fruit trees. Treat them just as you would any other plant. Just remember to avoid wet, heavy soils. When planting bare-root trees in loam, the soil does not have to be changed. Before planting, be sure to prune off all long or broken roots. Then set the tree in the planting hole so that the graft union

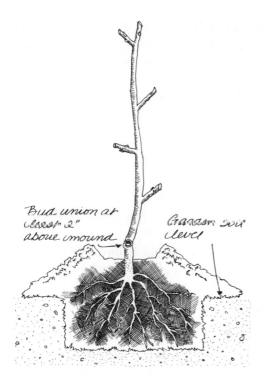

Bud union at
least 2"
above mound

Garden soil
level

When you plant any bare-root tree or shrub, set it so that its bud union is just above soil level.

remains about two inches above the soil level. Cover the roots with soil and tamp it down to get rid of air spaces. When the hole is filled, water the roots with a liquid fertilizer high in phosphorus to promote root growth.

The soil around the root system should be mulched. It is important to keep grass and weeds from growing up around young fruit trees. Weeds compete for water and nutrients and can slow the growth and development of the trees. Keep the mulch away from the tree trunks by several inches; mulch can be a good hiding place for a lot of pesky little rodents. If there are rodents in the area, it would be wise to use tree guards around the trunks.

Is it true that, when planting some fruit trees, two varieties of each are needed?

Most apples and several other fruits need two cultivars, or cultivated varieties, to produce fruit. This requirement has to do with pollination; the pollen they produce is incapable of fertilizing its own flowers. Some plants are self-pollinating, which means that the pollen they produce can be used to fertilize the egg cells found in the base of their own flowers. When plants are self-pollinating no other cultivar needs to be present. All sour cherries are self-pollinating as are most peaches, apricots, and some plums, apples, and pears.

All other tree fruits need to be cross-pollinated to bear fruit. In these cases a second cultivar—a pollinator—is needed. Sweet cherry, for example, needs a pollinator.

There are several ways of accomplishing pollination. The most common is to plant a second variety near the first. The two must be close enough for the insects, primarily honeybees, to carry the pollen. This is the primary means of pollen transfer among fruit trees. The two cultivars also must blossom at the same time. If they don't, cross-pollination cannot occur.

Bees are cold-blooded so they are active only in warm temperatures. It is not surprising, therefore, to find that the best temperatures for pollination are from seventy to eighty degrees. Temperatures below fifty degrees during pollination reduce the likelihood of good fruit set because of improper pollen-tube development or failure of pollen transfer.

A second way of providing a pollinator is to graft the branch of a different cultivar onto the existing tree. This should provide a sufficient quantity of pollen for pollination. Where space is limited, this is an ideal method.

Some nurseries carry what are known as "three-in-one" or "five-in-one" apple trees. These are trees that have been grafted with either two or four other cultivars of apples. These grafts make it possible to harvest several different kinds of apples from one tree.

Why do some tree fruits grow well in colder climates?

Certain types of fruit trees need periods of chilling weather before the flower and leaf buds can break dormancy. Usually the length of chill needed is expressed in a certain number of hours below forty-five degrees. This number varies with the type of fruit and the cultivar. The period of chill that peaches require ranges from 350 to about 1,200 hours.

Cultivars that need only a low number of chill hours can be grown farther south where temperatures are milder and winter doesn't linger. When the required number of chill hours is high, the cultivar must be grown where winters are long and cold.

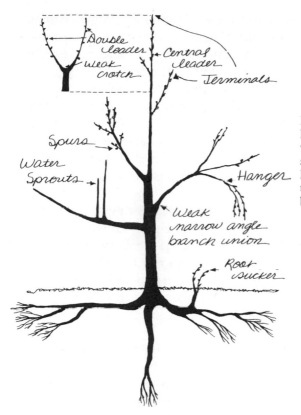

Prune fruit trees to a single leader. Remove hangers, weak branches, water sprouts, and root suckers. Narrow-angled branch unions make for weak branches.

How should fruit trees be pruned?

How fruit trees are pruned varies with variety, cultivar, rootstock, and amount of available growth space. Pruning is done in late winter or early spring and should be completed before the buds begin to swell and enlarge. Fruit tree pruning is almost an art, and proper pruning requires practice and more space for explanation than I have here. I highly recommend that you buy a book specifically on pruning to learn the various techniques that can be followed for the fruit trees you are growing. *Pruning Handbook*, published by Sunset Books, is an excellent reference.

Must fruit trees be sprayed to control pests?

Most fruits are prone to several insect and disease pests, so you may need to spray to ensure that the fruit stays healthy. Usually, the first application of pesticides is applied in late winter following pruning. This application, called dormant spraying, needs to be completed before the buds start to open. It should include a combination of liquid lime sulphur with a horticultural oil. It is a preventative spraying, and its object is to smother any disease spores and overwintering insects, whether they are adults, larvae, or eggs.

Sometimes you must spray throughout the growing season. A typical spraying schedule, after the application of dormant spray, would begin right before the flower buds open followed by an application after the flower petals drop. Thereafter, pesticides should be applied every two weeks until about a month before harvest. The type of pesticide used will be determined by the pest you are trying to control or prevent.

Problems can occur on fruits or on fruit trees even when you spray regularly. If this should happen, get help to see what is causing the problem and how it can be remedied. Remember this: it is much better to eat blemished fruit than to run the risk of eating more chemicals. When possible, therefore, try to find a nonchemical method of control. Insecticidal soap is effective in killing numerous insect pests, and insect traps and lures are inexpensive, nontoxic, and effective.

I should add that if I had an orchard and my livelihood depended on getting the best price I could for my fruit, my attitude might be different. As consumers we need to learn that, when buying fruit, the fruit's outward appearance is not the best criterion. How the fruit was grown and what chemicals were sprayed on it are more important.

How do I prevent deer from nibbling my young fruit trees?

Many of us who live in the country enjoy seeing deer in the backyard. I don't even mind sharing some of the garden's vegetables with them. Yet, they can be a real problem when it comes to fruit trees. How do we control them?

There are several deer repellents on the market. Have you ever smelled them? Some repel me! Universities have tested them, however, and found that they are not effective deterrents. I guess it's good they don't work or our yards would give off terrible odors. Other university research has shown that various types of fencing can be effective in keeping deer from fruit trees. Unless you are into fruit trees in a big way, though, the cost of putting up fencing is prohibitive.

Several novel approaches to deer control have been effective for some people. I use small bars of Ivory soap as a repellent. I place the bars in small mesh bags and hang one bag from each newly planted tree and several in larger trees. They have stopped my deer-nibbling problem.

Two similar methods have worked for friends. In both cases the people made bags out of old panty hose. One gardener placed mothballs in the bags and the other put human hair in the bags. The bags were then hung from the trees. Both people claimed it prevented further damage by deer. The only thing I don't like about these methods is that new mothballs must be added regularly and the hair must be replaced every few months.

What are *pome* fruits?

The three most common pomes are apple, quince, and pear. Pomes are fruits that have a rather paperlike core. Some fruits have a pit or stonelike center—cherries, plums, peaches, and apricots, for example. These fruits are referred to as *drupes*. (By the way, pomology is the study of fruit crops.)

What are some of the most popular apple cultivars?

Apples are considered the most important tree fruit in the United States (and probably the world). Apple trees have proven quite adaptable, and this attribute has led to the development of cultivars suited for many regions of the world. There are more than one thousand cultivars and new varieties are being produced every year. It is here in the United States that the most work is being done on apple development.

The world's most popular apple is the 'Delicious'. It was developed by Stark Nurseries and first appeared in Iowa in 1872. Other popular cultivars include 'Golden Delicious', 'Jonathan', 'McIntosh', 'Rome Beauty', and 'Granny Smith'. Of these, only the green apple 'Granny Smith' and the 'McIntosh' were developed outside this country.

There has been a trend away from growing these cultivars on standard-sized trees. Even orchardists are beginning to use semi-dwarf and dwarf trees, which are easier to care for and harvest from, and which produce good crops.

Are all apples equally good pollinators?

Definitely not! 'Gravenstein', 'Stayman', and 'Winesap' varieties should never be used as pollinators because their pollen is of poor quality. Let me again mention the importance of selecting cultivars that are in bloom at the same time. The 'Lodi' is a popular early blooming apple; 'Northern Spy', 'Granny Smith', and 'Rome Beauty' are late-season varieties.

What causes natural thinning of apples?

Natural thinning is also called natural drop. Apple trees that have a good fruit set can be expected to drop a few apples throughout the summer until harvest. A month or two after flowering, though, there is usually a large drop. This is known as the June drop and is important in controlling fruit load. Often there is a second major drop that occurs several weeks before harvest.

There are numerous reasons for fruit drop. Studies have shown that some cultivars are more prone to drop than others: 'McIntosh', 'Delicious', 'Stayman', and 'Winesap' are some of these. Weather conditions play a role in apple drop as do such factors as shade, nitrogen application, and pest damage.

Why don't my apple trees produce the same amount every year?

There are many reasons why apple trees do not always produce a bumper crop. Weather conditions, environment, and tree health all influence production. Some trees also have a tendency to bear heavily only every other year.

Alternate-year bearing can occur when the fruit is not thinned. Most apple trees set much more fruit than should be permitted to stay on the tree and mature. If the fruit is not thinned during years of heavy set, the fruit could be smaller and of poorer quality, and the branches could even break. Heavy fruit load will draw a large amount of the tree's food reserves, which will cause a light set the following year.

Therefore, if an apple tree has a large fruit set, you must remove some of the fruit while they are still small. If, after the natural fruit drop, which usually occurs in June, there is still too much fruit, thin again. There should be no more than one apple on every six to eight inches of branch. On spur trees there should be one fruit per spur.

Which apple cultivars are best for eating, best for baking, and best for making sauce?

The answer to this question is all a matter of taste, but I'll give you some of my favorites. 'Golden Delicious' is at the top of my list as an eating apple. It is spicy-sweet, juicy yet firm, and it does not brown when sliced for snacks or put in salads. I am looking forward to eating the fruit of the 'Ginger Gold', a new cultivar that is billed to be a better eating apple than 'Golden Delicious'. The world favorite is the 'Red Delicious'. This beautifully shaped red apple is crisp, juicy, and sweet. 'Jonagold' and 'Cortland' are two others that are good eating apples.

For baking three cultivars come to mind. 'McIntosh' is a good all-round apple, but I like it best in pies. The fruits are not the largest, but their white flesh is sweet. Some consider the 'Red Rome Beauty' to be the best baking apple. The medium-sized fruits have firm, tart flesh and a great shelf life. 'Granny Smith' is a cultivar that produces shiny, green apples. Its large, tart fruits are very good in pies and other desserts.

I'm no expert when it comes to making applesauce (and I'm really not that fond of it), but friends tell me the 'Lodi' is one of the best cultivars to use. The fruit flesh is sweet and tangy, and if you don't want to use it for applesauce, I understand it also makes good cider.

What is cedar-apple rust?

Cedar-apple rust is a fungal disease common in some parts of the country where red cedar and other evergreens grow wild. Both the apple and the cedar serve as hosts for the organism that causes the disease during certain parts of the organism's life cycle. The disease can make the fruit of affected trees inedible and cause spotting on the foliage.

Controlling the fungus is difficult. One method of preventing the disease is to destroy all red cedar or other host trees within a half-mile radius of your apple trees.

Apricot trees grow well where I live, but mine won't set fruit. What's the problem?

Apricot trees are very hardy and can be grown in the cold northeastern part of the country. Despite this ability to survive cold winters, many do not set fruit because they bloom too early in the year, and the spring frosts kill the flowers, destroying any possibility of fruit.

When selecting apricot trees for the home landscape, find cultivars that flower late. Probably the best northern apricot is the 'Goldcot'. Hardy to about twenty degrees below zero, it is sometimes called "super hardy." This self-pollinating cultivar produces fruits that are sweet, juicy, and firm. They are tasty fresh or dried and maintain their quality when canned.

Apricots are also great trees for the landscape. They have beautiful pink flowers, and their leaves are attractive in the spring and fall.

What conditions are best for planting and growing apricots?

Early spring is the best time of year to plant apricot trees. They should be planted in a rich, well-drained soil. If the soil in which an apricot tree is planted consists of a rather good but shallow topsoil overlaying a clay subsoil, the tree will not root deeply. This situation could lead to problems in a drought, when roots could dry out, or during thunderstorms, when trees could uproot. Apricot trees will not survive long in heavy soil, which becomes waterlogged. This is true for most stone fruits, the exception being plums.

Good air circulation is important to the health of apricot trees. It can usually be found on elevated areas, which are ideally suited for planting apricots. Cool air also settles on low ground so hilltops do not present the problems caused by low-lying areas, where frost is more likely.

When planting apricots, water the soil around the root system with a liquid fertilizer high in phosphorus. Be sure to keep grass and weeds from growing around the trunk; mulching helps take care of this problem. Remember, apricots have shallow roots and they do not compete well with grass for moisture.

Are all apricots self-pollinating?

Most apricots are self-pollinating. As with many other fruits, though, a heavier set of fruit can be expected when there is a second variety to permit cross-pollination. Most apricots are freestones, meaning that the flesh does not cling to the seed. Even if the cultivar you select is not, though, the fruit is enjoyable.

Do apricots need to be thinned?

Thinning is important on apricot trees, but it usually occurs naturally. Late spring frosts tend to take some fruit and there is also a June drop. If the fruit is not thinned sufficiently, the heavy fruit loads will cause the tree to bear only in alternate years.

What conditions are best for growing cherry trees?

As with the other drupes, a rich, well-drained soil is best. Spring planting is recommended and the planting site should be much the same as with apricots and peaches. Studies have shown that sour cherries are able to withstand temperature extremes better than sweet cherries. High summer temperatures are particularly hard on sweet cherries.

If you plant sweet cherries, expect to wait for as long as six years before harvesting any fruit. Sour cherries usually begin to set fruit a couple of years sooner.

Are all cherries good for making pies?

There are basically two types of cherries grown by the backyard gardener: sweet and sour. Sour cherries are used in pies. Sweet cherries are not considered baking cherries but are usually eaten fresh or in desserts, toppings, jams, and salads.

Three of the most popular sour cherries are the 'Montmorency', the 'North Star', and the 'Meteor'. The 'Montmorency' has been widely grown for years. Available as a semi-dwarf or a standard tree, it produces bright red fruit with a yellow flesh. Do not try to grow standard-sized cherry trees in a small backyard; they grow quite tall.

The 'North Star' is a natural dwarf. It might grow to a height of only nine feet, but it produces heavily each year. This sour cherry is red with red flesh. It is also considered by many to be the hardiest of the sour cherries.

'Meteor' is probably the most adaptable variety of sour cherry. It, too, is a dwarf that can be grown in almost any climate where cherries will grow. The large, red fruits have a yellow flesh.

What are some good cherry cultivars to eat fresh?

The cultivar that is grown more than any other is the 'Bing'. This is the one most of us buy at the grocery store. Considered a dark, or black, cherry (it actually is very dark red), it is large and sweet and one of the best eating cherries. Two good pollinators— 'Black Tartarian' and 'Sam'—are both excellent black cherries that are widely available.

'Royal Ann' is a red cherry with a hint of yellow. It is used to make maraschino cherries. It cannot be pollinated by 'Bing', but 'Windsor' will work. 'Van' is a red cherry that is very resistant to cracking and can be pollinated by 'Bing' or 'Royal Ann'.

There also are several cultivars of yellow cherries available to the gardener. The 'Stark Gold' is the hardiest and most disease-resistant sweet cherry one can buy. It is said to tolerate temperatures to thirty degrees below zero. Any other sweet cherry can serve as a pollinator for another. Another benefit of growing a yellow cherry tree is that the fruits are not eaten by the birds; they don't know that yellow cherries can be ripe!

Are there any self-pollinating sweet cherries?

I know of only two self-pollinating sweet cherries: 'Stella' and 'Lapins'. 'Stella' is a self-pollinator and is available as a dwarf or standard tree. This is not one of the hardiest varieties and probably should not be grown farther north than Zone 6. An interesting feature of this tree is that it can be used to pollinate any other sweet cherry.

The second tree is 'Lapins'. This cherry can be grown north to Zone 5 and is resistant to the cracking often brought on by spring rains. It is new to the marketplace, so I am not familiar with its quality as an eating cherry.

My cherry tree produces blooms but no fruit. What's wrong?

Cherry trees tend to blossom early, but cold temperatures can kill flowers and prevent a crop of cherries from forming. Cold temperatures also can affect the activity of the insects that carry the pollen. While the flowers are open, heavy rains can wash the pollen away before pollination occurs.

How do I stop birds from eating ripening cherries?

It is almost uncanny how birds know just when to eat the cherries. Often they do it the morning before we were going to pick them!

Fortunately, there are several ways to discourage birds from getting at the fruit. One method is to place netting over the trees. This works fairly well on dwarf or small trees but on big trees— forget it! A second deterrent is to place inflatable owls in the trees right before the fruit ripens. Owls are predators of small birds and their presence will discourage feathered pests from coming too close.

Do cherry trees need to be pruned regularly?

Cherries do not require much pruning after the first two years, and, in this way, they differ from many other fruit trees. The framework of the tree is established during these early years. Sweet-cherry trees should be pruned to have a strong central leader; sour cherries should be pruned to form a more open center. The early pruning also should include thinning out weak, deformed branches. Cherries tend to develop all along the tree's branches. It, therefore, must be pruned to allow sunlight to penetrate the canopy so that all the cherries can mature and ripen properly.

The pruning of mature trees should involve only the removal of any weak or dead wood and the heading back of terminal branches that are getting too long. Heavy pruning results in lower yields.

Should the fruit be thinned as it is on most other fruit trees?

The fruit on cherry trees does not need to be thinned. Cherries are much smaller than other fruits, and they are ready for harvest much earlier than are the larger tree fruits. An abundance of cherries on a tree will not stress it to the extent that would be expected with a tree full of apples or peaches. Of course, if drought conditions exist after fruit set, a natural fruit drop can occur.

Why did the bark crack on my cherry trees?

Bark splitting often occurs on young cherry trees in various parts of the country, usually during the winter. This is due in part to the texture of the bark, which is smooth, and to a rapid drop or rise in air temperature. If the cracks are shallow they can heal and will not damage the health of the tree. If the cracks are deep, the bark can split to the sapwood. This opens the tree to attacks by fungi, which in time can kill it.

Place tree guards around the trunks of all smooth-barked trees over the winter. This will help prevent bark cracking and also reduce the chances of rodent damage.

Do pests bother cherry trees?

There are some pests that damage cherries. The larvae of the cherry fruit fly burrow into the fruit to feed on the flesh. The entrance hole that remains is a sign to beware before biting into that cherry. Spray the cherries with insecticidal soap as they are developing to prevent this problem. Once the insect is inside the fruit, nothing can be done about it. Aphids and a few other insects can be a nuisance, but many of these critters also can be controlled by insecticidal soap.

Are peaches and nectarines closely related?

Peaches and nectarines are indeed closely related; they have the same scientific name: *Prunus persica*. Nectarines are also known as fuzzless peaches and are considered a variety of peach. Sports, or mutant stems, of nectarines are known to have been produced by peach trees. The skin is not the only difference between the two fruits; nectarines generally are smaller than peaches and usually firmer. They also are known to be more prone to the disease brown rot than are peaches.

In what part of the country do peaches grow best?

Peach trees can be found growing in much of the United States, excluding areas such as southern Florida, high-mountain areas, and places that receive extremely cold winters. California provides more than fifty percent of the peaches in this country, and much of that crop is used for canning. Georgia ("the Peach State") and South Carolina also are known for their peaches.

All varieties require a minimum number of hours of chilling to break flower-bud dormancy. Their adaptability can be seen in the range of chill hours. The cultivar 'Mayflower' needs 1,150 chill hours; the cultivar 'Ceylon' requires only fifty to one hundred hours. Most of the common cultivars require between 750 and 1,000 chill hours. When you select peach trees, particularly if you live in the South, be sure to consider the number of chill hours the cultivar requires.

Are there any unusual conditions needed for planting and growing peaches?

Plant peaches according to the recommendations for apricots, remembering that they do not grow well in wet soils. At planting time the trees should be pruned to form a strong framework of two or three branches. Like sour cherries, they should have an open-center form. Annual dormant pruning will keep peach trees productive and a reasonable size. Peaches need heavier pruning than do other fruit trees, and although this will decrease the quantity of fruit, it will increase the quality. Peaches grow on tree branches that were produced the previous year. With this in mind, you must maintain a fine balance between removing too much and removing too little. If you are growing peach and nectarine trees, be sure to follow proper pruning directions.

Peaches tend to set a lot of fruit, so the tree should be thinned often. Remember, however, that early-flowering peach varieties can have reduced yields as a result of late spring frosts. Unlike apples, peach trees can bear heavily every year even if the fruit is not thinned during years of heavy set. Too much fruit left on a tree, though, can break branches or stunt the fruit. Thin early peach cultivars well before the June drop while the fruit is small. Late-season cultivars can be thinned following the June drop if necessary. After thinning there should be about one fruit every six inches along the branch.

Thinning peaches also affects the flavor of the fruit. By removing some fruit, more leaves will be available to provide energy for the peaches that remain. The fewer leaves there are per fruit, the lower the fruit's sugar content and the poorer the flavor. About forty leaves per fruit provides the best flavor.

I want to make one more point about peach trees. Many cultivars of peaches are grown as standard-sized trees because there are few dwarfing rootstocks. Peach trees, though, do not grow as tall as most standard fruit trees, attaining a size of only fifteen to eighteen feet. There are several natural dwarfs that grow to a height of only eight feet. They are not grown commercially because their flavor is not as good as regular cultivars.

Do peach trees need to be fertilized?

Compared with many fruit trees, peaches are heavy feeders. Nitrogen is the nutrient the trees need the most. The best fertilizer to use, though, will be determined by the area's climate, the soil, and the trees' growth and productivity.

Fertilizer, when needed, should be applied in early spring, particularly if the fertilizer is high in nitrogen. The roots of peaches are quite near the surface and quickly benefit from the application. Contact your local agricultural extension office to determine the recommended rates for your area.

Are peaches self-pollinating or do two cultivars need to be planted?

Almost all peaches are self-pollinating. The only notable exception is the 'J. H. Hale'. Its flowers can be pollinated by any other peach cultivar in bloom at the same time. Despite the fact that most peach varieties are self-pollinating, they still rely on bees to help in the process. A poor peach set is not uncommon when spring is cold and bees are not active.

What are some good peach varieties to plant?

At one time the 'Elberta' was by far the most popular peach grown. It produces a large freestone fruit with yellow flesh. It is now being replaced by other varieties because its peaches do not have the best color, and it tends to drop fruit before maturity. Many cultivars of the original now exist. The 'Elberta Queen' is good for canning and freezing.

'Redskin' and 'Redhaven' are two red-skinned peaches that are becoming increasingly popular. Both are freestone and make great eating. 'Reliance' is a variety that can tolerate temperatures to about twenty-five degrees below zero. If you have trouble growing peaches because of the cold, use this variety. It is a freestone with red skin and a sweet, yellow flesh.

Some nurseries advertise that they sell the largest peaches grown, but don't be fooled into thinking that the best peaches are the largest ones. Stick to the tried and tested varieties if you are just beginning to grow peaches.

How should I select nectarines?

In areas that suffer harsh winters, I recommend planting the 'Mericrest'. Its fruit has red skin and a tasty, yellow flesh, and the tree is hardy to twenty-eight degrees below zero. 'Redgold' is another popular variety in the North; 'Redchief' is a good one to grow in the South.

What diseases are common to peaches and nectarines?

Peach-leaf curl is a common and serious disease of peach and nectarine trees. It appears early in the spring as the leaves open. The leaves look blistered and turn reddish. As the affected foliage matures, it thickens and becomes more deformed and lighter in color. By the time summer arrives, most of this foliage drops. Even though new leaves can develop, the tree has weakened and if any fruit was present, it usually drops.

Once the disease is present, it is hard to control. Sanitation—getting rid of affected leaves—is an important method of control. After the leaves drop in the fall, lime sulfur should be sprayed on the trees. Complete coverage is important. The affected trees should be sprayed again in late winter with lime sulfur and dormant oil.

Brown rot is a disease that can affect most drupes but can hit peaches and nectarines particularly hard. Although it can be found on the blossoms, it usually goes unnoticed until it is seen on the fruit. It begins as small brown spots, which gradually increase in size until the whole fruit is brown. All affected fruit should be removed from the tree to control the spread of the disease. Spraying the buds with Captan when they begin to show color can help prevent brown rot. Dormant spraying with a mix of lime sulfur and a horticultural oil is another means of control.

Oriental fruit moth larvae bore into the young stems of peaches, nectarines, apricots, and plums, causing the ends of the stems to wilt and then die. Later in the season, other, newly hatched larvae feed on both the stems and the fruit. Controlling this pest is difficult because it lives inside the tree, but you can eat the affected fruit. Just cut it open to remove the larvae first!

Borers also commonly infect peach trees. The flat-headed peach borer enters the tree at soil level. Gummy sap usually covers the entrance opening. Once found, the opening can serve as a method of doing away with the pest. The larva doing the damage often can be killed by pushing a wire into the entrance and along the tunnel. I have used a pocketknife to expose the tunnel and then have removed the pest by hand to be certain it would do no further damage. The borers are moth larvae, so mothballs placed around the tree and covered with two inches of soil often can prevent the problem.

Never use systemic insecticides on fruit trees to control borers because the insecticide goes to all parts of the trees, including the fruit. If you eat the fruit, you also eat the insecticide.

Are pears suited to home landscaping?

You bet they are! They have an abundance of color in the spring and attractive foliage in the fall, they bear fruit only a few years after planting, and they need little pruning when mature. What more could a gardener ask for? In addition, there are several dwarf varieties that respond well to espalier training. I have a pear tree that has borne fruit every year since it was first planted.

Do pears need special growing conditions?

If you can grow apples in the backyard, then you can grow pears. The soil requirements are the same, but pears can tolerate moist conditions better than apples. Wet soils, however, can affect the quality of the fruit produced. As with many other fruit trees, you need to plant two cultivars to set a good crop.

Pears seem to do best when there is permanent ground cover, such as grass, present. The cover helps prevent the loss of nitrogen, which the pear trees need. Pears also respond well when mulched with straw or other organic material.

Do I need to thin pears?

Some varieties of pear tend to set large crops. When this is the case, you might need to thin them to encourage larger fruit to grow. Pears are often produced on spurs, so the fruit should be thinned to only two pears per spur. If size is not important, though, you need not thin the fruit. Heavy-laden pear trees do not tend to bear only in alternate years as do heavy-laden apples.

What are some good pear varieties to try?

'Bartlett' is by far the most familiar pear. It is large, sweet, juicy, and tender and is a great eating and canning pear. The newer 'Starking Delicious' is a good all-purpose pear that produces large fruit. Stark Brothers advertises it as the best pear for the backyard gardener.

Another pear worthy of consideration is 'Moonglow'. This pear tree is resistant to the common disease fireblight. It also is a vigorously growing tree and a strong pollinator, and it has an upright growth habit. The fruit has blushes of red and is sweet and soft.

How do you recognize fireblight on pear trees? How is it controlled?

Fireblight is a bacterial disease carried by bees and a few other insects. It can affect apple trees, but pears are far more susceptible. Warm, humid spring weather seems to be conducive to the spread of the disease.

You will notice it first as a blight in the blossoms of affected trees. It usually spreads from there to vigorously growing shoots; the shoots will then bend over, brown, and die. The bacteria also can cause cankering on branches and the trunk.

To control the disease, prune to a few inches below shoots that are infected as soon as you see the symptoms. Clean all pruning tools so that the disease is not passed to other plants. To help prevent the disease, keep your pear trees healthy.

Do pears have any insect pests?

Like all fruit trees, pears are susceptible to pests. Pears, however, are not as bothered by insects as are other fruits. The pear psylla, related to the aphid, is one of the more common pests. The adults and nymphs suck juices from the leaves where they live. This often causes the affected leaves to curl; damage is similar to what aphids do to cherries and it generally reduces the tree's health and vigor. Using dormant-oil sprays in late winter prevents serious outbreaks of the pest. Spraying with insecticidal soap can take care of the problem when it is discovered.

Is it true that there are many kinds of plums?

Of all the fruits discussed, plums are the most varied. But we are going to discuss only the two most common varieties: the European and the Japanese. The European, or prune, plums were brought to this country first and are the hardiest. Their fruits have an oval shape, a blue or purple skin, a firm texture, and a very high sugar content. Most European plums are self-pollinating. Their growth habit is much like that of an apple tree, and the fruit needs to be thinned to about two fruits per spur.

When it comes to the best plums for eating, most of us are familiar with the Japanese varieties. These are round, sweet, and juicy with a red or yellow skin. Although these are the best eating plums, they are more difficult to grow in the Northeast than are the European varieties. All Japanese plums need a pollinator to set a crop; the 'Redheart' is a good variety for this purpose. Most Japanese plums bloom early, so they can suffer from late spring frosts. When frost does not thin the fruit, you will have to because the trees can be prolific bearers. Only one fruit should remain along every four or five inches of a branch.

How should plums be planted?

Plums are planted much as you would plant cherry, apricot, and peach trees. Plums tend to tolerate moist soil conditions better than do most stone fruits.

What are some of the best varieties of prune plums to plant?

Of all the European plums, the 'Stanley' is the most widely planted. It is great eaten fresh, canned, or dried, and the one plum sure to grow in the Northeast. The fruit has a dark blue skin and a yellow flesh.

'Earliblue' is another popular European plum. It is suggested that 'Earliblue' is easier to grow than 'Stanley' and is hardier because it blooms later in the spring. The fruit is much like that of 'Stanley', but the tree is not quite as productive. Don't exclude it for this reason, however, because it is so hardy.

A great prune plum for the South is the 'Italian Prune'. It is very sweet and great for drying.

What are some good Japanese plums for the garden?

'Redheart' is a good pollinator for all Japanese plums. Its fruit is juicy, sweet, and ideal for making jellies. The skin is deep red, as is the flesh. 'Methley' can be grown in the North and is self-pollinating, although a heavier crop is produced when planted with a pollinator, such as 'Shiro'. 'Shiro' is a yellow plum that looks as good as it tastes. 'Ozark Premier', which has a red skin and yellow flesh, is another variety that produces fairly well in the Northeast.

Two other varieties that I have tried but with which I am having little success are 'Santa Rosa' and 'Burbank Red Ace'. Both are known as excellent eating varieties, but frosts have taken the blooms every spring so far. They do better in warmer climates.

What problems can I expect with plum trees?

Black knot is the most troublesome disease. This fungus appears as large black growths on woody stems. The best control is to cut off the infected branches. Make the cut at least one foot below the growth because the fungus can spread beneath the bark. Burn the affected branches if possible. Little can be done if the black knot attacks the trunk, although the tree might linger for several years.

Spraying the trees during the dormant season with lime sulfur and a horticultural oil is one way to help prevent the problem. Black knot also can affect ornamental plum trees, so be certain they are dormant-sprayed if you find the disease.

One other disease that should be mentioned is leaf spot, which is common to Japanese plums grown in the East. It is most noticeable when there is a rainy spring. First, leaves are affected, then the infection spreads to the spurs that hold the fruit. Early fruit drop usually results.

Many of the insects that affect other stone fruits can injure plum trees, but the weevil called plum curculio prefers the fruit. The adult female weevil lays its eggs in the developing plum. The puncture in the fruit is crescent-shaped, a signature that a pest is present. The larvae feed on the flesh, then burrow out and fall to the ground to undergo metamorphosis. One of the best ways to control this pest is to put something sticky around the tree trunk because the adults crawl up the tree to mate and lay eggs. Tanglefoot, and even STP Oil Treatment, can present an effective barrier.

7

A Year's Worth of Color

When most of us think of flower gardening we think of annuals. Annual flowers provide almost-instant color, they are inexpensive to buy, and they last from spring until autumn's first frosts. Their diversity seems to be endless, with myriad colors, textures, and styles from which to select. In addition, annual flowers can be used along borders, in beds, in the vegetable garden, in window boxes, in barrels, and in pots. They are dazzling when used alone or when grown with perennials.

That annuals last only one year is really a plus for a gardener; because they're temporary, you can change color combinations and varieties every year. Planting annual flowers provides those of us not gifted in drawing or painting with an opportunity to be creative as we color the landscape with flowers. Our canvas can be large or small, depending on how much we want to plant.

Annuals are easy to grow. They were the first flowers many of us planted and cared for—and what a delight it was when they broke into flower. Those marigolds and petunias really did quite well considering they usually grew in the midst of weeds.

What are "warm" and "cool" colors?

Colors are described as warm or cool based on how they make us feel. What colors do we think of when we think of hot? Usually, the colors that come to mind are red, orange, and yellow, and all shades in between. Colors that have a cooling effect are green, blue, and violet, and their hues.

We can use this information in several ways. We all know that a southern exposure receives a lot of sunlight and is hot in the summer. Planting flowers that are red or orange make it seem hotter. A mixture of blue, violet, and white flowers will lend a cooling effect.

Warm colors tend to be bright and bold, so if you want to draw attention to some feature in the landscape, use warm-colored flowers. Cool colors seem to be more pleasing to the eye up close. So cool colors are better used along walks or along the edges of flower beds.

Is it hard to start annual flowers from seed?

There are several ways to start annuals from seed and none of them is difficult. Many varieties of flowers are started indoors and transplanted to the garden when the danger of frost has past in the spring. The most common method is to sow the seed in a container filled with about two inches of sterile potting mix. The container can be anything from an egg carton to a flower pot or an old tray. Be sure to make holes in the bottom of the container so that excess water can drain away.

Thinly scatter the seeds or space them evenly in shallow rows. The seed package will indicate whether or not the seed should be covered with soil. Then add water to the container to set the seed and ensure sufficient moisture for germination. The soil must be kept warm. A temperature of seventy-five degrees is ideal.

The seeds of some annuals need light to germinate. Do not cover them too deeply with soil, and set the seeded containers in sunlight. Examples of such annuals are ageratum, alyssum, coleus, gaillardia, impatiens, petunia, portulaca, snapdragon, and straw-flower. Several other varieties will germinate without light but have better germination rates when it is present. These include celosia, cockscomb, cosmos, monkey flower, nicotiana, and Transvaal daisy.

As soon as germination occurs, all seedlings need light; if there is not enough, they will develop spindly stems. Set the plants on a bright window sill or place them several inches from a light that encourages plant growth. When the young plants develop their second pair of leaves, transfer them to separate containers.

It is also possible to start seeds in peat-filled pots. Many of these pots are made of dried compressed peat and must be placed in water to expand before they can be used. When planting in individual peat pots, or any individual container, place two seeds in each container. This should ensure that at least one seed in each pot germinates. If both come up, select the healthier seedling and remove the other by cutting it off at soil level. Pulling it could disturb the root system of the other plant.

Some people prefer to sow the seed directly into the soil where the plant is to grow. This is the easiest method, but it is also the method over which there is the least control. The rate of germination is usually lower because of the vagaries of the outdoor environment. It can also be difficult to tell the seedlings from the weeds.

Before sowing annual flower seeds outside, you must prepare the soil. Add peat moss to improve the medium's quality, as well as the chances for success. When the soil is ready for planting, scatter the seed in the rows where you want the flowers to grow. Not all seeds will germinate, so sow more than you'll need. If, later, there are too many you can thin them out.

If the soil in the bed is heavy, germination might be better if you cover the seed with perlite or white sand. Plant seedlings are tough, but it is hard for them to push their way up through claylike soil. Last, water the newly planted seeds with a sprinkling can. Do not use a hose because the water's force could wash away the seeds or spread them to areas where you don't want the plants to grow.

If I want to start flowers from seed, when should I begin?

Not all annual seeds should be started at the same time. Many varieties germinate rapidly and should be started only four to six weeks before they will be transplanted outdoors. Others take a considerable amount of time to develop and need to be started very early. The back of the seed package should indicate the best time to start the seeds. In most cases, the instructions are to plant the seeds indoors so many weeks before the last anticipated frost date for your area. If you sow the seed directly into the flower bed, wait until all chance of frost has passed.

What are some annual seeds that are easy to start indoors?

Quite a few flowers can be started indoors with ease. The most common is the marigold, but dusty miller, petunia, coleus, snapdragon, sweet pea, bachelor's button, zinnia, strawflower, globe amaranth, nasturtium, and geranium are other possibilities.

Can seeds from annuals be saved in the fall for use the following year?

A few flowers, some marigolds, for example, produce seeds that can be saved and will grow if cared for properly. Most flower varieties, however, are hybrids—products of crosses between different flowers. When the seed is collected from hybrid flowers and planted, it often does not grow. If the seed does germinate, the resulting flower will probably not be like the parent flower, but like one of its "grandparents," because of genetics.

It is best, therefore, to always start with fresh seed of a named cultivar from a reputable seed company.

How close together can annuals be planted?

The growth habit of annuals determines how close together they can be planted. Some annuals grow tall rather than bushy; others stay low but become very full. Most of us tend to crowd flowers. The plants are so small when we transplant them that we overplant. Then we are disappointed when they don't grow properly or don't produce lots of flowers. By crowding them, we also encourage the spread of disease. Be sure to follow the directions on the nursery labels for how far apart to space your plants.

Do annuals ever need to be pruned?

Annuals can be pruned, but the word "pruning" might be a bit harsh for describing the care of these tender plants. A better term would be *pinched*. Pinching refers to the removal of plant parts from herbaceous plants. When setting in transplants, pinch off the growing tips of the plants. This step will encourage the growth of more stems, thus forming a fuller plant that can produce more flowers.

Pinching dead flowers off annuals will encourage the plants to set more flowers sooner than they would if the spent blooms were left on the plant. This will also keep the plant looking better. In some cases the flowers go to seed, which is a waste of the plant's energy.

Some plants, such as petunias, can become leggy as the summer progresses. Pinching them back can rejuvenate them and keep them more compact and more productive. But there is no one rule for all plants. You must determine which ones need to be pinched.

What fertilizer should I use when setting flower transplants in the ground?

The fertilizer used for transplants will depend to some extent on the soil in the beds. It is best to have the soil analyzed before planting so the pH and the level of available soil nutrients can be determined. Most annual flowers grow best in soils with a pH of 6.5 to 7.0. If your soil pH does not fall within that range, it should be corrected.

In most cases, a liquid fertilizer high in phosphorus works best. The plant uses it to grow roots at the time of planting. The percentage of phosphorus is indicated by the middle number of the three on the fertilizer container. Don't apply a fertilizer high in nitrogen, which causes the leaves to grow, until the roots are well established so that they can supply the water and nutrients necessary for the foliage growth. One of my favorite fertilizers for started plants is Peter's Root 'N Bloom.

What fertilizers are best to use on annuals during the growing season?

There is no one "best" fertilizer. Many people have their favorite and can give many reasons why they use it. What is crucial when selecting a fertilizer is that it be complete. Some common fertilizer formulas are 10–10–10, 5–10–10, and 5–10–5. Most fertilizers of this type are dry and granular. If rains are not forecast following the application of these fertilizers, soak the soil around the annuals to release the nutrients so they can be taken up by the flowers.

A popular product my friends recommend is Miracle-Gro, which must be mixed with water and applied as a liquid. I use fish emulsion on annuals. It's a natural product that also is applied as a liquid. The soil should already be moist when you apply any fertilizer, even one in liquid form, so that the plants can take it up more rapidly.

How often should annuals be fertilized?

Annuals do not need to be fertilized as often as do perennials and vegetables; they should be fertilized soon after planting and again in midseason. The plants might need a bit of a boost at other times if you don't think they are growing as they should. Just remember that plants use nitrogen to grow foliage. If you fertilize too often, the plants might grow lush and large but form few flowers. Remember, too, that plants growing in the shade generally need fewer applications of fertilizer than those in the sun.

A friend said that I shouldn't use tanbark around annuals. What about using other mulches?

Friends often share advice based on experiences they have had. Sometimes the advice has a basis in fact but is not entirely accurate. I believe it is beneficial to use mulch around annuals, and tanbark can be a good one to apply. It must be well cured, however. Fresh tanbark can burn plants, particularly tender annuals, but I have never heard of bagged, cured tanbark causing this problem. Place tanbark, or any mulch, an inch or two away from the plant stem because the heat generated by the mulch can hurt the plant.

The use of mulch around annuals serves the same purpose as it does when used around other plants. Two or three inches of mulch will help conserve soil moisture, prevent the soil temperature from getting too hot in the summer, and reduce the number of weeds that grow around the flowers.

Many types of mulch can be used. Actually, tanbark is the most common, but other favorites include pine bark nuggets and cocoa bean shells. The cocoa bean shells smell great, but, they weigh so little that they often scatter on the wind.

I have very little space in my yard. Can I grow annuals in hanging baskets?

Most certainly! The diversity of flower types is somewhat limited, but hanging baskets can add color in situations where no other container will work. Some varieties of flowers used in hanging baskets are geraniums, impatiens, lobelia, portulaca, sweet alyssum, coleus, petunias, nasturtiums, verbena, pansies, and fuchsias. When selecting plants for hanging baskets, look for the cultivars that are appropriate for the situation. For instance, if you like petunias, choose some from the 'Cascade' series. If you fancy geraniums, use the vining ivy geraniums.

Flowers that are grown in hanging baskets, or actually, any type of container, must be given special attention. Hot summer days tend to dry the soil in containers rapidly, so you must water those containers daily. Hanging baskets that are in the shade may not need to be watered as often, but check them each day to be certain. When watering, be careful not to wash the soil out of the basket. Use a gentle spray of water rather than a harsh stream.

Frequent watering quickly depletes the soil of nutrients, so use liquid fertilizer on a regular basis. With frequent use, however, dilute the fertilizer to about one-half the recommended rate.

Can some annual flowers be grown for use as cut flowers?

The beauty of some annuals can be enjoyed indoors as well as outside. In many cases, the cut flowers do not last as long as they would have had they remained on the plant, but having the beauty, and at times the fragrance, inside where we spend most of our time is worth that sacrifice.

Most of the annuals that are grown for cutting also look great in the flower bed, so don't plant them off by themselves; mix them with other annuals. The exception might be if you want to cut all the flowers daily. Then it might be wise to have a special cutting bed. Remember not to hide low flowers behind tall ones.

Flowers should always be cut in the early morning or in late evening. Use a sharp knife or cutting shears. Cut the stems at a slight angle and immediately place them in warm water for about an hour. When making an arrangement, use a container that has been cleaned with soap and water. Then fill the container with water and floral preservative. Next, remove the foliage from the part of the stems that will be under water and place the flowers in the container. If possible, change the water daily to keep the flowers looking fresh. If a flower starts to wilt early, recut the stem base and then replace it in the water. Keep the container in a cool but bright location to help prolong the life of the arrangement.

Asters, baby's-breath, candytufts, carnations, celosia, cosmos, dahlias, gazania, gladioluses, globe amaranth, marigolds, nicotiana (which is also fragrant), salvia, snapdragons, strawflowers, and zinnias can be used as fresh-cut flowers. Baby's-breath, globe amaranth, marigolds, and strawflowers also can be air-dried for several weeks for later use in natural dried arrangements.

Which flowers grow well in partially shaded areas?

Many more flowers will grow in sunny locations than in shaded ones. I define partially shaded areas as those that receive two to four hours of sun daily. Ageratum, alyssum, aster, wax or fibrous-rooted begonia, coleus, impatiens, nasturtium, and torenia, or wishbone flower, are some of the most popular annual flowers that tolerate partial shade. The wax begonia, coleus, and impatiens flower in shaded areas, as does fuchsia (fuschia should be used in hanging baskets because of the stems' natural tendency to hang down).

Are there any annuals that do well in dry weather?

I do not know of any flowering annuals that prefer drought conditions. There are, however, several that are persistent and productive even when summers are hot and dry. Many are old favorites, such as the petunia, marigold, and portulaca, or moss rose. Don't overlook alyssum, cleome, salvia, and zinnia; they too can survive in difficult situations. We must be realistic, though, when these flowers are stressed, they will not look as good as they do when conditions are normal.

Coleus is called a flowering plant, but it is grown for its foliage. What other plants are grown for foliage?

Coleus is indeed a flowering plant, but it and several other plants, such as dusty miller, have nicer foliage than flowers. I advise people to cut off the flowers of coleus so they don't distract from the foliage and waste the energy of the plant. Coleus are great in the flower garden because they offer a wide range of foliage colors, textures, and shapes. They are versatile and can grow indoors or out, in the sun or shade, in the garden or containers. They are easy to propagate from cuttings, and by taking cuttings you are assured of the colors you want. They also are easily grown from seed, although you can't choose the colors because they vary genetically from seed to seed.

Dusty miller is another plant grown for its foliage. Some varieties are considered perennials; in the Northeast, however, they are used as annuals. The silvery-colored leaves are a welcome addition to most flower beds with flowers that are bright and bold in color. Some of the varieties have lacy leaves. Pinch the plant to keep it compact and remove the flower buds before they open.

The kochia, or burning bush, is another foliage annual. This plant reaches a height of two to three feet. The tiny flowers it produces are usually not seen because they are green and blend in with the foliage. Kochias can be used in the landscape as temporary shrubs and hedges. In the fall their foliage turns a brilliant red.

The ornamental cabbage and the flowering kale also are good foliage annuals. These plants are usually started from seed in June and July for use in the fall and early winter. When grown in hot weather they tend to bolt like edible cabbage and kale. Their foliage can vary from white to pink, red, purple, and blue. You can eat them, but the leaves are tough and bitter. Such ornamentals are more suitable for the flower bed than for the vegetable garden.

Are there annuals that can be used as ground covers?

Some annuals can be used as ground covers, but unlike other ground covers, they should be considered temporary because they last only one year. Sometimes annuals are used as ground cover in a rock garden to lend color over the summer. A favorite of mine is portulaca. It grows only about four to eight inches high and will thrive in hot, dry conditions. The flowers come in red, yellow, white, pink, and purple. They open in the morning sun and close at night.

Other annual ground covers include the Madagascar periwinkle, which, like the portulaca, grows well in the heat of summer. In fact, it is sensitive to overwatering. The cultivar 'Polka Dot', which has white flowers with red centers, grows to a height of only six inches. Sweet William is a low grower that will perk up a rock garden or can be used in lightly shaded areas. The Dahlberg daisy, or golden fleece as it is sometimes known, produces small gold-colored flowers in the midst of dark green, feathery foliage. It tolerates high temperatures well, does not want much fertilizer, and grows to a height of four to six inches.

The sweet alyssum is a low grower that is used as a ground cover in areas that do not suffer from summer's heat. A good cultivar is 'Royal Carpet', which forms purple flowers. Where the ground is moist, forget-me-nots might be the preferred annual for a ground cover. They develop an abundance of blue flowers in early spring and again in the fall. Annual phlox and verbena are two others to consider. Both need well-drained soil and lots of fertilizer.

What are some tall annuals that can be used as a backdrop for other flowers?

One of my favorite tall-growing annuals is the hollyhock. The scientific name for all hollyhock is *Althaea rosea*. Some are listed as annual, others as perennial, and still others as biennial. I do not regard any as true perennials, only as annuals or biennials because in the Northeast, none that I have tried have come back after they bloom. Annual hollyhock begins blooming in August and does not suffer from rust, which is a common disease of the biennial hollyhock.

When you need tall flowers, grow the annual hollyhock 'Summer Carnival'. It grows to about five feet tall in either full sun or partial shade. It should be started early indoors and transplanted so that it has plenty of time to bloom before frosts arrive.

The other variety of Hollyhock I enjoy is the 'Fordhook', a giant biennial that grows to six feet. This cultivar produces double flowers that are four inches across and bloom in bright crimson, scarlet, or yellow. They remind me of the tissue carnations that girls made when I went to school. 'Fordhook' comes into bloom about June.

If you like bright color, plant amaranthus, or summer poinsettia. The foliage, not the flower, makes this plant so useful. This attractive annual is a sun lover that grows to about three feet in almost any soil. Summer poinsettia does not transplant well, so start it in the soil where it is to grow. Be sure not to overwater the plant; it responds best to dry conditions.

Joseph's coat is an unusually beautiful summer poinsettia. The top leaves are scarlet and gold, and the lower leaves have a mixture of green, yellow, and chocolate. Too much fertilizer will lessen the intensity of the foliage color. For bright red top foliage, try 'Illumination'. The bright top contrasts nicely with the chocolate and green lower leaves. Summer poinsettias are wonderful accent plants.

The sunflower is probably the tallest annual flower. Some sunflowers, such as 'Giant Sunflower', top off at about ten feet. Others struggle to grow to two feet. 'Teddy Bear' is one of the short varieties, but the flower is quite different from what you might expect; the large, ragged, double flowers are gold but lack a large center.

All sunflowers grow in a wide range of soils but need full sun. They also tolerate drought and heat. The worst problem with sunflowers is that they attract insects.

There seem to be many annuals with red, orange, or yellow flowers, but my favorite color is blue. What are some blue-flowering annuals?

There are quite a few blue-flowering annuals that are easy to grow. Several are low growing and stay rather compact. The ageratum 'Blue Danube' grows to only about six inches and there are other blue cultivars, such as 'Blue Lagoon', which grows a bit taller, and 'Blue Mink', which will grow to ten inches. Ageratum should be planted only after the last chance of spring frosts. It does not tolerate hot summers well. Don't be afraid to pinch it back to keep it compact.

The amethyst flower, or browallia, is a blue-flowering annual that grows to ten or fifteen inches tall. The cultivar 'Blue Bells' remains compact and reaches a height of ten inches. This variety is best grown in partial shade and can be brought indoors in the fall to be used as a houseplant. It often will bloom all winter when cared for properly.

Bachelor's button is a tall-growing blue flower. Some cultivars, such as 'Blue Boy', will grow to three feet. Others, such as 'Jubilee Gem', rarely exceed one foot. Bachelor's button likes full sun and will bloom even during droughts. If you are a bird lover, remember that the seed heads make good finch food. So save the flowers when they die.

The Chinese forget-me-not produces an abundance of attractive, small blue flowers with dark green foliage. 'Firmament' grows to around two feet and is tolerant of many soil conditions. It will do well throughout the summer if occasionally given a bit of liquid fertilizer. I should point out one problem with this plant: the seeds are sticky and can easily be carried into the house on dogs, cats, and kids.

Those living in cooler areas with an abundance of sun should consider the blue daisy. The 'Blue Marguerite' is a bushy annual that grows to about three feet. It is a striking plant that will bloom all summer in the proper conditions.

One of my favorite blue annuals is statice. This two-foot-tall plant is easy to start from seed, produces many spikes, and has a rosette of foliage at the base of the plant. 'Sky Blue' is one of my favorite varieties. The spikes can be dried for later use just by hanging them upside down.

One edging flower that the person who loves blue should not

overlook is lobelia. This plant is very compact and low growing, and it will bloom from spring until the frosts of fall. Lobelia can be grown in sun or partial shade and in most soils. Keep it moist in the summer or it might stop blooming until the temperatures cool. 'Crystal Palace' is unusual with its dark blue flowers and bronze foliage. 'Blue Moon' produces violet-blue flowers and bright green foliage. The intense blue of the lobelia makes it a must.

Two not-so-common blue annuals are the cupflower 'Purple Robe' and baby-blue-eyes. Both grow from six to twelve inches tall, tolerate sun or partial shade, and need to be watered during the heat of summer.

The old favorite, petunia, is available in several shades of blue. Some cultivars to look for include 'Sky Magic', 'Blue Frost', and that great giant, double, fringed hybrid, 'Blue Danube'. Remember that these are sun lovers and will need you to remove spent blooms so they can keep flowering.

We can't forget the salvia. Most of us know the red forms but do not realize that there are several cultivars that have blue flowers. The flower spikes open in early summer and last until fall. Some are rather short, growing to only about twelve inches; others can reach three feet. Check for 'Oxford Blue', which grows to about two feet and is easily dried, and look for 'Victoria' and 'Blue Queen'.

One other blue annual I must recommend is the pansy. This early spring bloomer needs a place in everyone's garden. I am not ready to recommend any one cultivar for planting, because I haven't found a pansy I didn't like. All pansies grow well in the spring when soils are moist. They do not like summer heat, but if kept watered, they often will rebloom in the fall.

I have a fence that needs some color. Are there any climbing annuals I can use?

There are indeed some annuals that vine and can be trained to grow on a fence or trellis. The first that comes to mind is the morning glory. The cultivar 'Heavenly Blue' probably is the most popular vining annual grown. Its flowers are quite large—about five inches in diameter. The petals are a rich blue and lead into a white throat. Other cultivars include 'Pearly Gates', which has a large white flower, and 'Scarlet Star', which is red with a white center. All of these are vigorous climbers, reaching a height of eight to ten feet. Be careful not to plant morning glories around small shrubs or other flowers. They can weaken the other plants by hiding them from the sun.

Another variety, a cousin of the morning glory, is the moonflower. The cultivar 'Giant White' seems to grow forever, often reaching fifteen feet in height. The flowers are about six inches across. Moonflower gets its name from the fact that it opens at night, when it releases a pleasing fragrance. By the following afternoon the flowers close. The dark green, heart-shaped foliage provides a beautiful backdrop to the flowers.

Another good climber is the sweet pea, which can reach about ten feet. Mind you, some sweet peas are not climbers, so be sure you select the right cultivars. 'Galaxy' and 'Gigantea' are two good multiflowering climbers. Both are resistant to heat and will flower throughout the summer if you remove spent flowers. The flowers come in blue, rose, scarlet, and white. It is recommended that sweet peas not be planted in the same area two years in a row because they deplete the nitrogen in the soil.

One more annual climber is the black-eyed-Susan vine. This vine does not grow as tall as the others, reaching only about six feet. The flowers, with orange and yellow petals and black centers, are very striking against the green, ivy-shaped foliage. This plant can be grown in a container and will thrive when brought indoors for the winter. It then can be set out again the following spring.

What are some annuals that can be grown for use in dried arrangements?

One of my favorite everlastings, as annuals dried for arrangements are known, is statice. It is available in yellow, blue, rose, lavender, and white. It is easy to grow and adds bright color to arrangements. The stiff stems make it easy to dry by hanging it upside down.

Globe amaranth is another plant that deserves attention for more than its use in dried arrangements. This bushy, compact plant is great as a bedding plant or in a container garden. It has few pests and can tolerate the worst that summer has in store. For drying, remove the flower head and force a wire up through it.

Strawflowers are also easy to grow because they enjoy the warmth of summer. 'Bright Bikinis' is a popular mix that will produce white, gold, red, pink, and purple flowers. Pick the stems before the flowers are fully open and remove the leaves. Then hang the stems upside down to dry. If you prefer, you can remove the heads and wire them.

The starflower is an everlasting that is not often used. The flower stem grows to about two feet and is topped with a round flower head that can be dried. The flower heads are about one and a half inches across and can be painted and used as Christmas ornaments or left natural for arrangements.

A few other annuals that can be dried are the bells of Ireland, annual baby's-breath, or gypsophila, annual delphinium, plume celosia, and cockscomb.

Geraniums and coleus can be kept alive indoors over the winter. Are they annuals or perennials?

In most parts of the country geraniums and coleus are considered annuals. Remember, annuals are plants that have a one-year life cycle—they grow, flower, set their seed, and die in less than twelve months. The plants die because they cannot tolerate temperatures below freezing. The only thing remaining to carry on the species is the seed. Thus, most annuals must be started from seed each spring when conditions are conducive to growth.

Some of us bring the plants in the house over the winter so they are not killed by the cold. Impatiens and wax begonias, as well as geraniums and coleuses, are some of the plants we dig up, put in pots, and bring inside. When the following spring arrives, we can plant them outside again. In most cases, though, the dim light of winter causes the plants to become spindly so they do not look very good when they are replanted. Cuttings, however, can be taken from these plants, and the cuttings will grow into a new generation of plants for the flower bed.

There are several other plants that we consider annuals even though we generally do not start them from seed or cuttings each year. Gladioluses, cannas, and tuberous-rooted begonias are a few. The corms or roots of these plants must be dug up and stored over the winter so they do not freeze.

Are there any annuals that can be grown from seed and enjoyed indoors over the winter?

Yes, there is a nice selection of annuals that can do well inside during the winter. As one might expect, however, it is not always easy to keep them healthy. Our homes are usually very dry in winter, and low humidity causes many annuals to drop their leaves. Gravel-filled pans or a humidifier can solve this problem. Limited amounts of light can also complicate the situation, so you must augment the available light with an appropriate lamp. You can place fluorescent grow-lamps several inches from the plants. If the plants are long-day plants, they will need about fourteen hours of light daily.

Annuals that are used in the house should be compact varieties; tall plants need large containers and too much space. Use pots that are two and one-half to four inches in diameter, and sow the seed directly into the containers. Do not overfertilize the plants, because that can cause them to stop blooming.

If you would like to grow annuals for winter color indoors, try small varieties of ageratum, lobelia, marigold, snapdragon, and zinnia.

How should gladioluses be grown? How should they be cared for over the winter?

I treat gladiolus as an annual rather than as a perennial because it must be dug from the ground each fall if the plant is to survive. The corm, which produces the leaves and flowers, is, in a sense, perennial. When the corm is properly cared for over the winter, it can be planted in spring and will grow a new plant.

Gladiolus corms are sold at nurseries during the spring. They can be planted a week or two before the last frost in the area. It is probably best to plant only several of the corms then and continue to plant more every two weeks until the end of June. This schedule will assure you a continuous array of flowers over the summer.

Plant the corms in a good garden soil about four inches apart and two to three inches deep. Mix a fertilizer rich in bone meal with the soil before planting. The concave side of the gladiolus corm is the bottom, so orient it accordingly.

After the first fall frost blackens the flower's leaves, lift them from the ground and cut the foliage back to about one-half inch from the top of the corm. Then dry the corms by laying them on a screen in the sun for about two weeks. Break off the old, shriveled parent corm and discard it. Then remove the little cormels that have formed at the junction between the old and new large corms. Dust these and the large corms with benomyl to prevent disease

Gladiolus (Corm)

and hang them in the cellar in an onion bag or in an old nylon stocking. The best storage temperature for them is in the range of forty to fifty degrees.

How do I care for dahlias?

Dahlias grow from tubers, not corms. They are treated like gladioluses, though, because their tubers are not hardy. Dahlia tubers are available in the spring, or you can plant tubers saved from the previous season. The first thing you must do when you plant wintered-over dahlias is to cut apart the individual tubers. Be certain that each has a section of crown with eyes or buds. Be sure your knife is clean to prevent the spread of disease.

After the danger of frost has passed, set the tubers in the garden or in individual eight-inch pots. Mix in some bone meal and cover them with two inches of soil. Add water to settle the soil around the tuber, but be careful not to overwater.

As soon as the first frost takes the foliage in fall, cut the stems back to about four inches from the ground. Use a garden fork to lift the tuber clusters that have formed over the summer. Wash the soil from them and set them upside down in a shaded area to dry for several hours.

When dry, place the clusters in a plastic-lined box that is large enough to accommodate them so they do not touch one another.

Fill the box with peat moss or vermiculite to prevent the tubers from drying out and store it in a cool cellar. Check the tubers midway through the winter to be sure they are not shrivelling or decaying. If they have started to shrivel, add a little water to the filler.

Do any other plants need similar winter care?

Several plants need similar care over the winter. Caladium grows from tubers and is treated like the dahlias. The canna also grows much like the dahlia and is treated the same way in the fall and winter.

Which pests attack annual flowers?

As with almost any plant alive, there is always something that will live on it, in it, or off it! When starting annual flowers from seed, the first problem is damping-off. This is a fungus disease that causes seedlings to topple over soon after emerging. Overly moist soil seems to precipitate it. You can discourage the disease by using a sterile potting mix, by not overwatering, and by sprinkling a thin layer of white sand over the soil surface after the seed is sown.

Numerous other fungus diseases can affect annuals. Gray mold attacks the buds and flowers and appears as a fuzzy growth. Powdery mildew and rust affect the foliage. For all these problems, it is best to remove the parts of the plants that are affected. If the problem persists, apply a fungicide to help control the spread of the disease. When the frosts kill the foliage in the fall, remove the infected plants along with any fallen leaves.

Many plant cultivars are now resistant to diseases, so try to select those that are less prone to problems.

Seedlings and young annual plants seem to suffer most from insect damage and predation. Slugs gorge themselves on the foliage of young marigolds, yet all we usually see is the damage. Slugs are nocturnal feeders, hiding by day to avoid the drying heat of the sun as well as watchful eyes. A night walk with the flashlight should reveal these guys if they are active in the flower bed. You can control them with a salt shaker.

The pillbug, also called the sowbug, is another common pest. This critter feeds on the roots of many plants. A pesticide such as diazinon is effective in controlling such soilborne pests. Some caterpillars will destroy the leaves and, in some cases, the flowers of many plants before the pests are even noticed. Aphids, Japanese beetles, and whiteflies are other insects that enjoy our annuals almost as much as we do. Insecticidal soap or Sevin should be used to keep these pests in check.

8

Color That Comes Back

Some of the most attractive flowers you can use in the landscape are perennials—plants that come back year after year. They include trees, shrubs, and some herbaceous plants. (Herbaceous plants are those that are not woody.) They die back to ground level, usually in the fall, and survive the winter underground as bulbs, corms, rhizomes, tubers, or roots. Common examples of perennials are the peony, iris, crocus, and bleeding-heart.

Many herbaceous perennials are not intentionally planted; most of them are called weeds. The classic example is the common dandelion. It is not native to this country but was brought here as a culinary herb. Today much time and money are used to eradicate this perennial from our landscapes. Other wild perennials, however, are being used in flower beds, and many new horticultural varieties of these are now available.

In recent years perennials have been touted as the perfect solution for the gardener who is tired of planting flowers each spring. The thinking is that all you need to do is plant the varieties that you like and let them grow. But perennial gardening is not that easy. I am quick to remind folks that perennials often require more attention than do annuals. Gardeners sometimes have trouble growing perennials or even lose them because of improper soil conditions, inappropriate light, winters that are too cold, incorrect amounts of water, or lack of care. Problems also can result from disease and insect pests and too much competition from weeds and other plants.

At the opposite end of the spectrum are the perennials that take over and "can't be killed." These are plants that grow so well they need to be divided regularly to keep them in bounds. When time is not taken to control the growth of these plants, they become weeds.

Another reason perennials are not the perfect answer is that no perennial blooms all summer. Most have a short blooming period followed by a period of foliage growth. This means that if you use only perennials in the landscape, you must plant many varieties to have color throughout the summer.

I am not trying to discourage anyone from using perennials because I believe that more of them should be included in the landscape. They do require some care, however, and they should not supplant the use of annual flowers.

What are some perennials that can provide continuous color?

Look at the chart of perennial flower blooming times for suggestions. Keep in mind the conditions each variety needs to grow properly. Be sure to find out all you can about the plants before you buy them to ensure they are appropriate to your plans. In no way is the list comprehensive; it just covers some of the perennials I like. Remember that in most cases the blooming periods overlap months and the varieties of particular plants bloom at different times.

Are there any perennial flowers that will add a nice fragrance to the garden?

There are flowers that add a good scent to the garden, but don't count on these few plants to provide their fragrance throughout the summer. As with other perennials, they only stay in bloom for a short time. Plant them with annual flowers that have a fragrance, such as sweet alyssum, sweet pea, heliotrope, and some of the nasturtiums.

Things smell differently to different people, so to say a plant smells good depends on the nose of the beholder. However, the list of perennials that I think smell good includes peony, bearded iris, bee balm, lily-of-the-valley, lavender, hyacinth, various lilies, and daffodil. The peony, iris, lavender, and daffodil can also be cut and dried for potpourri. Of course, such shrubs as lilac, mock orange,

PERENNIAL FLOWER BLOOMING TIMES

March:
Christmas rose
Crocus
Daffodil
Reticulate iris
Squill
Winter aconite

April:
Bleeding-heart
Candytuft
Columbine
Grape hyacinth
Hyacinth
Violet
Virginia bluebells
Windflower

May:
Bearded iris
Cranesbill
Globeflower
Maltese cross
Leopard's bane
Lily-of-the-valley
Painted daisy
Peony
Perennial flax
Sweet William
Veronica

June:
Avens
Bellflower
Butterfly weed
Coralbells
Day lily
Foxglove
Larkspur

July:
Meadow sweet
Monkshood
Shasta daisy
Spiderwort
Stoke's aster
Yarrow

August:
Bee balm
Cardinal flower
Gayflower
Rose mallow
Silver mound
Turtlehead

September:
Blanket flower
Chrysanthemum
Purple coneflower
Sage
Sedum

fragrant viburnum, and the rose could be counted on for more pleasant smells.

How much light do perennials require?

Most perennials flower best when they are planted in full sunlight. The more heavily shaded an area, the more difficulty you'll have growing any plant—including perennials. Flowering perennials that do grow in the shade generally are not vigorous, their flowering is not profuse, and, at times, the color of the flowers is not as intense as in those growing in brighter locations. Few flowering perennials can be grown in heavy shade, and many of those that will grow there are not grown for the beauty of their flowers. As a matter of fact, the flowers are often removed so that the energy of the plant is applied to the foliage, which is of more interest.

Which flowering perennials can be expected to grow in heavy shade?

The first flowering perennial for shade that comes to mind is the hosta, which is also one of my favorites. A common variety, *Hosta undulata,* with which most of us are familiar, has twisted, lance-shaped, cream and olive-green foliage. It is extremely hardy and easily divided in the spring. It is not the most attractive hosta, but it is fairly trouble-free. One of the few pests to bother it is the slug, but remember, you can easily control this guy by stalking him at night with a salt shaker.

Don't limit yourself to the *Hosta undulata.* There are now a dozen or so varieties from which to select, and more are developed every year. Some grow to only about six inches high and can be used as ground cover. Others will grow to about three feet tall, not including the flower stalk. The foliage also varies in color from shades of green to yellow or gray to bluish. The leaf edges of some are tinged with white, cream, or yellow. Leaf textures vary as well. Some are smooth, others ribbed; some are waxy, others twisted. The shape of leaves ranges from extremely lance-shaped to quite oval-shaped.

One of my favorite varieties is 'Frances Williams'. This is one of the larger varieties and a description of the foliage cannot do it justice. The center of the leaf is olive green and is edged in a yellowish green. The rough texture of the leaves adds to its beauty.

Hosta will grow in many soils, but it prefers a rich soil that is a bit moist. It can be grown in full sunlight but does best in light shade. Many varieties have been tested in heavily shaded situations and have proven to be very adaptable. Once established, they require next to no care. The hosta clumps can grow to five feet in diameter, so they might need to be divided occasionally. But the procedure, best done in the spring, is not difficult.

The flowers, which develop on stalks to five feet tall on some varieties are not showy. The flower color varies from white to purple and violet. You can leave the flowers on the plant, but I think they detract from its appearance. I remove the stalks as they start to form.

A few other perennials that I have seen growing in medium shade are the fringed bleeding-heart, which has delicate foliage; lily-of-the-valley, which has a lovely, light fragrance; liriope, which has variegated leaves; trillium, which has large, showy flowers; cardinal flower, most varieties of which have red flowers, and Virginia bluebells, which blooms early with blue flowers.

Which perennials grow well in partial shade?

There are a surprising number of perennials that can thrive in lightly shaded areas of the landscape. Some are short and can be used as groundcover; others tend to be tall, growing to four or five feet. Most plants require some sunlight to grow and flower. This might be two or three hours of morning sun or just filtered sunlight. Some areas receive more sun in the early spring than in any other time of year and thus can be planted for early season color. Such bulbs as daffodil, crocus, snowdrop, and winter aconite, can be planted in areas that are covered by tree canopies much of the year. Most of the bulbs' growth will be complete before the tree's foliage emerges to block out the sunlight.

Aren't ferns a type of flowering perennial that will grow in heavy shade?

Yes, some varieties indeed can be grown where there is little sunlight. Ferns are not flowering perennials. A fern is more primitive than the flowering plants. Unlike flowering plants, ferns never form seed but reproduce by releasing spores, which develop on the underside of the fronds, or foliage.

The fronds emerge from underground stems called rhizomes. In some cases, the fronds appear at regular intervals from a rhi-

Bloom Times of Perennials for Partial Shade

March–April:
Christmas rose
Lenten rose

April:
Cranebill
Hepatica
Jacob's ladder
May apple

April–May:
Heart-leaved bergenia
Spring beauty
Trillium
Windflower

April–June:
Primrose
Purple rockcress
Violet

May:
Foam flower
Lily-of-the-valley
Marsh marigold

May–June:
Avens
Bishop's hat
Brunnera
Bugleweed
Candytuft
Columbine

(May–June cont'd:)
Leopard's bane
Shooting star
Siberian iris
Veronica

May–July:
Coralbells
Lungwort

May–August:
Forget-me-not

May–September:
Allium
Knotweed
Bleeding-heart

June:
Solomon's seal

June–July:
Astilbe
Cardinal flower
Foxglove
Goatsbeard
Lupine
Meadowsweet
Wild indigo

June–August:
Bellflower
Meadow rue

(June–August cont'd:)
Ragwort
Spurge

June–September:
Day lily
Fleabane
Mallow
Sedum
Spiderwort

July:
Lady's mantle

July–August:
Bee balm
Bishop's weed
(Goutweed)
Garden phlox
Sage

July–September:
Gentian
Pearly everlasting

July–October:
Heliopsis
Stoke's aster

August–September:
False dragonhead
Monkshood
Turtlehead

133

zome that creeps along just at or under the soil surface. In other cases, the fronds arise from a rhizome that is rather concentrated and forms a crown.

Ferns are best planted in spring, after the soil warms, or in early fall. They need a soil that is rich in organic matter and is fairly moist while they are growing. As with most plants, it is important to adjust the soil when planting and to fertilize with bone meal or a bone meal-rich fertilizer. You must not set the plants too deep in the ground. The crown should be just below the soil surface. Cool soil conditions are more conducive to summer growth, so mulching can be a benefit. If the soil gets too warm or too dry, the plants often will go dormant early.

Many ferns grow wild. Although they are not difficult to transplant, I do not recommend removing them from their habitat. Some species of fern are becoming harder to find in the wild because they are being dug up for home gardens. Nurseries are now growing many varieties for home use.

Which ferns grow in heavy shade?

One of the largest ferns to grow in shade is Goldie's wood fern. It needs a rich, cool soil, and its fronds can grow to three or four feet in height. The 'English Crested' male fern, which grows to three feet in height, is harder to find but would make a great addition to any shaded landscape.

Other ferns to consider are the maidenhair fern, lady fern, Christmas fern, and the small rock polypody. One that I have recently grown in full shade is the Japanese painted fern and it is doing extremely well.

There are many other varieties of ferns that can be used in the landscape. Some grow well in full sun and others in light shade. If the ferns you want are not available from a local nursery, check the mail-order catalogs.

Are bulbs considered perennials?

Bulbs and corms that can remain in the ground all year are indeed perennial. Not all perennial bulbs, however, will successfully rebloom. A good example of this is the tulip. Many tulips should be treated as annuals because they do not flower well after their first year in the ground. Many gardeners dig up tulip bulbs after the foliage dies, dry the bulbs, and store them in the refrigerator until late fall when they replant them. But other folks don't care for all that work. They just replant new tulip bulbs every fall. I have been successful in getting the Kaufmanniana tulips, early bloomers that grow to only about six inches high, to rebloom for many years.

A new class of tulips is being developed that will be a true perennial. These tulips will last for many years and increase in numbers without our having to dig them up. The Greigii tulips are generally thought of as perennial. Some early bloomers are 'Toronto', 'Red Emperor', and 'Showwinner', all red; 'Plaisir' and 'Stresa', both red and white; and 'Orange Emperor'. Midseason varieties include 'Peerless Pink', 'Golden Melody', the red-orange-and-yellow 'Apeldoorn Elite', and orange 'Holland's Glorie'. For late-season tulips try 'White Triumphator', the violet 'Ballad', and 'Burgundy Lace'.

To encourage perennial tulips and other bulbs to come back, remove the spent flowers so that seed pods do not develop, and keep the foliage growing as long as possible. In the fall add some Bulb-tone or bone meal to the soil.

Why is it that my tulips either don't come up or come up but don't flower?

Several problems can prevent bulbs from flowering, but first let me go over the planting instructions for tulips so you are sure you are planting them correctly.

Tulips need to be planted where winter temperatures drop to twenty degrees or colder. In warmer areas of the country, the bulbs can be planted but they must have been precooled, a condition you should check for before you buy them. About October, plant the bulbs in a sunny or lightly shaded area. The soil should be well drained and rich in organic matter, and should have a pH of about 6.0 to 6.5. If the soil is heavy, add sufficient peat moss or compost so the soil will drain properly. Add a fertilizer rich in bone meal to the bottom of the planting hole, which should be six to eight inches deep. Bulbs look better planted in clusters rather than in rows, and this arrangement minimizes the visual effect of a bulb that fails to bloom. Remember to plant tall varieties behind short ones so no flowers are obscured. You might find it helpful to write on each bag you buy the name of the variety as well as its average height.

Now about the problems. Many rodents enjoy tulip bulbs. Squirrels will frequently dig them from the ground. Voles will tunnel through the soil to find bulbs and then will eat them where they were planted. Deer are fond of tulips and can easily find them among many other types of bulbs. The deer eat the foliage and may root up the bulb. Placing mothballs just under the soil around the bulbs is often enough to discourage small-mammal damage. To prevent deer problems, I sprinkle small pieces of bar soap where I plant tulips.

Botrytis blight is a common disease that affects the foliage as well as the tulip bulb. Many other fungus diseases can cause the bulbs to rot in the ground. To prevent rotting, handle the bulbs carefully to prevent bruising them; treat them with a fungicide before planting, and never plant them in a soil that does not drain well.

A few other factors can hinder blooming during the first year: planting the bulbs too deep or too shallow, planting them too early in the season, or planting them in heavily shaded locations.

What is the difference between daffodils and narcissus?

In horticulture, as in many professions or fields of study, words are commonly used that have somewhat clouded meanings, and the confusion between daffodils and narcissus is such a case. The situation can be made more confusing by saying that daffodils are narcissus but not all narcissus are daffodils. Let's try to straighten out the mess.

Narcissus is the botanical name given to a genus of plants that grow from bulbs, which are in the Amaryllis family. The genus *Narcissus* is broken down into two groups: the daffodils and the jonquils. The word *daffodil* can be used when describing all narcissus except one group known as *Narcissus jonquilla,* the jonquils. The word *jonquil* is used more often in the South than in any other part of the country. So, the word *daffodil* is often used interchangeably with the word *narcissus.*

For lovers of trivia, the American Daffodil Society has decided that *narcissus* is both singular and plural.

My bearded irises occasionally rot and die. How should they be planted? What is killing them?

The bearded iris has been around a long time. The flower has six petals: three outer petals, called falls, that hang down, and three inner petals, termed standards, that stand upright. The beards of the iris are in the center of the falls. An artist could hardly create a color that is not already found in some iris; breeders have developed myriad colors and shades.

When planting any iris, find a location in full sunlight. Of soil, bearded irises require only that it not be too moist. Dwarf-bearded irises get only eight inches tall; the tallest can grow to thirty inches and need to be staked when in flower. (Plant the dwarf varieties near the front of the beds so you can see them.)

Never set iris plants too deep in the soil, and don't use mulch. Irises grow from rhizomes, which should be set so they are just covered, not buried. Many problems can arise when they are set too deep.

The plants can be propagated by cutting the rhizome into sections and replanting them. Do this after blooming. Late July is the best time of year. Before replanting, dust with a fungicide and check for iris borer. Fertilize twice a year with a side dressing.

The iris borer, a moth larva, is the major insect pest of the iris. The eggs of the moth overwinter. Then sometime in May or June, the eggs hatch and the larvae begin to feed on the iris foliage, or fans, so-called because of their growth and arrangement on the rhizome. The larvae eat holes in the leaves and chew the leaf edges. If you notice this damage, spray with malathion.

After about two weeks the larvae tunnel into the rhizome where they do their worst damage. Now unseen, they are more difficult to control. The larvae grow to about three inches long and can completely consume the rhizome, causing the foliage to die. Systemic sprays are the usual chemical means of control, but use them with great caution. One of the best ways to deal with this pest is to prevent it from attacking. The eggs overwinter in the debris around the iris, so each fall cut and remove the foliage and flower stems from the area. If the iris borer is an annual problem, place moth balls just under the soil by the plants to discourage the moths from laying eggs.

Several fungus diseases can destroy iris beds, and several rots can attack the rhizomes. A fungicide will control these diseases. Leaf spot is a common foliage disease. The spots are usually reddish brown in color and affect the plant by reducing its vigor. Cut away diseased foliage when you see it and use the fungicide benomyl.

Do not let the potential problems of the iris stop you from planting some. As far as I am concerned, every garden needs them.

What are minor bulbs?

I have never seen a good definition of *minor bulb,* but the term refers to the smaller, less showy spring-flowering bulbs, corms, or tubers that are planted in the fall. Not only are the flowers smaller, but so are the bulbs. There are many minor bulbs that can be included in the landscape, a few of which are fairly common—crocus, snowdrop, and grape hyacinth. Others that I am fond of are winter aconite, anemone, various alliums, trout lily, reticulate and Siberian irises, and squill.

How do I plant and care for peonies?

The peony is another perennial that should be in everyone's landscape. Peonies get rather large, spreading to about three feet in diameter. They come in a variety of colors and bloom at various times during the summer. By selecting several—some that bloom early, some during midseason, and others late—you can have peonies in bloom for about six weeks.

Peonies are best planted in early fall. Choose a location that receives full sun, then dig a hole about two feet deep and place six to eight inches of manure in the hole. Cover the manure with about six inches of soil so the peony's roots aren't burned. Then set the plant into the hole so that its eyes are not more than one inch below the soil surface. If possible, buy plants that have more than two eyes. Often, the fewer the eyes, the longer the plant will take to bloom. Peonies do not need to be divided more often than every eight to ten years. When you do divide them, be sure each section has about five eyes.

Many things can prevent a peony from blooming. Commonly the problem is that the plant was set too deep in the ground. If the eyes are much more than an inch below the soil, the plant will not bloom. Other factors that will hinder blooming are that the plant is too young, the ground is too dry, the area is too shaded, the plant is competing with too many other plants for the resources, there is not enough fertilizer, the roots are diseased, the soil is too wet, insects are feeding on the buds, or any combination of these problems.

Is it true that the buds of peonies only open properly if ants are around?

This question has been asked many times. No, ants are not needed and do not aid in the flowering of peonies. Let me add that ants do not harm the developing bud either. They are not eating the buds but instead are feeding on the sweet fluid that the flower releases.

However, ants have been known to spread the disease botrytis blight, which causes the buds to either wither or turn black. If you find it, apply the fungicide benomyl every ten days to two weeks until after the flowers open. In the fall, cut away all the foliage and remove it to help prevent a recurrence.

Are tree peonies planted and cared for like regular peonies?

Tree peonies are among the most attractive perennials. They grow from five to eight feet tall, depending on the type, and produce flowers that are four to eight inches across. Their bright colors include shades of red, deep maroon, orange, yellow, and white. They are also winter-hardy and can survive temperatures of fifteen to twenty degrees below zero.

The best time to plant tree peonies is fall, but you also can set them very early in the spring. Tree peonies do their best when planted in a rich loam soil with a pH of 5.5 to 6.5. Before planting them, add a handful or two of composted manure or peat moss to the soil, and work in half a cup of bone meal or 5–10–10 fertilizer.

Plant tree peonies deeper than you would regular peonies; the eyes should be covered with four to six inches of soil. Don't expect newly planted tree peonies to flower the first year. Flowering usually begins about the third year following planting.

Are day lilies edible?

The buds of the day lily are indeed edible. I've tried them but do not think they're very tasty. There are many better foods and the day lily has a much better purpose.

This plant has been around a long time and has probably been hybridized more than any other perennial flower. There are close to fifty thousand named cultivars, and many new ones are introduced each year. With so many varieties, it is no wonder that this is such a popular plant.

Another reason for its popularity is that it is easy to grow. It likes a soil that is slightly acidic and rich in organic matter, and that drains well. The day lily grows well in full sun but doesn't mind some afternoon shade. It has a large root system and thus needs a considerable amount of water in the spring as it grows. It can be planted in either the spring or fall, and clusters need to be divided only about every eight years. Divide them after they bloom.

How long do day lilies bloom?

The individual flower of the day lily lasts only one day, hence the plant's name. The blossom opens in the morning and closes between dusk and midnight, depending on the variety. Each plant produces many flower buds, so one plant can have flowers opening over several days. For this reason, day lilies bloom longer than other types of perennials. To keep some varieties blooming, you might need to pick off the dead blooms, or "dead-head" them, daily. Different varieties bloom at various times throughout the summer and early fall. Creative planning can ensure that you have day lilies in flower for several months and in a multitude of colors, which include orange, yellow, gold, red, pink, and lemon yellow. Day lilies also come in mixed colors.

One new variety, 'Stella de Oro', is a must for everyone who enjoys day lilies. The plant is not spectacular. It grows to two feet and has golden flowers, which are not that large. However, it is the only day lily that will bloom all summer. The blooms start opening in late spring, and buds continue to form and open through about the end of September.

It seems as though blue-flowering perennials are hard to find. Can you suggest some?

Spring begins with several blue-flowering perennials. Crocus, reticulate iris, hyacinth, grape hyacinth, and scilla are the first. Then throughout the spring and summer, more bloom: windflower, forget-me-not, Virginia bluebells, spiderwort, blue cardinal flower, blue columbine, delphinium, iris, mountain bluet, wild indigo, bell-flower, flax, cornflower aster, hosta, globe thistle, and perennial sage. Most of these are easy to grow in northern climates. It is important to know the necessary growing conditions for those perennials you want to plant.

Each fall I buy hardy chrysanthemums and plant them as directed. Yet, in the spring many do not come back. What could be the problem?

When it comes to fall color, nothing can compare with the beauty of mums, but not all varieties are equally hardy. You must find out from your nurseryman which are the hardiest for your area. In many areas of the country, mums should be treated as tender perennials, meaning they might come back yearly or they might not. Winter's cold temperatures greatly affect the degree of hardiness. Regardless of their hardiness, though, mums should be planted for all the beauty they bring to the landscape.

Chrysanthemums come in a wide variety of flower types as well as colors. The more familiar types are the pompons, which are rounded and less than two inches across; cushions, which have large three-inch flowers on compact plants; buttons, which look like little pompons; rayonetees, or spider mums; singles, or daisy types; and spoons, which have tubular petals that open to a spoon-like end.

As with most perennials, mums need at least six hours of sunlight daily or they will become leggy. They need a well-drained soil that is high in organic material. Fall is the best time of year to plant them, and I recommend you plant them by mid-September. This should give the roots time to start knitting into the soil, preparing them for winter.

Liquid-feed your mums after planting and continue to water them if there is insufficient rain in the fall. Then feed them at least one more time while they are in bloom. When the frosts of fall kill the foliage, cut the tops to the ground. If the foliage is diseased, remove it. If not, leave it over the crown of the plant and add more mulch, such as straw, oak leaves, or evergreen boughs. The mulch will help keep the winter winds from drying the crowns. The mum crown is alive and needs oxygen, so never use maple leaves because they compact and can smother the plant. Do not uncover the crowns of the plants too early in spring. The early growth is tender and frost can kill it.

Mums should be divided every two to three years, depending on how well they are growing. Divide the plant in early spring and replant immediately. Add some superphosphate to the planting hole. Chrysanthemums are heavy feeders, so use 5–10–5 fertilizer monthly throughout the summer.

To help keep mums from becoming leggy, pinch back the growing tips. This should begin when the plants reach a height of about eight inches. As the plant grows, continue pinching until about July 15. By then the plant should be bushy, compact, and ready to form buds. If any buds form before this, remove them.

Few insects other than aphids and caterpillars bother chrysanthemums. Use insecticidal soap to control aphids and Sevin to take care of caterpillars. Powdery mildew and gray mold are the two most persistent diseases, and benomyl is effective in managing both.

What perennials can be used to attract hummingbirds to the landscape?

In the East, ruby-throated hummingbirds often visit our yards. Hummingbird feeders provide one method of attracting them, of course, and for many people this works fine. Many of us, though, use plants to bring them to the yard, and I believe hummingbirds fancy the natural food, which is usually found in red flowers with deep throats. There are two perennials that are a must for attracting hummingbirds: bee balm and coralbells.

Bee balm, or monarda, is easy to grow and needs little care. The biggest problem is that it tries to take over flower beds, so keep after it. Coralbells is also care-free, but it is not invasive. Both plants come in colors other than red, so be sure you select red cultivars. Hummingbirds will also visit foxglove, columbine, lupine, butterfly weed, day lily, and loosestrife.

Use perennials in concert with other plants that hummingbirds regularly visit, such as red salvia, snapdragon, and geranium. Woody perennials, such as trumpet vine, azalea, and beautybush, also provide the nectar hummingbirds need.

Of course, there is no guarantee that you will have hummingbirds in your yard just because you plant the flowers they are known to visit, but you certainly increase the likelihood of attracting them.

Which perennials can be cut and used in fresh arrangements?

There is a great pleasure in walking around the landscape and enjoying the various perennials in bloom. But there is something special about having a house full of fresh-cut flowers. As a child, I remember peonies being cut and brought inside to brighten the table. I later learned that the stems of peonies can be cut very short and the flowers floated in a brandy snifter.

There are quite a number of perennials that maintain their beauty after they are cut. I'm sure we have all had the experience of cutting some perennials only to have them wilt in a matter of minutes. Here are some that you might consider for indoor use: baby's-breath, gayflower, various irises, shasta and painted daisies, globeflower, torch lily, lily-of-the-valley, delphinium, blanketflower, chrysanthemum, sage, and yarrow.

Cut the flowers early in the morning, selecting those that just opened or are about to open. Use a sharp knife or scissors and be sure to clean the blades with alcohol to prevent the spread of disease. Cut the stems at a slight angle to increase the surface area for water absorption. Carry a container of warm water with you and place the cut stems in it immediately. When you are ready to arrange the flowers, recut the stems to the length you want while you hold them under water. And remember, you don't have to be an expert when it comes to arranging!

Are there perennial flowers that can be grown for drying?

There are flowers that look great in the garden and keep their color after drying. Yarrow is one, and the money plant, actually a biennial, is another. The list of perennials I have dried includes giant allium, lamb's-ears, delphinium, purple loosestrife, gayflower, pearly everlasting, sea lavender, baby's-breath, sea holly, Chinese lantern, globe thistle, lavender, and several of the grasses.

There are various ways of drying perennials. The most common method is to cut the flowers in the morning and then hang them upside down and air-dry them in a dark room. Cut the flower stems long and remove any leaves that could interfere with the flower. In some cases, the flowers can be bunched together with a rubber band. Drying should be complete in about three weeks. Be careful when you handle dried flowers because they are brittle.

Can any perennials be grown in containers? If so, how?

There are places in the landscape where only containers will work: patios, decks, walks, and sunrooms, for example. The containers can be wood, concrete, clay, or plastic. Old whiskey barrels, urns, iron kettles, hollow stumps or logs, even old bathtubs can make interesting gardens.

Make drainage holes in the bottom of any container you use so excess water drains away. Put in some gravel to keep soil from clogging the openings.

There are many commercial sterilized soils available. For container gardening, I recommend a mix of three parts soil to one part composted cow manure. Fill the container with this mixture, leaving enough room that, when watered, the soil does not spill out. Thoroughly soak the soil to compact it before you set in the plants.

You will need to water frequently throughout the season because containers tend to dry out rapidly. During the heat of summer they probably will require daily watering. Check the soil before adding water, though. Water in the morning and try to keep water off the foliage to help prevent diseases. Do not use a high-pressure sprayer; it can wash out the soil and damage the plants.

Because you are constantly adding water to the container, nutrients are leaching from the soil. A liquid fertilizer replaces these nutrients whenever the plants are watered. Be sure to know if the plants prefer an acid or alkaline fertilizer.

Most early spring-flowering bulbs can be used in containers. When they have finished blooming, you can plant annuals over the bulbs. Other perennial flowers that can be used in containers include coralbells, bee balm, bleeding-heart, yarrow, violet, sedum, day lily, gayflower, loosestrife, torch lily, shasta and painted daisies, monkshood, cranesbill, blanketflower, chrysanthemum, and phlox. If you mix some annuals with the perennials, you can have continuous color. The size and type of container will determine how many plants can be used and, to some extent, their size.

Container gardens of perennials need special care during the winter. After fall frosts have taken the last of the summer foliage, remove the annuals and prepare the container and plants for winter. Never bring planted containers into a heated greenhouse for the winter because the perennials must go dormant, and they need cold temperatures to do so. You can bury the containers in the ground or put them in an unheated shed or porch. Or you can gather them on the ground and cover them with evergreen boughs or surround them with chicken wire and mulch them with straw or leaves. This will prevent drastic fluctuations in temperature.

Are there any perennials that should be avoided because they tend to take over the landscape?

Some plants are invasive, but I am not sure I should tell you not to include them. Some have pretty flowers, others have nice foliage. Be aware, though, that they can easily get out of bounds and end up being weeds if you do not keep after them.

Two very common ground covers are the bugle weed, or ajuga, and bishop's weed. Both have their good points, but if they escape, look out! Certain violets go wild in the lawn, and purple and yellow loosestrife will overwhelm all other plants in moist soil. Mint is fine in the garden but keep it there. Actually, if you like mint you're probably better off growing it in a container, which will control it. Common tansy and creeping bellflower are two others that need to be added to the list of invading perennials.

Can wildflowers be included in perennial beds?

Many native wildflowers are perennial and can be used among horticultural perennials, or you can create a special area and incorporate them into the landscape. There are some showy wildflowers, such as lady's slipper and trillium, but most do not produce flowers that are particularly large. However, they are beautiful and worthy of our attention. Many of the perennials that are now common in the garden had their origins in the wild, and many wildflowers are now horticulturally grown so you can buy them from catalog companies and garden centers.

Never remove wildflowers from the wild. Many wildflowers are becoming rare because people have transplanted them from their natural settings. We must do all we can to discourage this practice. Buy wildflowers from a nursery, but be sure the supplier is getting the plants from a legitimate grower.

Some wildflowers that I have found available are Virginia bluebells, wild columbine, cardinal flower, and butterfly weed. These are a few of my favorites. Others that are available include spring beauty, bloodroot, Solomon's seal, and Dutchman's-breeches. Jack-in-the-pulpit, trout lily, and wild ginger are three others that are growing well for me.

What are some good perennials for the person who does not have a green thumb?

I don't believe there is anyone who doesn't have a green thumb. There are people who don't take time to plant things properly, water plants when needed, and pull weeds. There are many who try to plant a variety in the wrong place and then overwater it to make it grow. All this has nothing to do with the color of one's thumb; it has to do with time, knowledge, and effort.

Nothing can replace good planting techniques and choosing

the right plant for the habitat. Excluding these two exceptions, however, there are a number of perennials that seem to thrive with little attention. These are plants that don't grow too tall, so they don't need to be staked. Most of them do not have to be divided or, if they do, not very often, and none try to take over the yard. All are winter hardy and need no special attention to get them ready for cold weather. Most are bothered by few pests. But when plants are given a bit of care, they will do better than when left to themselves.

Let's start with some spring bulbs: daffodil, crocus, snowdrop, and grape hyacinth all do their own thing after they are planted, and all will increase in number over the succeeding years. Put them out in the fall. For a shaded area, try hosta. Remember that there are many great varieties from which to select. Then there are a number of old favorites, such as bleeding-heart, peony, day lily, black-eyed Susan, and coralbells. For something different try gayflower, cardinal flower, coneflower, liriope, and astilbe.

What are some of the common insects and diseases that affect perennials and how can they be controlled?

There are several things we can do to prevent many pests from becoming serious problems. One of the most important is to keep the plants healthy—feed and water them properly—because healthy plants are less susceptible to insects and diseases. Weeds attract many pests, so keep weeds out of the perennial beds. Clean the beds in the fall, because the debris often harbors disease carriers and dormant insects.

Examine your plants frequently for disease. When you discover a disease on a leaf or stem, remove the affected part. Leaf spot, a common name for several infections, can attack many plants, particularly chrysanthemums. Damp weather can bring on blights, rots, and molds. Rusts, mildew, and canker are a few more troublesome diseases. There are few natural products on the market to fight all these diseases. If a fungicide is needed, I recommend benomyl. Tests have shown that it is effective at controlling more diseases than any other single product. Safer now has a natural fungicide available, but I am not sure of its effectiveness. If there is a plant in the garden that is particularly predisposed to disease, either apply a fungicide in spring before you notice the problem or remove the plant after it has been infected.

Insects can seem to enjoy almost every plant. If you find insects or their eggs, remove them by hand and destroy them. If you think that the pest is eating at night, head to the garden with a flashlight and destroy the critter.

You may think the bugs have gotten the better of you, but before you apply any pesticide, carefully identify the critter you find. You don't want to unwittingly destroy a beneficial insect that is trying to control those that are doing the damage. By spraying you would kill your insect allies.

Common problem insects are whitefly, aphid, leaf hopper, mealybug, thrip, and scale. These are difficult to remove by hand, but insecticidal soap is effective in controlling them. Carry a bottle of it whenever you visit the flower bed. It's also effective on mites, which are so tiny that their populations seem to explode almost overnight in the flower garden. Sevin is effective for beetles and caterpillars.

Borers and miners are more difficult to control because they live inside plants. If possible, remove the leaf or stem to get rid of the pests. Remember that removing debris in the fall can help prevent these pests from causing problems. Placing mothballs, in early spring, around plants attractive to these pests will help prevent future problems, too.

If slugs and snails are troublesome, go out at night with a salt shaker or set out a saucer of beer. For earwigs, put on the gloves and go after them. No, they cannot pinch very hard!

Is it true that some perennials are poisonous and should not be used around homes?

Some perennials, or parts of them, contain natural chemicals that are poisonous. There are also plants in our homes that have toxins, as well as woody plants used in landscaping that are poisonous. Some vegetable plants also have parts that contain poisons. I do not feel that all of these plants should be avoided in the landscape. Instead, we must teach children not to remove leaves and flowers from plants and put them in their mouths.

Some perennial flowering plants that are known to contain poisons are lily-of-the-valley, Christmas rose, monkshood, foxglove, autumn crocus, lobelia, delphinium, tansy, bleeding-heart, bloodroot, buttercup, daffodil, Dutchman's-breeches, Jack-in-the-pulpit, lupine, squirrel corn, May apple, and larkspur. None of these plants has a taste that would appeal to anyone, but if you think that someone has eaten any of them, call the doctor or hospital emergency room immediately. Local poison-control centers can supply you with a list of all poisonous plants.

Are grasses considered perennial?
Will they take over perennial beds in
which they have been planted?

Grasses are flowering plants. They are monocots and are related to corn, cereal grains, and plants such as lily and spiderwort. Many of the grasses—both turf and ornamental—are perennial. Some grasses are annual, such as crabgrass and annual bluegrass. The grasses used in perennial plantings are ornamental grasses.

Ornamental grasses are available in many colors, including red and blue. They vary in both texture and size, ranging in length from just a few inches to twenty feet. Some ornamentals with long stems, or culms, arch; others form mounds. Ornamental grasses do not have to be cut or staked, and they flourish with little care. Most have few pests about which to be concerned. Ornamental grasses can be used as accents, in a grouping, or in beds or borders. Unlike perennial flowers, they do not die back to the ground in the fall, so they keep the landscape interesting throughout the winter.

Ornamental grasses are best planted in spring. Some cannot be planted bare root, so it is always best to use those grown in containers. The various grasses differ in soil requirements, spacing, and fertilizer needs. Overfeeding can provoke trouble; if the grass grows too rapidly, it becomes weak and prone to problems.

Few ornamental grasses are invasive, and therefore few are of much concern when used in the landscape. Two of them, bamboo and ribbon grass, however, are strongly rhizomatic and thus need to be restricted.

Could you suggest some grass varieties that
are easy to grow for the beginning gardener?

Many ornamental grasses are rather care-free if they are planted in the proper environment. Trying to force a grass to perform in conditions that are not to its liking can be frustrating. So when selecting grasses, you must understand what they need. Some interesting low-growing grasses are Japanese sedge grass and wide-leaf sedge. Autumn moor grass and Maires fescue are nice, but my favorite low grower is blue fescue. Taller grasses worth considering are the tuber oat grass 'Variegatum', squirreltail grass, Japanese blood grass 'Red Baron', porcupine grass 'Strictus', zebra grass 'Zebrinus', and Chinese silver grass.

9

Woody Plants

When I first became professionally involved in horticulture, I worked in a nursery. My main duty was to sell landscape plants to homeowners. Part of the job entailed helping people select the proper plants for their site. Before I would recommend a shrub I would ask the patron several questions. One was always, "How tall do you want the shrub to grow?" A common response was, "I want a plant that will get only two feet tall because I hate to prune." The only plant I know of that, in some cases, gets only two feet tall and never needs pruning is what I term the "everbrown." It never needs fertilizer, never needs water, and never needs pruning. If you want it green, though, you have to paint it; it's dead.

Too bad plants don't grow more like people do. We reach a certain height, then stop. Often we continue to grow out, but not up. As long as plants are alive, however, they grow up. No plant will stop growing at two feet, but many plants can be maintained at that height by pruning.

In this chapter, I deal with shrubs, those woody plants that generally lack a central trunk, and dwarf conifers, small cousins of the forest evergreens. (Having one main trunk, dwarf conifers actually are trees.) Some shrubs are evergreen; others drop their leaves in the fall. Some of the evergreens have broad leaves; others have needle-shaped or scalelike leaves. There are evergreens that are used in the landscape because they produce beautiful flowers, whereas others are often used as a backdrop for shorter shrubs and flowers.

Many of the deciduous shrubs we plant in our yards provide color. In most, the color results from flowers that form in spring and, in a few cases, over the summer. The flowers of some shrubs, rose, lilac, and mock orange, for example, provide fragrance as a bonus. But it is the foliage and even the stems that are the main interest on many shrubs. The fall color of burning bush's foliage, holly and viburnum berries, and even the stems of the red- and yellow-twig dogwoods all contribute their unusual qualities to the landscape.

Some woody plants that are not shrubs will also receive some attention here. Woody vines and ground covers are often used with shrubs to create a certain effect. Vines can hide unsightly walls and fences and serve as a pleasant backdrop for shrubs and flowers. Some of the vines are used to create shade and, in most cases, they also provide colorful flowers.

I know of a lot of trees that are conifers. Could you list some conifers that are shrubs?

Indeed, many of the conifers we find around houses are trees, and most of the conifers that we call shrubs are, in reality, just small trees. A good example of this is the very common American arborvitae. Is the pyramidal form a tree or shrub? It usually has only one main trunk, and it can get to be sixty feet tall. Yet, in most nurseries it is sold as a shrub and it is used in the landscape as a shrub. For our purposes then, let's consider these species as shrubs: arborvitae, yew, and juniper; several pines, such as Mugo pine and dwarf blue Scotch pine; hemlocks, such as weeping 'Sargentii' and 'Cole's Prostrate'; and several plants that we call cypress, although they are not true cypresses, such as 'Hinoki', 'Boulevard', and 'Goldthread'.

What are dwarf conifers?

Dwarf conifers, which need little if any pruning to stay small, are the slow-growing cultivars of many common conifers. Being slow growers, they tend to be expensive if they are very large. They often are used as specimen plants in the landscape, and most certainly are worth the attention they receive.

All of us are familiar with the pyramidal and global arborvitae—they're two of the most overused plants in the home landscape. Several arborvitae that are considered dwarf conifers have more interesting characteristics than the typical varieties we so often see, and they grow at a much slower rate. The 'Hetz Midget' has a globe shape and will rarely grow taller than three feet. 'Holm-strup' is a dwarf pyramidal form that does not grow taller than nine feet. One of my favorite arborvitae is 'Rheingold'. This small conical shrub has foliage with a rich gold color. The 'Westmont', another globe-shaped cultivar, has unusual yellow-tipped branches.

Some varieties of false cypress which are just called cypress, are dwarfs. The 'Nana Gracilis', or dwarf 'Hinoki', cypress is one of the most distinguished of the dwarf conifers. It grows to only six feet, and its flat branchlets are a rich dark green. The silver-green foliage of the 'Boulevard' cypress turns gray-blue in late fall. The 'Goldthread' cypress has a yellow-gold color year round but is brighter in the spring.

Some varieties of hemlock are also dwarfed. The 'Sargentii' is a cultivar that remains low and has a weeping form. It is one of the most spectacular of the conifers. Two other dwarf hemlocks are 'Bennet' and 'Cole's Prostrate'.

Several pines are considered dwarf conifers, and there are several 'Compacta' forms of eastern white pine available. The Japanese stone pine is extremely dwarfed: it grows to only about seven feet. Another common dwarf conifer is the Mugo pine 'Compacta', which is maintained at only about three feet. Two other pines to consider, because of their unusual characteristics, are the dwarf blue Scotch pine and the 'Tanyosho' pine.

If you fancy spruce then consider the pyramidal dwarf Alberta spruce, a variety of white spruce. A beautifully shaped shrub that grows only about three inches a year, this spruce is at home in almost any landscape. A dwarf conifer that can easily be maintained at two feet is the bird's nest spruce. This is a low, round, compact shrub, with a depression in the center of the plant. Bird's nest is actually a variety of Norway spruce.

Is there some special way dwarf conifers should be planted?

All dwarf conifers prefer a slightly acid soil that is rich and well drained. If the pH becomes alkaline, the foliage tends to yellow. Most dwarf conifers do best when planted in full sunlight, but they will tolerate light shade. Those that have normally yellow foliage need full sun because their color fades in the shade.

Most dwarf conifers should be planted in the spring. They are available at nurseries either in containers or balled and burlapped.

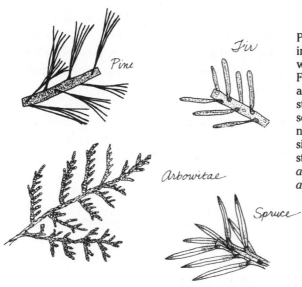

Pine needles are arranged in bundles of two to five with a sheath-covered base. Fir needles are singular and attached directly to the stem. Arborvitae have scalelike leaves rather than needles. Spruce needles are single and attached to the stem by a "peg." *Pine, fir, and spruce illustrated by author*

If you are planting in heavy soil, add peat moss. Some dwarf conifers, such as the pines and hemlocks, are more susceptible to wind than the others. None do well in moist or wet areas.

Can arborvitae be used as a windbreak to protect the house?

A windbreak is probably the best use there is for the pyramidal arborvitae. This species is found much too often around homes and is usually left to grow too tall. Windbreaks need to be tall, though, and pyramidal arborvitae grow fast enough to soon be effective in this function.

Arborvitae is not the first choice of many folks for a screen or wind barrier. Hemlock and white pine are often selected for this purpose. These trees make poor windbreaks, however, because they are weak-wooded and shallow-rooted, and they do not tolerate winter winds very well. The arborvitae, on the other hand, seems to be more suited to windy situations.

When planting a windbreak with arborvitae, set the plants in two rows that are four feet apart. Set the trees four feet apart within each row and stagger the rows so that the front row does not hide the one behind it. Although arborvitae prefers a slightly acid soil, it grows well even in limestone soils, which are alkaline. Full sun is the best situation for planting, but light shade does not seem to be much of a problem.

Few pests bother the arborvitae, but look out for bagworms. When discovered, remove the pests by hand. The larvae are well protected inside the little "house" of needles they carry along with them. I do not recommend spraying them with a systemic pesticide. Yet that is one of the few ways to control another pest called the arborvitae leaf miner. These larvae feed on the new growth, turning it brown. With enough damage, the trees will die.

It is normal for the inner foliage of the arborvitae to brown and shed its leaves in the fall of the year because of stress brought on by the climate. The browning is much more apparent in some years than in others. Keeping the plants healthy prevents excess shedding. Fertilize arborvitae in the spring and fall with Holly-tone and water the plants if there is little rain.

What juniper cultivars would you advise for landscaping around a house?

Many juniper varieties grow in diverse sizes and shapes, and you can use many of them effectively around your home. The question is how the plant is to be used. Several junipers make good ground cover. 'Blue Rug' is a trailing form that grows to only about six inches in height but can spread to about eight feet. Its silver-blue, dense foliage is very attractive. If you want a ground cover that is slightly taller, try 'Bar Harbor'. It grows to nearly one foot and spreads to eight feet. Another handsome cover is 'Blue Chip', which grows to ten inches. The 'Broadmoor' is a low-growing spreader that reaches a height of about thirty inches but spreads to ten feet. One other cultivar that can be used as a ground cover is 'Blue Pacific'. It is extremely hardy, grows about ten inches high, and has beautiful blue-green foliage. It is my favorite juniper ground cover.

If you want a juniper that is taller and more shrublike, there are several varieties to consider, but please do not plant the 'Hetzii'. This old variety is very hardy, but it grows too fast, reaching a size of about twelve by twelve feet. It needs almost constant pruning.

For use around the house foundation, consider the following varieties. 'Armstrong' reaches about four feet high and has light green foliage. For some golden color, try 'Gold Coast' or 'Old Gold' junipers; both stay compact and will not grow out of hand. To keep their nice gold color, though, they need to be planted in the sun. (Remember, colors fade in the shade.) 'Mint Julep' is mint green in color and is a compact grower. 'Sea Green' has compact growth and dark green foliage.

If you need tall, treelike junipers, consider 'Spartan', which grows fast and has a columnar shape. 'Robusta' has an irregular, upright growth habit and will reach twelve to fifteen feet if not pruned. 'Hollywood' also has an irregular upright shape but grows faster and will get taller and wider than 'Robusta'. One of my favorite upright junipers is 'Gray Gleam', which will reach ten or twelve feet but will maintain a tight pyramidal shape. Its silver-gray foliage really make this one a prize. Probably the narrowest and tallest of the junipers that I would recommend is the 'Skyrocket'. This plant looks great when planted next to a tall, contemporary home. The foliage is a blue-green color.

All of these junipers are easily grown in almost any soil; some even tolerate moist soil. To help them do their best, plant them in full sun and keep the soil acidic. Junipers suffer from very few pests.

What type of shrubs are broadleaf evergreens?

All shrubs that keep their leaves over the winter are termed evergreens. In reality, some of the leaves do drop, but most of the foliage remains on the plant. Broadleaf evergreens are those that have broad foliage, that is, not needlelike, scalelike, or awllike shapes that refer to the leaves of conifers. Broadleaf evergreens are flowering plants, not conifers.

Broadleaf evergreens produce some of the most striking flowers found in the landscape. Rhododendrons and azaleas are good examples of this. Others, such as holly, exhibit flowers that are quite inconspicuous. Many folks regard the plant's retention of its foliage throughout the winter as an added benefit. They're more interested in the flowers or fruit.

There are numerous broadleaf evergreens besides the popular rhododendron, azalea, and holly. There is wintergreen barberry, certain cotoneasters, mountain laurel, leucothoi, Scotch heather, many wintergreen euonymus cultivars, Japanese holly, leatherleaf and burkwood viburnums, Japanese pieris, and some pyracanthas. One of my favorite is the Oregon grapeholly; its shiny, bronzish spring foliage changes to green and then to purple-bronze by fall. It forms bright yellow flowers in the spring, which develop into small, blue, grapelike clusters in autumn. This slow grower should be maintained at a height of three to six feet in shaded areas with acidic soil. Two other broadleaf evergreens are pachysandra and the vine English ivy, which can also be used for ground cover.

Do broadleaf evergreens need special winter care?

Care given to broadleaf evergreens will vary with the plant's location and hardiness. Some varieties are much tougher than others. If you want to give the plants some protection and, more important, give yourself some peace of mind, you can do several things.

Mulch around all evergreens. Plants that keep their leaves over the winter constantly lose water due to evaporation, which is made worse by winter wind. Mulch will prevent the soil from drying and thus retain the water for the evergreens' use. It is very important to water these plants until the ground freezes. (I have watered rhododendrons on Christmas Day.)

Apply an antidesiccant to both sides of the foliage of broadleaf evergreens to help cut the rate of transpiration. The product coats the leaf with a waxlike layer. Wilt-Pruf is one such product and should be applied in early winter and again during the midwinter thaw. This is just another way of protecting those beautiful and expensive rhododendrons, azaleas, and hollies.

Putting burlap around newly planted evergreens protects them from the wind and also slows both transpiration of moisture from the leaves and evaporation of moisture from the soil.

I love rhododendron flowers. What are some pointers for growing this part?

The rhododendron family is large and includes azaleas. There are about a thousand species and more than ten thousand hybrids of rhododendrons and azaleas. The conditions needed for proper growth are the same for all members of the family.

Rhododendrons prefer partial shade, or if planted beside the house, an eastern location where they get morning sun and afternoon shade. These are acid-loving plants, and they will not grow well in limestone soils. If you have alkaline soil and want rhododendrons, you can build raised beds filled with a soil more to their liking. Raised beds can also solve the problem of soils that do not drain well. When planting a rhododendron, set the plant in the ground so that the top of the root ball is an inch above the soil level. Setting it in too high is better than setting it too deep; in most cases, the soil will later compact under the plant, lowering it into the ground.

Rhododendrons are shallow-rooted plants and can suffer during the summer if the soil dries out. You might need to water frequently if rainfall is insufficient, particularly in the first summer following planting. To help the soil retain moisture, apply about three inches of tanbark, or hardwood mulch, over the root zone of the plant. Mound it so that water will drain toward the root system—not away from it.

Fertilize rhododendrons with Holly-tone in early April and again in early July.

What are some good rhododendron cultivars to plant?

Not all rhododendrons grow to be large plants. The 'Purple Gem' is a dwarf variety with small, azalea-like leaves. It blooms early and is winter hardy to fifteen degrees below zero. 'P. J. M.' has deep pink flowers, is taller, and is maintained at about four feet. The leaves are larger than those of the 'Purple Gem' but smaller than most, and they take on a mahogany cast during the winter, which adds some color that the others don't. The old favorite, 'Roseum Elegans', has lavender flowers and seems to bloom prolifically almost every year. Often this variety grows to eight or ten feet tall.

A very winter-hardy rhododendron is the 'Nova Zembla'. The leaves of this variety are very glossy and the flowers are about as red as any found on rhododendrons. If you want to think pink, then 'Scintillation' might be more to your liking. This adaptable plant is not quite as winter hardy as the others; it survives to only fifteen degrees below zero rather than twenty-five below, but its beautiful flowers make it worth trying. 'Chionoides' is the most popular white-flowering cultivar and is most attractive when mixed with other colors.

Could you suggest some azaleas that need little care?

A recent survey conducted among the nation's nurserymen asked them to list their favorite azalea cultivar, as well as many other types of plants. Altogether, ninety-one varieties of azalea were listed by the one hundred sixty-seven people who responded. Obviously, there are many favorite azaleas.

Azaleas are commonly divided into two major groups: evergreen and deciduous. Most people are familiar with the evergreens, which keep most of their leaves during winter, and they are the most popular azaleas. The deciduous forms are referred to as Exbury and Mollis hybrids. Both have colorful flowers, but the Exbury are hardier and their flowers are somewhat larger.

Let me list some of the more popular evergreen azaleas. I think the 'Delaware Valley White' is the most commonly sold azalea. You can rely on this plant for color every year, and it is hardy to twenty degrees below zero. For red flowers try 'Hino Crimson', which grows three to four feet tall. The dwarf 'Hershey Red', which has bright red double flowers, grows to about two feet. The 'Stewartstonian' has a brick-red flower, and 'Coral Bells' has a pink flower. 'Herbert' is a very hardy purple-flowering azalea.

The deciduous azaleas are ideal plants to use in a naturalized situation. They grow taller than do the evergreens, and they are very hardy. They are also some of the most underused plants in the landscape. They drop their leaves in the fall so there is little chance of winter-wind damage to the plant. One drawback is that the foliage is susceptible to powdery mildew in the fall.

The flowers of these plants are bold and bright. Flowers may be brilliant orange, salmon, gold, yellow, pink, or white. My favorite cultivar is 'Gibraltar,' which has red-orange flowers.

Do azaleas and rhododendrons have many insect pests?

Unfortunately, quite a number of pests affect azaleas and rhododendrons. Lace bug can devastate the foliage of azaleas, rhododendrons, laurel, pyracantha, and Japanese pieris. Azaleas and rhododendrons in sunny locations are most affected. Lace bugs— small, clear-winged insects—live on the underside of the foliage and suck the juices out of the leaves. The upper side of the foliage reveals the presence of the pest. The green foliage quickly appears stippled because of the constant probing of the insect. In time the foliage yellows because the chlorophyll has been removed, and often the leaves drop. Another sign of the insect's presence can be found on the underside of the leaves; it leaves small brown drops of excrement as it feeds.

Using dormant spray can help control this pest, which over-winters in eggs attached to the leaves. If azaleas and rhododendrons were heavily damaged during the previous season, Sevin or insecticidal soap should be applied beginning in May to prevent future problems.

The black vine weevil preys on rhododendrons, azaleas, yews, and hemlocks. The adults, which are all females, are nocturnal feeders and thus are not often seen. They hide in the mulch around the plant by day and climb the plant by night to feed on the foliage. Their presence can be spotted by their feeding habits: they feed along the leaf margin and leave a notched edge. This feeding does not hurt the plant.

However, the feeding by the larvae can kill the plant. The larvae feed from summer through fall and then again the following spring when they metamorphose into adult beetles. Most damage is done to the plant in May and June just before the larvae change into adults. They feed on roots and underground bark of rhododendron, destroying a connection to the soil and causing the plant to wilt and die. Control of larvae is difficult. Diazinon applied to the soil can be helpful in eradicating the larvae or, if damage from adults is noticed on the foliage, a night stroll with a flashlight would be helpful. Remove them by hand and dispose of them.

The rhododendron borer also presents trouble to rhododendrons, azaleas, and mountain laurel. The adult, a clear-winged moth, lays its eggs under the bark of the host plant. Upon hatching, the larvae, or borers, tunnel into the bark, eating as they go. This can wilt leaves and young branches, reduce the rate of growth, and eventually kill the branches and plants. Systemic chemicals have been used to control this pest in the past. There are now synthetic pheromone traps available to lure adults before they can lay eggs. The adults begin to appear about mid-June.

Other insects use azaleas and rhododendrons as their hosts, but those pests already mentioned are the ones you should be most concerned about.

I also want to remind you that voles feed on the roots and bark of rhododendrons and azaleas. Voles certainly aren't insects, but these little rodents can kill an azalea quicker than any insect.

What diseases are common to azaleas and rhododendrons?

When spring weather is wet and warm, a disease called azalea gall often occurs. The fungus causes the leaves to thicken, twist, and turn to pale green and then to white. The same disease will cause the petals of rhododendron to thicken and galls to develop. The disease will not kill the plants, so the best control is simply to remove the affected parts by hand and destroy them.

The most serious rhododendron disease is *Phytophthora* dieback. This fungus causes the flower buds to pale, then brown, and the leaves to turn brown, curl, and droop. Soon the affected stem starts to turn pale green and a canker will appear. To prevent the disease from spreading, the affected part must be pruned away. Nothing will cure a plant when it is infected, but spraying with bordeaux mixture as the leaves open can help prevent the disease.

Winter injury can lead to several problems, the most common of which is botrytis blotch. Winter's cold winds kill the tips or margins of leaves. The disease affects these dead areas by turning them gray. If the spring is damp, the disease will affect other parts of the leaves and more dead areas will form. Botrytis blotch does not normally threaten the life of the plant so no control is needed.

The environment can cause problems to rhododendrons and azaleas at times. These are acid-loving plants and if planted in alkaline soil, their foliage can yellow because the high pH prevents the plants from receiving iron. You can spray the foliage with iron to green up the leaves and use an acid-formulated fertilizer to acidify the soil.

Do not plant azaleas and rhododendrons near walnut trees. The toxins given off by the trees' roots will kill many plants, including these species. Remember that winter weather, too, can cause foliage to brown and flower buds to freeze and die. You can give plants a bit of protection by spraying them with Wilt-Pruf.

Are hollies easy to grow?

Hollies are no more difficult to grow than any other plant, provided they have the proper growing conditions. They need an acid, well-drained soil that is somewhat sandy. They can be grown in full sun but prefer partial shade or an eastern exposure near the house. Winter winds tend to dry out the leaves, which turn them brown in late winter or early spring.

Hollies should be fed with an acid fertilizer in the spring and fall. They do not tolerate dry soils well, so mulch the root zone with tanbark to help reduce the evaporation of moisture from the soil. If there is a summer drought, water hollies every week.

Can I plant a holly that will be winter hardy and not grow like a tree?

The genus *Ilex,* or holly, is a diverse group of plants. It includes those with spiny leaves that have red berries, inkberry, and the Japanese holly, which have small oval leaves and dark black berries.

When a holly tree is mentioned, I assume it is American holly— the plant that provides us with the green leaves and red berries at Christmas. It can get tall, growing to about forty feet. Remember that nearly all holly plants are either male or female. If the female is to have berries, a male plant must be nearby. Two good female cultivars of American holly are 'Jersey Princess' and 'Wyetta'. A good pollinating male is 'Jersey Knight'.

There is a self-pollinating holly: 'Nellie R. Stevens'. This is a fast-growing holly but is not as winter hardy as the others.

If you prefer shrublike hollies, then I suggest the Meserve hollies, named after the man who developed them. They are more commonly called blue hollies. These plants can be maintained at a height of three to six feet, although some cultivars can grow from eight to fifteen feet tall. The foliage of most of these hollies is a lustrous dark green, sometimes with a bluish sheen.

Of the many blue hollies on the market, the 'Blue Princess' and the 'Blue Prince' are the most popular. Many people also think that they are the hardiest. 'Blue Angel' is slow growing and more compact; she can be pollinated by any of the blue males. 'Blue Maid' is a very hardy female that grows fast. Two newer varieties are the 'China Boy' and 'China Girl'. One male plant produces enough pollen for all the females in a large area.

Are Japanese hollies hardy?

Most Japanese hollies generally are hardy to Zone 6 and can be grown in Zone 5 if they are protected. The Japanese holly has small oval leaves with a toothed margin. One very compact variety that has been sold for years is 'Helleri'. It can easily be maintained at two feet. When winter is severe, however, it can die back if not protected from the cold wind. A tall-growing variety is the 'Convexa', which is not any hardier.

More recently, the 'Schwoebels Compacta' and 'Schwoebels Upright' have been made available. The only difference between these two is their growth habit, indicated by their names. These are the most winter hardy of the Japanese hollies.

Are there holly varieties that have yellow berries?

There are yellow-berried varieties of holly. They certainly are not as common as the red-berry forms, but they are attractive. The American holly 'Xanthocarpa' is by far the most frequently seen. Recently, 'Golden Girl', a blue holly with yellow berries, was introduced. As with other blues, this one is more shrublike and can be pollinated by any blue male.

What causes the leaves to yellow on holly?

Even though holly is an evergreen, some of its leaves naturally turn yellow and drop. But several diseases can also cause them to yellow. Tar spot causes yellow spotting on the leaves of American holly. The spots gradually turn black over the summer. This is not a life-threatening problem, so a fungicide need not be applied unless the disease affects most of the foliage. Instead, gather and remove the affected foliage as early in the season as possible.

Other leaf spot diseases can affect holly, and here, too, removing the affected leaves is probably the best control. To help prevent yellowing due to disease, bordeaux mixture is sometimes effective. If summers are dry, be sure to water the plants regularly to reduce leaf drop.

The holly leaf miner, the larva of a small black fly, can form yellow tunnels in the leaves. If the tunneling is extensive, the entire leaf can yellow. At the beginning of May, the female fly makes openings on the underside of the leaves, where she lays eggs. Upon hatching, the larvae, or miners, start feeding on the tissue between the leaf's upper and lower layers. Once inside the leaf, the miners are relatively safe. Only handpicking infected leaves or spraying with a systemic chemical are effective controls.

My holly develops berries, but they don't turn red. Why?

If the berries on your holly don't turn red, as they should, you may have a problem with holly-berry midge. The larvae of this fly enter the berries, then overwinter. As many as three larvae can live in one berry. Their infestation somehow prevents the berries from turning red. By removing the infected berries in late fall, the problem can be prevented the next year. Sevin will kill the adults if they can be found. The best time of year to spray for them is mid-May to mid-June.

I thought euonymus held its leaves in the winter, but the leaves on mine turn red in the fall and drop. Is there a problem?

Yes, there is a problem, but only with terms. *Euonymus* is a genus of plants that has many species and varieties. The type you have is called winged euonymus and is probably the variety 'Compactus', or the dwarf-winged euonymus. The more common name is burning bush, so-called because the foliage turns a brilliant red in the fall before dropping. The bark of the plant has corky wings, which give it a nice appearance even during the winter. This makes a great specimen or foundation plant, and it can be very effective when used as a hedge.

Wintercreeper euonymus, however, keeps its foliage over the winter. The early cultivars of the wintercreeper were all low growing, getting to only about six inches high but spreading nearly fifty feet when provided with support. Today there are some shrub varieties. One of the most popular is 'Emerald Gaiety'. This very dense, upright wintercreeper is maintained at two to three feet. Its somewhat-rounded leaves are dark green with a white margin. 'Emerald and Gold' is much more compact, reaching only about two feet tall, with leaves similar to those of 'Emerald Gaiety'. The main difference is that the leaves of 'Emerald and Gold' have a yellow margin.

The major pest of the euonymus is the euonymus scale, which can kill the plant if left unchecked. This pest also attacks holly, boxwood, English ivy, and pachysandra. Most folks don't realize there is a problem until leaves begin to drop on the evergreen varieties. Then they notice the brown and white bumps on the stems and leaves. The small, oyster shell-shaped, brown bumps are the female scales, and they are larger than the males, which are white. In many cases they completely cover the stems. The adults, which are sessile, or fixed to one location, adhere tightly to the stems, and are not affected by most contact insecticides. Control at this point is difficult.

If possible, remove the most heavily affected stems. Some folks use a systemic pesticide at seven-day intervals for three weeks to control the pests. I have heard of others trying a mixture of rubbing alcohol and insecticidal soap—one cup of alcohol and two tablespoons of insecticidal soap in a quart of water. Spraying dormant oil in late winter is most effective in controlling scale populations.

Another way to deal with scale is to understand their life cycle. The adults overwinter and the females lay eggs under their protective scale in spring. In the Northeast, the eggs hatch over a couple of weeks in June, and start crawling to other parts of the plants. It is during this crawler stage, when they have not yet formed the protective scale, that they are susceptible to insecticides such as Sevin or insecticidal soap.

I thought pyracantha was a hardy plant, but mine has died back a couple of times. What could be the problem?

There are several species of pyracantha, but the most common is the scarlet firethorn. Numerous varieties are available as well as many hybrids. 'Mohave' is readily available but is only hardy to about five degrees below zero. This means that when winters are very cold, you can expect dieback in the spring. In some cases the entire plant might be killed. 'Mohave', however, is one of the most spectacular of the pyracantha; it produces large quantities of white blooms in spring and orange fruit during fall, and it often keeps its fruit well into winter.

The hardiest cultivar I am familiar with is 'Yukon Belle'. It can be grown as far north as Zone 4. Other cultivars to consider are 'Low Boy' and 'Kasan'. 'Fiery Cascade' and 'Rutgers' are two cultivars that are resistant to scab.

Firethorn should be planted in the spring. It needs a well-drained soil with a pH of 5.5 to 7.0. It tolerates dry soil well during the summer and likes full sun or light shade. Make sure you put the plant where you want it, because it is difficult to transplant. Firethorn is a great plant to espalier on a wall, but be sure you have a hardy variety. Be careful when pruning firethorn, as it has rather large spines along the stems. Many birds love its berries.

You need to watch for two diseases on firethorn. One, a fungus called scab, attacks the leaves and berries, which causes black sooty spots. The affected foliage turns yellow and eventually drops. The diseased fruit often turns black and will either persist for a while or drop. The variety 'Lalandei' is particularly susceptible to scab. Keeping firethorn healthy helps it resist the disease. Dormant spraying with a lime-sulphur mixture can help prevent the problem.

The second major problem is fireblight, which also affects many other plants, such as pear trees, mountain ash, hawthorns, and cotoneasters. The disease is caused by a bacterium and usually is transmitted by insects. We often notice the first symptom in late spring when the new growth suddenly wilts and becomes brown. It is best to cut off and remove affected parts.

I need a tall shrub for the landscape. Someone suggested using a leatherleaf viburnum because it stays green during the winter. Is this a good choice?

Leatherleaf viburnum is a good selection for the landscape if you have the space. It does get to be about fifteen feet tall and twelve feet wide. There are many good viburnums available, but few evergreen varieties will survive in the North. The leaves of the leatherleaf are green, long, wrinkled, and leathery, with light-colored fuzz on the underside. The flowers of this viburnum are not spectacular and there is little fruit. Being evergreen is a plus during the winter, but if winters are cold, some of the foliage will dry out and turn brown.

Another evergreen is the burkwood viburnum. This variety grows to only ten feet, and the leaves are not as large as those on the leatherleaf. The flowers are white and have a spicy fragrance. The fruit, if it forms, is red at first, then turns black in August. This plant is very hardy, tolerates hot summer weather, and should be used in the landscape more than it is.

I believe viburnums are one of the most underused plants in the landscape. Let me suggest a few more varieties that need our attention. The viburnum 'Carlesii', or Koreanspice (also called fragrant viburnum in the North), is one of the more compact viburnums; it grows only about six feet tall. The plant's fruit is not particularly attractive but the white flowers in spring have a wonderful fragrance.

Probably the best flowering viburnum is the double-file. This plant will grow to ten feet and is hardy to Zone 5. In May, the double-file is covered with masses of white, nonfragrant flowers and is a sight to behold. The foliage is dark green and turns to a red-purple color in the fall. If you want only one viburnum in the landscape, this is the one to select. Birds love its fruit.

Another of my favorites is the tea viburnum. At one time, its leaves were used to make tea. The growth habit of the plant is somewhat spindly, and the flowers are white but not spectacular. In October, though, when the fruit turns bright red and the leaves change to red-purple, the plant is outstanding.

My experience with viburnums has been great. They grow well, have few pests, and add much beauty to the landscape.

I understand that some dogwoods grow like shrubs and not trees. Do they have the same type of flower as the tree?

Shrub dogwoods do not have the same flower as the trees. They cannot take the place of the flowering dogwood, which, unfortunately, is in a state of decline due to disease.

There are many shrub dogwoods, and all get clusters of small, yellowish white flowers in spring. The value of most of these shrubs is not in the flowers they produce but in the color of their stems. The red-twig and yellow-twig dogwoods lend some needed color to dull winter days. The colors are bright and most effective when there are evergreens to serve as a backdrop. The plants are very hardy and produce a whitish fruit that some birds enjoy, but the berries are of little aesthetic value.

The silky dogwood is another popular shrub dogwood. It can tolerate moist soil conditions and is best used in shrub borders. The stems are greenish red and grow to about nine feet long. The flowers are not outstanding, but the shrub produces berries that many wildlife species like to eat.

One last dogwood I must mention is one that I cannot grow because I live too far south. It is actually a ground cover that grows only six to eight inches tall. The *Cornus canadensis,* or bunchberry, is a most attractive plant with only one whorl of four or five leaves. Flowers form in June, and they look very much like those on the flowering dogwood tree. Each plant produces four white bracts with a cluster of yellow flowers in the center. If the flowers are fertilized, scarlet berries will form in August. Unfortunately for me, the bunchberry needs moist, acid, organically rich soil. It also likes cool weather and a shaded environment and grows from Zone 4 north. Boy, what a great ground cover!

What are some spring-flowering shrubs you would recommend for use around the house or in the yard?

Before suggesting plants for use around the house, or what are called foundation plants, I must caution you to consider exposure of the site to sun and wind, type of soil, and location and size of windows, doors, porches, and walks. These factors will determine which plants can be used, and where.

There are many spring-flowering plants that can be used as foundation plants or at other locations in the landscape. I have already discussed spring-flowering evergreens, but there also are many deciduous flowering shrubs. One of the first to flower is the dwarf flowering almond, which grows to about four feet tall. This inexpensive little shrub has flowers that look like miniature paper carnations. Small, usually pink and double, they bloom along the stems in April or early May. Unfortunately this shrub has many weak branches. It is grown mainly for the beauty of the flowers; otherwise, it has little value.

I must mention forsythia, which blooms in April. The forsythia is not meant as a foundation plant and looks best growing along the border of the property or on a bank. It grows to about eight feet and can spread to twelve feet. It does well in almost any soil and is easily propagated by cuttings, which are rooted in water. One problem is that its flowers can be taken by a hard frost. Look for the cultivar 'Lynwood', which I think is the best.

Lilac is another early spring bloomer. This tall-growing shrub needs to be planted in full sun to flower well. Common lilac is the most popular type, the varieties of which produce flowers of many colors: white, pink, violet, blue, lilac, and purple. To be honest, I can't tell some of those flower colors apart! The flowers can also be singles or doubles. Lilac should be in the landscape because the flowers are attractive and fragrant, and they can be used in cut arrangements.

The old-fashioned weigela is another plant that, like the forsythia, should be planted away from the house. It grows to nine feet tall and ten feet wide and flowers in May. Varieties can be found that flower in colors from white to red. Weigela adapts well to different soils.

One of my favorites is the sweet mock orange. This should not be used along the foundation either, because it can get as large as the forsythia. Many cultivars of this plant produce an abundance of fragrant flowers—and the fragrance is the reason to include it in the landscape. Make sure the variety you select is fragrant; many of the cultivars are not.

Spring bloomers that can be used as foundation plants are viburnum, deutzia, broom, flowering quince, spirea, cinquefoil, and, for those of us lucky enough to be able to grow it, crape myrtle.

When should flowering shrubs be pruned?

Some flowering shrubs need to be pruned in late winter or very early spring. Many others should not be pruned until after they flower. The following lists indicate when to prune various shrubs.

How should roses be planted?

Spring is the best season during which to plant roses. They can be purchased bare root or in containers. The bare-root roses are usually available earlier. Roses you order from a mail-order company will be bare root; if they arrive before you can plant them, be sure to heel them into the ground. Cover the roots and several inches of the canes with soil to prevent freezing. Try to get them planted within two weeks of delivery.

You should plant roses in full sun or where they will receive at least six hours of sunlight daily. Keep in mind, too, that roses like an acid soil.

When you plant bare-root roses, dig a hole about eighteen inches deep and eighteen inches wide. If the soil is heavy, cut it with peat moss to a fifty–fifty mix. Lighter soils need less peat moss. Some folks like to place composted manure in the bottom of the planting hole. If you do this, be sure to cover it with four to six inches of soil to protect the roots. Then make a small mound of soil in the center of the planting hole over which to spread the roots. Cut off any broken or diseased roots and set the plant into the ground.

Rose specialists disagree about the depth at which roses should be planted. I recommend planting deep enough that the graft, or bud, union—the bump above the roots—is just above ground level. Keeping it slightly above ground level helps prevent several problems, and the graft union can be temporarily covered with soil to protect it against the harshness of winter weather. Once the rose is

When to Prune Flowering Shrubs

Very Early Spring

Butterfly bush

Clematis

Crape myrtle

Currant

Hibiscus

Honeysuckle

Kerria

Lilac tree

Privet

Spirea (summer-flowering)

Trumpet vine

Viburnum (except 'Carlesii')

Virginia creeper

Wisteria

After Flowering

Azalea

Bittersweet

Bush honeysuckle

Broom

Cinquefoil

Deutzia

Flowering almond

Japanese pieris

Laurel

Lilac

Mock orange

Rhododendron

Spirea (summer-flowering)

Viburnum 'Carlesii'

Weigela

in the ground, backfill with the soil mix. Fill the hole two-thirds full with soil and add water to settle the soil. Fill the hole with the soil and water again. If there is still a chance of frost after planting, mound about eight inches of soil around the plant. Remove the mound as the temperatures warm and the buds open.

Potted roses are planted in much the same way as bare-root roses. If the pot is paper, remove the lip of the container and the bottom before planting, and cut some openings in the sides. If the container is plastic, you'll have to take the rose out of it. Be careful not to bare-root the plant, especially if it already has foliage.

Most roses should be planted at least two to three feet apart. Miniature roses need a spacing of only one foot; climbers should be spaced every six to eight feet.

How and when should roses be pruned?

Newly planted roses generally do not need any pruning. The grower has already taken care of that. All established roses should be pruned in the spring. You can do minor pruning in late fall to prevent tall canes from being whipped by winter winds. Secure climbing roses to prevent them from breaking off.

The pruning of roses consists of shortening the canes and removing any dead wood or excess canes. When pruning, remember to use sharp hand-pruning shears, and be sure the blades are clean and free of disease. The pruning cut should be made at a forty-five-degree angle and about one-fourth inch above a bud. Wipe the blades with alcohol before going to a new plant.

How "hard" roses should be pruned depends on the type of rose and the extent of winter damage. If there was a lot of dieback, prune them to just below the dead tissue. Under more normal conditions, most rose bushes should be pruned to a height of twelve to eighteen inches. Pruning canes shorter will result in plants that produce fewer, but larger roses. Miniature roses usually need only very light pruning but can be pruned more heavily if necessary. Prune tree roses so that the canes are about eight inches long. Remember, tree roses need to be completely buried for the winter if they are to survive in many areas. When planted in containers, the container can be brought into a garage. Where winters are not severe, tree roses can be wrapped in burlap filled with straw or oak leaves.

What should roses be fertilized with and how often?

Most rose experts I know have their own opinions about what fertilizer to use and how often to fertilize. Some switch between liquid and dry fertilizers. Newly planted roses should be given a liquid fertilizer high in phosphorus after planting. Wait about two months to begin a regular program of feeding.

I think Rose-tone is the best rose fertilizer. It is organic and comes in a granular form. Feed established roses in early spring, in June as they are blooming, and again in late July or early August. If the foliage looks a bit pale at other times, you can give them a foliar feeding. Miracle-Gro makes a product for this purpose.

If the leaves start to yellow but the veins in the leaves remain green, the plant needs iron because the soil pH is too high. Work at lowering the pH by adding aluminum sulphate to the soil, and apply an iron supplement in the meanwhile.

Are there many pests found on roses?

Unfortunately, many pests like roses. Japanese beetles, aphids, thrips, and leaf hoppers are several of the worst insect pests, and black spot and mildew are two prevalent diseases. Insecticidal soap or Sevin will control most of the insects. Benomyl is the most effective fungicide for controlling and preventing disease. Most rosarians practice preventive maintenance on roses. You must decide if you have the time and want to use the chemicals needed to prevent problems on roses.

There are some roses that are nearly pest-free. Miniature roses do not attract nearly as many pests as full-sized roses. I never use a pesticide on my miniatures. There are also some new care-free roses available. The 'Meidiland' is a shrub rose. All of the varieties are very hardy, almost pest-free, and when in bloom, are full of flowers. These roses require little pruning and their foliage is quite attractive. Remember, these are shrub roses, and they cannot be confined to small spaces.

What are some good varieties of
roses for cutting?

This is a tough question to answer because everyone has a favorite. When it comes to red roses, which happen to be my favorite, try 'Mr. Lincoln', a hybrid tea. There are several pink roses, but remember that there are different hues and shades of pink. The hybrid teas 'Touch of Class' and 'Color Magic' are recommended, as is the grandiflora 'Sonia'. 'Paradise' is a great purple hybrid tea, and the hybrid tea 'White Masterpiece' is another suggestion.

I have an old grape arbor over a patio, but I
would like to use some other type of vine.
What are some hardy vines for the Northeast?

There are several vines that would do nicely for this purpose. Wisteria is the first one to consider. The vine can grow to thirty feet but can be pruned shorter. At times, it can be difficult to get blooming but the results are worth it. It prefers a moist, well-drained soil that is slightly alkaline. The flowers are purple and carried on clusters that are up to twenty inches long. They bloom between April and May.

If the wisteria fails to bloom after three years, prune the roots by digging straight down in the soil around the plant about eighteen inches from the trunk. Check the soil pH, too. Do not over-fertilize with nitrogen, because that encourages foliage growth rather than flower development. Instead, add some phosphorus. Consider an additional pruning in midsummer to slow the growth.

Trumpet vine is another hardy flowering vine. It grows to forty feet and will grow in almost any soil. The scarlet-orange flowers are borne on the new wood and are attractive to hummingbirds. Trumpet vines bloom from July through September. It is aggressive and needs to be pruned regularly.

Virginia creeper and Boston ivy are attractive. They produce inconspicuous flowers, but the foliage of both vines has a beautiful color in autumn.

How should clematis be planted?

Clematis is one of the most beautiful flowering vines, yet for some it is very troublesome to get growing and flowering. The pH of the soil does not seem to be critical, but other details are important. Plant clematis in the spring in a loamy and moist, but well-drained, soil. If the soil is heavy, amend it to one part sand, one part peat moss, and one part soil. The roots must be kept cool, so mulch with several inches of tanbark. Clematis does best when planted where it will be shaded from the hot afternoon sun.

There are at least three different types of clematis, and they are each pruned differently. The most popular clematis is *Clematis jackmanii,* which has large blue, purple, deep red, or pink flowers. Early spring is the best time for pruning this clematis. Cut back all the growth to the lowest pair of strong buds on the wood produced during the previous year.

10

Branching Out

The largest organisms that have ever lived on Earth are trees. The General Sherman Tree, a giant sequoia in Sequoia National Park, is more than two hundred seventy-two feet tall. Not only is it one of the largest trees alive, but also it is one of the oldest, estimated to be more than 3,800 years old. At the other extreme are the bonsais, some of which are hundreds of years old but only a few feet tall.

Few plants or animals have received the recognition that trees have. Today, all fifty states have Arbor Day festivities, when people plant trees and take time to appreciate the value of trees in their lives. Julius Sterling Morton of Nebraska first proposed the notion of setting aside a day to plant trees, and on that very first Arbor Day in 1872, more than a million trees were planted.

But man's interest in trees began much earlier than the first Arbor Day. More than four hundred years ago, the Egyptians were planting trees in gardens and transplanting them to new locations, sometimes hundreds of miles away. Theophrastus of ancient Greece wrote a complete guide to the planting and care of trees. And when the early settlers came to the Americas, they brought with them trees from their homelands.

Today most of us understand the importance of trees to our existence. We know that weather patterns are controlled, to some extent, by trees. Much of the oxygen in the air we breathe is produced by trees. They provide shade from the sun, cut the winds of winter, screen out noise, hide unsightly areas, and help remove pollutants from the air. The pages in this book, the studs in the walls, the furniture we sit on, even the rubber in our car tires, all come from trees. And what would life be without cherry-crumb pie, fresh orange juice, or maple candy, all made from products of trees? Or, can you imagine a bright fall day without the beauty of the colorful foliage?

Trees are a diverse group of plants. Some are evergreen; others drop their leaves in the winter and become dormant. Many trees grow very tall and provide shade; still others are used as ornamentals. We like some trees because they flower beautifully. Others that do not have showy flowers in the spring provide brilliantly colored fall foliage.

Is there any special way to plant trees?

Unfortunately, the way most of us have learned to plant trees is probably not the proper way to do the job.

Spring is the best time of year to plant both deciduous and evergreen trees that are either in containers or balled and burlapped. Deciduous trees can also be planted in the fall. Evergreens that are planted in autumn often suffer from winter dieback because the roots have had insufficient time to develop. Bare-root trees are safely planted only when they are dormant, that is, before the leaves start to grow or after they drop. Never transplant trees during the growing season.

The recommended advice for planting a tree used to be to treat it like a baby—handle it gently, feed it well, and protect it from the environment. I used to advise people to dig a large hole for the root ball and then mix a lot of peat moss, or other supplement, with the soil from the hole. Next, they were to set the tree in without disturbing the roots. Then they were to add some fertilizer around the roots, then the soil mix. The last two steps were to wrap the trunk of the tree to protect it and then stake the tree to prevent wind damage.

Now we know that much of this advice is incorrect. In reality what we were doing was creating an underground container for the tree, particularly in clay soils. Recent research reveals that this old method of planting actually is of little, if any, benefit and that trees planted without soil amendments or fertilizer outperform those planted with them.

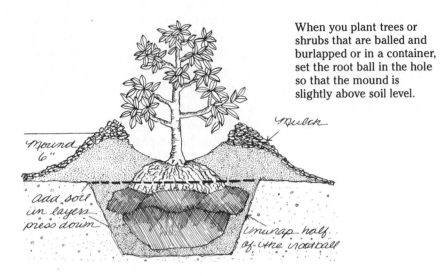

When you plant trees or shrubs that are balled and burlapped or in a container, set the root ball in the hole so that the mound is slightly above soil level.

Instead, proper planting technique begins with the selection of a tree that is suited to the conditions in which it is to grow. For instance, few trees grow well in soil that is not well drained. If you want to plant a tree in a soggy spot, you need to select a species, such as a willow, that will tolerate that soil type. Or you can bring in soil and create a raised bed so you can use a different tree.

Once you have selected the appropriate tree, dig the planting hole. The width of the hole should be two to three times that of the root ball and the hole should be shaped like a saucer or satellite dish, rather than a straight-walled pit. The depth of the hole should be only a few inches deeper than the tree is to be planted.

After digging the hole, backfill so that when the root ball is set in the ground, the top of the root ball will be a couple of inches above ground level. Remember, the soil under the tree will compact, lowering the plant into the ground. A tree planted too deep will be more prone to disease problems and its roots can grow toward the surface.

If the tree was growing in a container, remove it from the container before planting. If any of the roots are growing around in the container, spread them out. When planting trees that are in burlap, set the tree in the planting hole, untie the burlap and roll it down to the bottom of the root ball. Then backfill with the soil that was taken from the hole. Do not add anything to the soil—no amendments and no fertilizers! The amendments do more harm than good, and research shows that fertilizers high in nitrogen can cause more growth than the root system can support. Wait until the second year to fertilize with nitrogen, and then apply it to the edge of the planting hole to encourage the roots to spread. In subsequent years, fertilize at the drip edge of the tree. (The drip edge is the rim of ground under the outer ends of the limbs.)

Once planted, soak the root ball with water. I believe that a liquid fertilizer high in phosphorus can be helpful for getting roots to grow, especially if the soil is deficient in phosphorus. Place several inches of mulch over the surface of the planting hole. This will help the soil retain moisture as well as prevent "mower blight," a pseudo-technical term for the damage you do when you hit the trunk with the lawn mower. Water the tree as needed. If, when you check the soil under the mulch, it is still moist, do not water.

Should new trees be pruned and do they need to be staked?

Recently much has been written about how much trees should be pruned at planting time. When trees are purchased from a nursery they generally need no pruning. Even bare-root trees generally need only light pruning to remove diseased or broken branches. If the tree you buy has two leaders or main stems, prune off the weaker of the two.

There is also considerable debate about the value of staking trees after planting. Trees used to be staked so that they could not bend in the wind. Now the advice is to place stakes in the ground about ten inches away from the trunk, then fasten the wire to the stake and trunk low enough that the top of the tree can bend in the wind. (Run the wire through old garden hose so that it does not cut into the tree bark.) Some studies have shown that unstaked trees developed a better taper, the proportion of top to base of trunk, and a stronger root system than those that had been staked.

When should mature shade trees and evergreens be pruned?

Most shade trees should be pruned while they are dormant. Late winter and early spring, before the buds open, seem to be when most pruning is done. However, it can be done at other times. Summer pruning should consist only of the removal of new growth

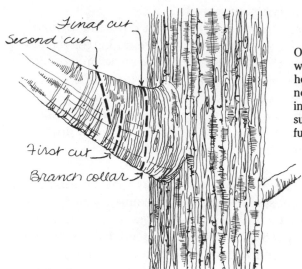

Final cut
Second cut
First cut
Branch collar

On most trees, dressings for wounds slow the natural healing process. Only oaks need a dressing for a pruning wound because they are susceptible to oak-wilt fungus.

that is not wanted. Extensive summer pruning can be stressful to trees. Researchers have found that wounds from spring pruning heal better than those made any other time of the year. Do not prune from mid-July until the trees go dormant. Late summer pruning can cause buds to open and new branches to form, and they will not have enough time to harden off before the cold of winter sets in.

One of the main reasons for pruning deciduous trees while they are dormant is that you can see the structure of the tree, which is hidden during the summer by the foliage. When pruned in early spring, some trees, such as maples, bleed profusely. This does little damage to the tree.

Coniferous evergreens usually are not pruned as often as deciduous trees; they simply don't need it. You should rarely need to "hard" prune common evergreen trees. Most lack lateral buds on the older wood that has no foliage. Generally, this means that you cannot severely reduce the size of a conifer.

The pruning of most conifers consists of heading back growing tips in the spring. This will maintain the size of the tree and make it fuller. To control the size of whorl-branching conifers, such as pine, fir, and spruce, cut back the new growth just after it has fully formed.

What type of pruning seal should be used to cover pruning wounds?

You may be surprised by my answer: Don't cover the pruning wounds on most trees. Tree-wound dressings are no longer recommended, because, in most cases, they have been found to slow trees' natural healing process. As far as I know, only oaks need a dressing, because they are susceptible to oak-wilt fungus.

Always use clean tools when you prune. The blades of pruners and saws should be sharp to avoid ragged cuts. And when pruning large limbs, avoid ripping the bark on the trunk.

Does it help to mulch over the roots of trees?

The results of a recent study reveal that it is much better to use mulch over the trees' root zone than to allow grass to grow. In the study, the researcher looked at the growth of feeder roots, which are those that supply the tree with most of its water and nutrients. The root zone of each tree was divided into thirds. Over one third, the soil was left bare; over the second third, grass was grown; and over the final third, four inches of mulch was applied. After several years the root zone was checked for the growth of feeder roots. The area that had a covering of mulch produced far more of these fine roots than either of the others. This proved true with all trees that were tested. The worst production of roots was found in the area covered with grass.

It would appear that the grass competes with the tree for the moisture, and wins. Many times we have difficulty growing grass under shade trees. Maybe this is their way of dealing with this competitor. So instead of grass, mulch with three or four inches of tanbark.

The black locust sends up suckers from its roots in the yard and the crab apples send up sprouts at their base. Can I use an herbicide to control these?

Suckers and sprouts are part of the tree from which they are growing. If you apply an herbicide, it will travel through the system of the sprout or sucker to the trunk or roots of the parent tree and could kill the tree itself. It is best to mow off the root suckers and prune off the sprouts.

You should also be careful when applying herbicides to the

lawn. If weather conditions are right, the herbicide can deform tree leaves or kill the tree. Remember, use herbicides as infrequently as possible.

I just moved into a new house and would like some shade out front. What fast-growing tree can I plant?

There are at least two questions I need to ask before you run out and buy a fast-growing tree. The first question is: Are you sure you want shade at the front of the house? When I think of planting trees for shade I think of trees that get tall and have a broad canopy. This type of tree will hide a house, which is not good. If the home is rather low, like a ranch style, the larger trees should be used behind the house to frame it. Smaller, ornamental trees, because of their growth habit, are better for the front. So consider what the tree will look like in ten or fifteen years and be certain you are not planting a tree that will overwhelm the location.

The second question is: Should this be a fast-growing tree? All of us want trees to grow fast to provide instant shade or color. Most folks, though, don't want to prune trees, and a fast-growing tree must be pruned often. Fast-growing trees also are weak-wooded. They tend to break easily in the wind, which means you will spend a lot of time cleaning up after them, and because their limbs break, these trees often do not have good shapes. They also are shallow-rooted, which suggests that they can be uprooted in a storm. Shallow roots are also troublesome when you have to mow around them. Many a blade has been bent or dulled by the roots of a silver maple.

Now, after reading all that, if you still want a fast-growing tree for the front of the house, try 'Red Sunset' red maple. I do not recommend silver maples or poplars, particularly the hybrid poplars, for a home landscape! The 'Red Sunset' does not grow quite as fast as the silver maple, but it does grow rapidly. The wood is stronger, the roots are deeper, and the brilliant, red fall color is spectacular. This tree will tolerate moist soils but is not good in urban settings.

There is one other fast-growing ornamental that I think also should be avoided in the landscape. The silktree, also called mimosa, is prone to many problems. Despite the pretty, pink, brushlike flowers, it is not worth planting.

What are some trees that can be used along the street?

In reality, trees used along the street will vary from one community to another. Most townships and municipalities have ordinances that govern the kinds of trees that can be used along streets. You must find out which trees they permit to be planted. If you plant the wrong kind, they can have it removed.

I have seen the lists of trees several neighboring townships recommend for street planting, and I am amazed at how different they are. If you find that the tree you would like to plant is not on your community's list, find out when the list was last updated. Perhaps your tree should be included. But don't expect to find trees like silver maple on the list.

Let me suggest some trees that are rather tall and make good street trees. The Norway maple is one commonly found in landscapes in both urban and rural areas and is often used along streets. It has a spreading crown equal to its height, which can be forty to fifty feet, so it needs considerable space. The cultivar 'Crimson King', with its burgundy leaves, is the most widely used. I think there are better selections than this one, though, because it is already overused.

The other maple that can make a good street tree is the red maple, but it should not be used in cities because it does not tolerate pollution well. 'Red Sunset' and 'October Glory' are two of the more attractive cultivars.

The green ash is adaptable to street use and has been used extensively in parks and the home landscape. It is, however, a fast-growing tree and often produces an abundance of seeds, which, to many folks, makes it a "dirty" tree. If you plant a green ash, be certain to select the variety 'Marshall's Seedless'. This is a male tree so there will be no seeds to clean up. In addition, this variety has yellow foliage in fall and is resistant to insect pests.

Two oaks are also commonly used along streets. My favorite is the red oak, which gets its name from the color of its fall foliage. This strong, tall tree is very handsome and should be considered. The other oak I have seen used along highways is the pin oak. This oak retains its foliage through the winter, but it is less desirable than the red oak because it lacks fall color and develops more problems when planted in limestone soils.

There are some other tall trees to consider. The ginkgo has

an open form and fan-shaped leaves. Sweet gum has star-shaped leaves. Zelkova is an elmlike tree with an interesting, asymmetrical shape. The littleleaf linden, a handsome tree, has dark green foliage.

Are there any ornamental trees that can be used along streets?

I would again caution that it is best to first check the local ordinances to see what trees are legally permitted for street planting. When I think of ornamentals for street planting, my mind immediately goes to two varieties of callery pear: 'Bradford' and 'Redspire'. They are about the finest street trees that can be used. My only reservation is that they are such great trees, they soon will be overused. They both produce a profusion of white spring flowers. The 'Bradford' has reddish purple fall foliage. Another nice feature of callery pears is that they color up in the fall later than most other trees. Of all the ornamentals, these are the only ones I would suggest for street planting. This is not to say that I have never seen others used. The flowering dogwood, kousa dogwood, crab apple, and flowering cherry can all be found along streets in developments. However, these trees can develop problems, so I do not think they are suitable.

There is a moist area in the front corner of my property. Will any trees grow there?

There are several trees that can be planted in poorly drained areas. As one might expect they are not the most attractive species, but you must select from those that will survive. Don't plant a tree that has little chance to succeed.

The green ash is probably the best of the lot. I would suggest the cultivar 'Marshall's Seedless', which does not develop seed and thus does not create much of a mess. The American sweet gum tolerates moist soils. The star-shaped leaves are very attractive in the fall as they change to shades of red, burgundy, orange, and yellow. It can be a "dirty" tree, because it drops its fruit, which looks like golfball-sized burrs.

Another less common tree is the black gum or black tupelo. It is a native tree that prefers an acid soil and a location sheltered from winter's wind. Its spring flowers are not showy. Neither are the blue berries it develops in the fall, but the birds love them. Its fall foliage, however, is always outstanding, with colors of red, yellow, and orange.

Several other less attractive trees that will survive in moist soils are the thornless honey locust, sycamore, hackberry, and weeping willow.

Can any of the smaller, native flowering trees be useful in the home landscape?

There are several of these trees that can be included in the landscape when conditions are suitable. Of course, the most common is the flowering dogwood. This tree has been used for years and remains the favorite ornamental flowering tree. It is losing its popularity quickly, however, due to the outbreak of the disease anthracnose, which is killing thousands of trees annually. At this point, the native dogwood seem more prone to the disease than those growing in home landscapes. It is too bad this problem has developed; the flowering dogwood is so beautiful.

The American yellowwood is a native tree that for some reason has never been very abundant. It has beautiful foliage and flowers and can be grown from Maine to Alabama. It likes limestone soils and prefers the sun. Growing to thirty-five feet tall, the tree develops chains of white, fragrant, wisteria-like blooms in late May and early June. The foliage is bright green in the summer and changes to yellow in the fall. The tree does best when protected from the wind. Pruning, if needed, should be done in the summer.

Another of my favorite native trees is the eastern redbud, which is often seen growing in the wild with the flowering dogwood. The redbud is a low-growing tree and has rather large heart-shaped leaves and often a divided trunk. Its rosy-pink flowers open in April. The tree grows well in sun or light shade and likes a slightly acid soil. It is ideal for a naturalized setting or as a specimen tree.

Sourwood is another native tree that is rarely seen in the landscape, although many gardeners consider it the most attractive native tree. The leaves are long and bright green in spring, dark green in summer, and yellow, red, or purple in the fall. Often all of these colors are on the same tree. Small, urn-shaped, fragrant, white flower clusters appear in June. The fruit is not showy but is an interesting characteristic of the tree in winter.

One last tree I will mention is the serviceberry. One of the shortest natives, it grows to only about twenty feet high. The gray-ish foliage of spring turns green in summer and then yellow to orange in the fall. In April, white clusters of flowers cover the foliage that is just opening. Serviceberry can be grown in sun or light shade and looks best in naturalized situations. In addition, the tree rarely needs to be pruned.

Are there any trees that can add a pleasant fragrance to the landscape?

Some trees do produce flowers that have a nice fragrance, but I don't know of any that are as effective as the various fragrant shrubs and annual and perennial flowers. Nevertheless, one of my favorites is the star magnolia. This small shrublike tree flowers in early spring, well before its leaves are out. It grows best in an acid soil that is rich in organic material. Place it in the sun or light shade and protect it from the winter wind.

The southern magnolia is another beautiful tree that has fragrant flowers in May and June. As its name indicates, this is a tree of the South, but it can grow and flower in protected areas of Zone 5. In northern limits, it must be protected during winter if it is expected to survive. Plant it in locations similar to those of the star magnolia and in the winter spray it with Wilt-Pruf. Place burlap around this, and other small trees, to help protect them from the wind as well.

Japanese snowbell is a small tree that is hardy to Zone 5 and is easy to grow. The fragrant, white, bell-shaped flowers open in late May. The tree needs an acid, well-drained soil and lots of sun, although it cannot tolerate dry soils. The Japanese snowbell is one of the few trees that is almost pest-free. I have a weeping variety and just love the little tree.

Other more common trees that might be considered are the black locust, yellowwood, sourwood, and various cherries, crab apples, and plums.

What are some trees that can be used to capture people's attention?

The type of tree being referred to is what I call a specimen tree, and there are many to recommend. Let me stress the importance of knowing the physical conditions of the site where you want a tree and then matching the tree to those conditions. Don't buy a tree and then hope it can grow where you plant it.

Some conifers are outstanding specimen plants. There are several weeping forms of rather common conifers, such as weeping white pine, weeping Norway and Serbian spruces, and the weeping blue atlas cedar. All are very hardy and have no growing requirements different from other conifers. Most do require some training to get them to grow in the desired form. If left alone most would develop a horizontal trunk, so they need to be staked.

Other conifers with a more traditional form are the 'Hoopsii' Colorado blue spruce, which is almost white in color, the Korean pine, the 'Glauca' Japanese white pine, and the Bhutan pine.

One very pretty tree is the common China fir, but it is not very winter hardy. I have seen it growing successfully in Ohio and southern Pennsylvania. It needs a moist, acid, well-drained soil and some protection from winter wind in the northern part of its range.

There are many deciduous trees to add to the list of specimen trees. We can start with maples, among which is an abundance of what are frequently called the Japanese maples. Some develop burgundy leaves. The 'Bloodgood' is the most common Japanese maple, and it keeps its burgundy foliage all summer. 'Burgundy Lace' has foliage that is much more finely divided than that of the 'Bloodgood'. The most outstanding of the Japanese maples for specimen use is the 'Dissectum Atropurpureum'. Growing to about ten feet, the drooping branches and finely divided, lacy, burgundy leaves seem to flow to the ground, forming a large mound.

Another type of tree that has many fine cultivars is the European beech. A few cultivars to check are the 'Aurea Pendula', 'Laciniata Pendula', 'Purpurea Pendula', and 'Rohanii'. All do best when planted in full sun and in a well-drained, acid soil. These often do better in varying soil types than does the native American beech.

There are many more common trees with weeping forms that also make good specimen trees. Weeping cherry and weeping crab apple are two. There is even a weeping arborvitae that is suitable as a specimen tree.

What are some shade trees that offer good fall color?

There are many trees that provide color. The sugar maple, with its fall colors of yellow, burnt orange, and various hues of red, is one of my favorites. Another maple worth considering is the red maple. Some red maples turn yellow but most change to shades of red. The 'Red Sunset' guarantees you orange to red color. The red oak is faithful in producing red to brown-red fall foliage. Most American sweet gum can be counted on for multicolored foliage of yellow, red, and orange. Green ash color up the landscape early with bright yellows. I can't forget the tulip poplar, or tulip tree. This is one of my favorites for many reasons: the flowers it produces in late May, its straight trunk, and the rich yellow color of its fall foliage.

Some smaller trees that color up nicely are the sourwood, zelkova, 'Bradford' pear, franklinia, katsura, dogwood, and birch.

Which trees will attract birds to the yard during the winter?

Birds need two things during the winter that trees can provide: shelter and food. Evergreens provide excellent shelter. Some of the taller evergreen shrubs can serve as places for birds to escape from winter's cold winds. Taller trees such as Norway and Colorado blue spruces, Douglas fir, hemlock, and various pines also can provide the shelter needed for their survival.

Then there are several trees that provide an abundance of fruit to supply the birds with the energy they need to survive the season. In reality, all trees that produce seed have the potential of being food sources for birds, but some trees have fruit that birds find especially appealing. The American holly, which can be treated as a large shrub or a small tree, provides both berries and shelter. I have watched eastern bluebirds gorge themselves on its fruit.

Crab apples are a favorite for attracting many birds. In late fall and again in early spring, I can always count on visits from the cedar waxwings as they stop to feed on these small pomes. Crab apples are also useful in providing a bounty of spring color. Their white, pink, or red flowers add to the beauty of any landscape, and the fall fruit can be red, orange, green, or yellow. Before buying a crab apple, be sure to check its resistance to apple scab and other diseases. Some of the old standards such as 'Hopa', 'Radiant', and 'Almey' are very susceptible to scab. Instead, look for 'Sargentii' and 'Snowdrift'.

The European mountain ash is often planted to attract birds in the fall. This rather low-growing tree has large clusters of white flowers in May and, if pollinated, will produce orange-red berries in

September. The fall display of fruit is spectacular. Do not count on keeping the tree for long, however. It is very vulnerable to pests and does not last more than about fifteen years. But it is worth planting for the enjoyment of the birds.

Hawthorns and the flowering dogwood are two others that brighten the landscape in the fall with their fruit, and the birds love it. Both have severe disease problems, however, so I would not recommend them.

What type of evergreen would you suggest for use in the house as a live Christmas tree?

The answer to this question depends on where you live and the location's soil. My favorite is the Fraser fir. I must admit that I use a cut tree at Christmas, and I always select a Fraser or a concolor fir. The problem with using the Fraser fir as a live tree is that, when planted outside, it does not grow well in most soils. It needs a moist loam in which to grow and flourish and will not respond when planted in clay soils that dry during the summer. I find that high summer temperatures can also be a problem.

The concolor, or white fir, will tolerate most soils, with the exception of clay. It also adapts to most weather conditions and has few pests. If you can get a concolor for use indoors, do. I say "if you can get it" because some form a deep taproot, which makes them more difficult to successfully unearth. Therefore, there are fewer live concolors than other trees available at Christmas.

Several evergreens that seem to grow well when planted after Christmas are the Douglas fir, white pine, and Norway and white spruces.

Live Christmas trees will grow well when planted outdoors, if they were cared for properly indoors. A live tree should not stay inside for more than ten days. If it remains inside longer than that, it will assume winter is over and will start to push buds. Then when planted in the yard, the buds could freeze, and the tree would die.

Just as important to remember is that the tree is alive and needs water. Do not allow it to stand in water, but be sure the root ball does not dry out. When you bring the tree home, put the root ball in a bucket and add water. Homes tend to be hot and dry in the winter, so check the roots daily and add water if needed.

Do not take the tree right from the house and plant it in the yard, particularly if the temperature is really cold. First, move it to a porch or the garage for a few days to gradually acclimate it to the cold weather. Dig the planting hole before the ground freezes and then keep the soil you removed from the hole in the garage, or covered, so it does not freeze.

Why are so many flowering dogwoods dying?

The flowering dogwood is, unfortunately, extremely susceptible to insect and disease pests. Probably the worst insect pests are the borers, larvae of several species of moth. The female moths often lay their eggs in wounds on the tree, which sometimes causes knots to form. The borers tunnel into the wood of the tree, which kills the branches and, in some cases, the entire tree.

There are two approaches to dealing with the borers. One is to use a systemic insecticide to kill them. This involves spraying the tree, beginning in mid-May, every two weeks until mid-June. The other control method is to either dig into the borer tunnel with a pocketknife to find and kill the critter or to insert a wire into the hole to kill the larva. Then the hole should be sealed with wood filler or pruning seal.

The most serious problem facing the flowering dogwood is the fungus disease anthracnose. It was first discovered in New York state in the late 1970s, and it is now found in most of the northeastern and several northwestern states. Some people think that all native dogwoods will succumb to this disease within the next twenty years if a cure is not found.

It appears that all flowering dogwoods are susceptible to the disease. The symptoms first appear as purple-outlined spots on the foliage, and then larger brown areas appear. Purplish spots can be found on the white bracts around the flowers if they are blooming. Soon lower branches die. Sometimes watersprouts start to grow and cankers form, killing branches.

It used to be thought that by keeping flowering dogwoods healthy and free of stress, they would be resistant to diseases. Both stressed and unstressed trees, however, are affected by anthracnose. What is more unfortunate is that there is no control for the disease. Recommendations are to remove affected branches and watersprouts. Other than that, the only thing to do is dig out the flowering dogwood and replace it with the kousa, or Japanese, dogwood, which seems to be resistant to the disease. The kousa is an attractive tree, but it can never replace the native flowering dogwood.

The leaves of my white birch are turning brown. This seems to happen every year. What could be the problem?

Mature birch trees, with their white papery bark, are beautiful trees. There are several species that we call white birch and they are all similar; all of these happen to attract the birch leaf miner. The leaf miner is the larva of a sawfly that was accidentally introduced into this country from Europe. It can now be found in most of the Northeast.

About the beginning of May, the overwintering pupae finish their development, emerging as adults. The females, which are small and black, lay eggs on the surface of developing leaves. Upon hatching, the larvae tunnel into the leaves and begin feeding between the upper and lower layers of the leaves. Several miners are usually found in each leaf, and as they tunnel and eat the chlorophyll-containing cells, the leaf quickly becomes brown. After about two weeks, the larvae cut their way out of the leaf and fall to the ground to complete their life cycle. In about eighteen days they are adults, and they continue the cycle on new leaves. This can occur up to four times over the summer. The first brood does the worst damage. The brown leaves eventually drop and the tree develops new leaves. Although no immediate damage is done to the tree, after a few years the tree becomes stressed and begins to die.

To control the problem, Sevin, malathion, or insecticidal soap should be sprayed on the foliage at the beginning of May. Apply it three times at ten-day intervals. To help eradicate the pest, spray again July first and again ten days later. Systemic insecticides can be used. Regardless of what you use, always read and follow label directions.

What caused my birch tree to die after only ten years? It seemed to die from the top down.

Few white-barked birch trees die of old age. Most last only fifteen to twenty years in the landscape and die as a consequence of the damage caused by the bronze birch borer. This beetle is found across Canada and as far south as New Jersey and Ohio. It is most commonly found on birch trees weakened by other pests, such as the birch leaf miner, and various diseases, as well as on trees suffering from a lack of water or nutrients.

Larvae overwinter under the bark of the tree. There are various sizes of larvae present, and those that are smaller begin to feed again while the mature larvae pupate. In about mid-June, adults begin to emerge. They immediately mate, and the females then begin laying eggs where they can find cracks in the bark. Fresh wounds, such as pruning cuts, seem to be a favorite place to lay eggs. Upon hatching, the larvae bore into the cambium under the bark where they begin feeding. The larvae can remain in the tree for up to two years before completing development. The adult beetles will eat foliage on the tree, but they seem to do little damage.

The constant tunneling girdles the branches. Leaves begin to yellow and soon upper branches begin to die. In time, the entire tree will die. If woodpeckers are in the area where the trees are growing they will often find the larvae and eat them. The presence of the larvae can be detected by the presence of bumps that appear just under the bark on the trunk and branches.

Although systemic pesticides can be used on the tree to control this critter, I recommend they be used sparingly. If you see holes in the trunk, dig the pest out with a knife or insert a wire to destroy the borer in its tunnel.

The key to warding off this pest is to keep your birch tree healthy. Feed it regularly and add water over the summer if rainfall is insufficient.

A new cultivar of birch is making its way to the market. The 'Heritage' birch is touted as being resistant to bronze birch borer.

My Colorado blue spruce develops curved, swollen growths every fall. What is this and can it harm the tree?

The growths are caused by the Cooley spruce gall aphid, which is not a true aphid. This pest often uses an alternate host, the Douglas fir, and the galls that you describe can also occur on the white and Englemann spruces.

The adults are about the size of gnats and are most often found on the Douglas fir, where the females form cottony, white egg sacs as part of the life cycle. The complete life cycle can take up to two years to complete. What we commonly see, however, are the pineapple-like galls that are formed as a result of crawlers, which hatch from the eggs, and inject saliva into the base of newly forming

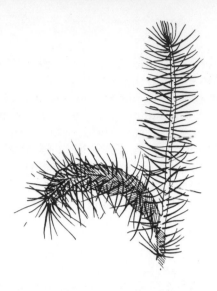

Cooley Spruce Gall aphid

needles in the spring. As a result, galls grow around the crawlers. The galls enlarge and remain green until they die and turn brown at the end of summer. While green they are rarely noticed.

Heavy infestation of this pest over several years can kill a tree. Douglas firs generally do not die, but their needles can become twisted and chlorotic. Control of the pest must be directed at the nymphs, which overwinter on the tree. Dormant oil spray should be applied in the fall, after most of the deciduous trees drop their leaves, and again in about April before the buds on the evergreen open. Applying insecticidal soap in early May also can help control this pest.

Why do the tips of Norway spruce branches sometimes die in the fall?

The pest that causes this problem—the eastern spruce gall aphid—is similar to the pest that damages the Colorado blue spruce. The insect is actually called an adelgid. Females overwinter and, in the spring, begin laying masses of eggs on the Norway, and sometimes red and white, spruce trees. After the eggs hatch, the nymphs begin feeding at the base of newly forming needles at the buds, and a cone-shaped gall develops. A short twig generally grows beyond the end of the gall. By the end of summer everything from the gall to the stem tip dies and turns brown.

The method of control is the same as that for the Cooley spruce gall aphid.

There is a lot of talk about problems caused by the gypsy moth. What does the moth look like?

The gypsy moth is one of those pests that should not be here in the first place. It was intentionally introduced into Massachusetts in 1869 because the caterpillar form was thought to be a source of silk. Guess what. It not only didn't make silk, but it also escaped the lab and began defoliating the local trees. Efforts were made to control the pest but all failed. The gypsy moth chewed its way to Pennsylvania in 1932 and by the late 1970s, it could be found in every county of the state.

The eggs of the gypsy moth begin hatching in late April and the larvae begin feeding on the developing foliage. Each female lays one hundred to eight hundred eggs, and when the moth population levels are high, there could be several thousand egg masses per acre. That represents a lot of munching. In residential areas, the number of egg masses could be only a few hundred per acre but still produce enough larvae to defoliate the trees.

The caterpillars of the gypsy moth grow to about two inches long, are dark gray in color, and have two rows of spots on their back. The spots are two colors: the first five pairs are blue and the last six pairs are orange-red. The larvae feed for about eight weeks, then pupate and emerge two weeks later as adults. The male moths are dark brown and the females are white with black markings on the wings. They live only about a week, just enough time, however, to lay eggs—usually about mid-July—and keep the cycle going.

Do gypsy moths attack all trees, or are there some they will not destroy?

The caterpillars prefer white and chestnut oak but also will eat the foliage of other oaks, as well as apple, birch, box elder, larch, mountain ash, basswood, and sumac. Older larvae also savor beech, hemlock, and all types of pine and spruce. The foliage of many other trees such as maples, sweet gum, cherry, hickory, pear, and hackberry also appeals to the pests.

Most deciduous trees can withstand two years of defoliation. Usually a new crop of leaves will form following defoliation, but this effort weakens the tree, which must use food reserves to produce the leaves. Conifers often die after they are defoliated.

There are indeed some trees that the gypsy moth will not eat: mulberry, sycamore, tulip poplar, black locust, arborvitae, catalpa, ash, and dogwood. They also will not eat the vine poison ivy! But

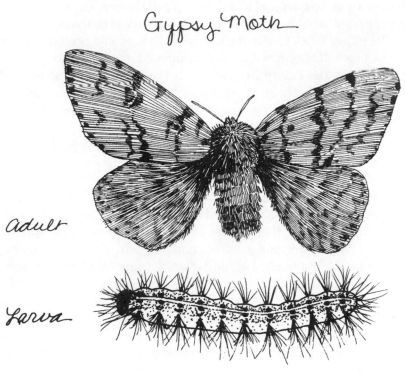

Gypsy Moth

adult

larva

The wingspread of the gypsy moth is about 2 inches. The larva, which does the damage we see, is about 2 inches long. *Larva illustrated by author*

most of these are not trees we want to plant.

I would not let the presence of the gypsy moth in your area deter you from planting any tree you want. Just be on the lookout for this pest and keep it under control.

How do I control gypsy moth?

Sevin and insecticidal soap are effective in controlling the larvae in the home landscape. Another method is to take a piece of tree-wrap and place it around the tree trunk. Fasten it with string placed in the middle of the wrap and then fold the wrap down over the bottom half. Larvae are night feeders and crawl down the tree in the morning to find shelter from the sun and heat. The folded band makes a nice home. Check the bands daily to remove the pests.

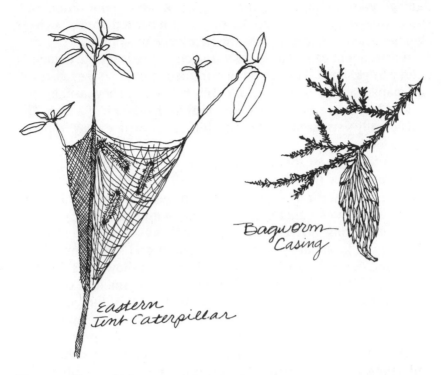

Eastern Tent Caterpillar

Bagworm Casing

Tent caterpillars, which grow to 1¼ inches long, eat the foliage of deciduous trees. Bagworms prefer conifers. The bagworm's casing is 1 to 2 inches long.

Scientists have been experimenting with a fungus, *Entomophaga maimaiga,* that attacks and kills the larvae of the gypsy moth. The results of the tests are promising, so a natural control soon may be available to us as well.

Last spring I noticed tent caterpillars in the Kwanzan cherry tree and then I also saw a large, vertical split in the bark. Did the caterpillars cause the split?

No, the split in the bark was not caused by the tent caterpillars. The split is probably what is called a frost crack. Smooth-barked trees are affected more often than those with a textured surface. Frost cracks are caused by the rapid cooling of the bark in winter. When the bark contracts too rapidly, a split can result. Often the damage goes unnoticed until spring when we are out and about. Using tree-wrap on the trunks of smooth-barked trees, such as cherries and birch, can reduce the incidence of splitting.

Eastern tent caterpillars are voracious feeders on the foliage of cherry trees. Their damage is not confined to cherry; they also will eat maple, apple, oak, ash, and birch leaves. They usually are noticed by the presence of a silken tent in the crotch of a tree. The tent actually gets larger as the caterpillars go farther away from the tent to feed.

It is the eggs of the tent caterpillar that overwinter. They are laid in masses by the female around small twigs of a host tree. The eggs are black and look as though they have been varnished. There can be up to three hundred fifty of them in a mass.

When spring arrives, the eggs hatch into small caterpillars, which grow to about two inches in length and are black with a white line down the back, and blue dots and yellow lines on each side. The caterpillars seem to gather together in the fork or crotch of the tree and then start to build their tent. As they forage beyond the tent they put down silk strands which increase the size of the tent.

After reaching a certain size, the caterpillars leave the trees, find a protected spot where each forms a cocoon, and finally in late June emerge as adults. Mating occurs shortly after they emerge and the females lay the eggs, which will hatch about nine months later.

The most effective control is also very safe. When you see the tent, spray with Bt, the bacteria *Bacillus thuringienses*. Repeat the spraying two more times at seven-day intervals. Sevin is also effective in controlling this pest.

There are round golfball-sized growths on some of my oak leaves. Is this a serious problem?

The growths, called galls, on the leaves are not serious and do not endanger the health of the tree. This particular type is the apple gall and is formed by the leaf in reaction to a wasp laying an egg in the leaf tissue. The gall is very fibrous and in the center is the developing larva. Later in the season the green galls turn brown and dry.

There are many types, shapes, textures, and sizes of galls found on oak trees. Actually, galls are very common on most parts of the oak: bark, roots, leaves, stems, even the acorns. Galls form in response to plant growth-regulating chemicals that insects somehow inject into the plant. The gall is primarily protein, so the larvae inside the gall find themselves surrounded by a large supply of food and protected from would-be attackers.

Most of the insects that cause galls are not harmful to the tree, so no control measures need to be taken. The exceptions are the horned oak gall and the gouty oak gall. The horned oak gall affects the twigs of pin and black oaks and can even kill the trees. The gouty oak gall attacks the pin, red, scarlet, and black oaks with similar effects. The wasps that cause these galls have a complicated life cycle, which can take a couple of years to complete. Infestations can get so bad that branches droop because of the weight of the galls.

Dormant spraying with lime sulfur and dormant oil can destroy most of these overwintering pests. When twig galls are found, though, they should be removed immediately.

Galls are also common on maples, hackberry, and many other trees, but in most cases they cause little or no harm. However, all the galls that form on stems and twigs are harmful and should be cut off and disposed of.

The earth's vegetation is part of a web of life in which there are intimate and essential relations between plants and the earth, between plants and other plants, between plants and animals. Sometimes we have no choice but to disturb these relationships, but we should do so thoughtfully, with full awareness that what we do may have consequences remote in time and place.

Rachel Carson, *Silent Spring*

Index

Italicized page numbers refer to illustrations.

Acidity, 4–5
Aconite, winter, 132, 138
Adelgid, 190
Ageratum, 111, 117, 120, 124
Ajuga, 145
Alkalinity, 4–5
Allium, 138
  giant, 143
Almond, dwarf flowering, 167
Aluminum sulfate for lowering
    soil pH, 5
Amaranth, globe, 112, 116, 122
Amaranthus, 119
Amethyst flower, 120
Anemone, 138
Animal pests, 36–37
  see also individual names
Annuals, definition of, 123
  see also individual names
Anthracnose, 182, 187
Ants, 138–39
Aphids, 26, 31, 50, 52, 71, 102, 127,
    142, 147, 171
  Cooley spruce gall, 189–90, 190
  eastern spruce gall, 190
Apple trees, 95–97
  amount of water needed for, 8
  cedar-apple rust, 97
  pests of, 191, 194
  pollination of, 91, 92
  see also Crab apple trees
Apricot trees, 97–99, 105
  cross-pollinating, 92, 98
Aquatic plants, 8
Arborvitae, 153–54, 191
  dwarf varieties of, 151–52
  excess shedding of, 154
  needles, 153
  pests of, 154
  weeping, 184
Arborvitae leaf miner. See Leaf
    miners

Ash trees:
  European mountain, 185–86
  green, 180, 181, 185
  pests of, 165, 191, 194
Asparagus, 44–45
  as a companion plant, 23
  white, 45
Asparagus beetles. See Beetles
Asparagus rust. See Rusts
Asters, 116, 117
  cornflower, 140
Astilbe, 146
Azalea gall. See Galls
Azaleas, 14, 155, 157–60
  for attracting hummingbirds, 142

Baby-blue-eyes, 121
Baby's-breath, 143
Baby's-breath, annual, 116, 123
Bachelor's button, 112, 120
Bacillus thuringiensis, 51, 194
Bacteria, nitrogen-fixing, 7
Bacterial wilt. See Wilts
Bagworms, 154
Bamboo, 148
Barberry, wintergreen, 155
Basswood trees, 191
Bean beetles. See Beetles
Beans, 11, 12, 16, 37, 38, 48–49, 61
Beautybush, 142
Bee balm, 129, 142, 144
Beech trees:
  European varieties, 184
  pest of, 191
Beer for controlling slugs and
    snails, 147
Bees, 35
Beetles, 147
  asparagus, 31, 45

bean, 26, *31,* 48–49
  Colorado potato, 26, *30,* 52, 56–57
  control methods for, 23, 33
  cucumber, spotted, 26, *29,* 59
  cucumber, striped, 59
  flea, 45, 50, 52
  Japanese, *29,* 71, 85, 127, 171
  larvae, 7
Beets, 16, 41, 53
Begonias, 117, 123
Bellflower, 140
  creeping, 145
Bells of Ireland, 123
Belly rot. *See* Rots
Benomyl, 146
Birch leaf miner. *See* Leaf miners
Birch trees, 185, 188–89, 191, 194
Birds:
  deterrents for, 70–71, 100–101
  trees that attract, 185–86
  see also Hummingbirds, attracting
Bishop's weed, 145
Black-eyed Susan, 146
  vine, 122
Black gum trees, 181–82
Black knot, 109
Black leg, 47
Black rot. *See* Rots
Black spot, 171
Black tupelo trees. *See* Black
  gum trees
Black vine weevils. *See* Root weevils
Blackberries, 75–76
Blanketflower, 143, 144
Bleeding-hearts, 144, 146, 147
  fringed, 132
Blights, 36, 48, 146
  botrytis, 136, 139
Blood meal, 6
Bloodroot, 145, 147
Blossom-end rot. *See* Rots
Blue-flowering plants:
  annuals, 120–21
  perennials, 140
Blueberries, 76–78
Bone meal, 5, 6
Borax solution, 53
Borers, 147
  bronze birch, 188–89
  corn, 26
  flat-headed peach, 105

iris, 137
  rednecked cane, 74
  rhododendron, 159
  squash vine, 59–60
Botrytis blight. *See* Blights
Botrytis blotch, 160
Botrytis neck rot. *See* Rots
Box elder, 191
Boxwood, 163
Boysenberries. *See* Blackberries
Brambles, 14
  see also individual names
Broccoli, 19, 40, 46–47, 61
Bromeliads, 1
Bronze birch borer. *See* Borers
Broom, 168
Browallia. *See* Amethyst flower
Brown rot. *See* Rots
Brussels sprouts, 40, 46–47
Bugle weed. *See* Ajuga
Bulbs, 13, *14,* 134
  how to encourage to come
    back, 135
  minor, 138
  rotting, 136
  see also individual names
Bumblebee, *35*
Bunchberry, 166
Burning bush. *See* Euonymus; Kochia
Buttercup, 147
Butterflies, life stages of, 26, *27*
Butterfly weed, 142, 145

Cabbage, 12, 19, 23, 40, 61
  diseases of, 46–47
  ornamental, 118
Cabbage looper, 26
Cabbage maggot. *See* Maggots
Caladium, 126
Candytufts, 116
Canker, 146
Canna lilies. *See* Lilies
Cantaloupe, 16, 38, 40, 41, 58–59
  see also Watermelons
Cardinal flower, 132, 140, 146
  wild, 145
Carnations, 116
Carrot rust fly, 53
Carrots, 16, 37, 41, 52–53, 61
Catalpa trees, 191

Caterpillars, 126–27, 142, 147
 tent, Eastern, *193,* 194
Cauliflower, 19, 41, 46–47, 61
Cedar-apple rust. *See* Rusts
Cedar, weeping blue atlas, 184
Celosia, plume, 111, 116, 123
Centipede, *36*
Cherry fruit fly, 102
Cherry trees, 99–102, 183
 flowering, 181
 pests of, 102, 191, 194
 sour, 92, 99
 sweet, 92, 99–100
 weeping, 184
Chill hours, 92, 102
Chinese lantern, 143
Chives for pest control, 23
Christmas trees, 186–87
Chrysanthemums, 9, 13, 140–42,
 143, 144
Cicadas, *32*
Cinquefoil, 168
Clay-colored root weevils. *See* Root
 weevils
Clematis, 172
Cleome, 117
Click beetles. *See* Wireworms
Club root, 47
Cockscomb, 111, 123
Coleus, 111, 112, 115, 117, 123
Colorado potato beetles. *See* Beetles
Colors, flower, 110–11
Columbine, 142
 blue, 140
 wild, 145
Common vetch, 3
Companion planting, 23
Compost, 2, 3, 5, 26
Coneflower, 146
Conifers, dwarf, 151–53
Container gardens, 37–39
 annual, 115–16
 perennial, 143–44
 vegetable, 37–38
Cool-season crops, 10, 40–41
Coralbells, 142, 144, 146
Corms, 124–25, *125,* 134
Corn, 10, 11, 12, 16, 41
 as a companion plant, 23
Corn borer. *See* Borers
Cornus canadensis. See Bunchberry

Cosmos, 111, 116
Cotoneasters, 155, 165
Cottony leak, 59
Cotyledons, 11
Cover crops, 22
Crab apple trees, 181, 183, 185
 weeping, 184
Crape myrtle, 168
Cranesbill, 144
Crimson clover, 3
Crocus, 132, 138, 140, 146
 autumn, 147
Crop rotation, 22–23
Cucumber beetles. *See* Beetles
Cucumbers, 10, 16, 38, 41, 57–59
Cultivation, 18
Cupflower, 121
Curly-top virus, 53
Currants, 79–80
 black, 79
Cutting flowers:
 annual varieties of, 116
 how to cut, 116, 143
 perennial varieties of, 142–43
 rose varieties of, 171
Cuttings, propagating from, 14
Cutworms, 26, *29*
 controlling, 7, 33
Cypress, dwarf varieties of, 152

Daffodils, 129, 132, 136, 146, 147
Dahlias, 13, *14,* 116, 125–26
Daisies:
 blue, 120
 Dahlberg, 118
 painted, 143, 144
 shasta, 143, 144
 Transvaal, 111
Damping-off, 126
Dandelions, 10, 128
Day lilies. *See* Lilies
Day-neutral plants, 9
Deer repellents, 94–95, 135–36
Delphinium, 140, 143, 147
Delphinium, annual, 123
Deutzia, 168
Dewberries. *See* Blackberries
Dicots, 11, *12*
Disease control, 36, 146
 see also individual names of
 diseases

Dogwood trees, 181, 182, 185, 186, 187, 191
　Kousa (Japanese), 181, 187
　shrub varieties of, 166
Downy mildew. *See* Mildew
Drupe fruits, 95
Drying flowers:
　annual varieties of, 122–23
　how to dry, 122–23, 143
　perennial varieties of, 143
　potpourri, 129
Dusty miller, 112, 117
Dutchman's breeches, 145, 147

Earthworms, 7
Earwigs, *32*, 147
Edible plants, 139
Eggplant, 10, 19, 38, 52, 56
　Japanese, 52
Elephant garlic. *See* Garlic
English peas. *See* Peas
Entomophaga maimaiga, 193
Epsom salts for peppers, 51
Espalier training, *89*
Euonymus, 163–64
　wintergreen, 155
Euonymus scale. *See* Scale
Evergreens:
　broadleaf, 155–56
　pruning, 177
　see also Conifers, dwarf; Fir trees;
　　Pine trees; Spruce trees;
　　individual names

False cypress. *See* Cypress, dwarf
　varieties of
Ferns, 132–34
Fertilizers, 6
　fish emulsion as foliar, 25
　methods of applying, 25
Fir trees:
　China, 184
　concolor (white), 186
　Douglas, 185, 186, 189
　Fraser, 186
　needles, *153*
Fireblight, 107, 165
Firethorn, 155, 158, 164–65
Fish emulsion, 6, 25, 114
Fish meal, 6

Flat-headed peach borer. *See* Borers
Flax, 140
Flea beetles. *See* Beetles
Flower parts, 10–11, *11*
Foliage plants, 117–18
Forget-me-nots, 118, 140
　Chinese, 120
Forsythia, 167
Foxglove, 142, 147
Fragrant flowers:
　annual varieties of, 129
　perennial varieties of, 129–31
Franklinia, 185
Freestones, 98
Frost cracks, 193–94
Fruit fly, cherry, 102
Fruit moth, Oriental, 105
Fruit trees:
　bare-root, planting, 90, *91*
　drupe, 95
　dwarf, 88–89
　espalier training of, *89*
　period of chilling, 9–10
　pome, 95
　semi-dwarf, 89
　using systemic insecticides on,
　　105–106
　see also individual names
Fruitworm, raspberry, 74
Fuchsias, 115, 117
Fungicides, 36
　benomyl, 146
　natural, 146
　see also Herbicides; Pesticides
Fusarium wilt. *See* Wilts

Gaillardia, 111
Galls, 194–95
　azalea, 160
　gouty oak, 195
　horned oak, 195
　twig, 195
Garlic, 13, 23, 33, 55
Gayflower, 143, 144, 146
Gazania, 116
General Sherman Tree, 173
Geraniums, 14, 112, 115, 123, 142
Ginger, wild, 145
Ginkgo trees, 180–81
Gladiolus, 116, 123, 124–25
　corm, *125*

Globe amaranth, 112, 116, 122
Globe thistle, 140, 143
Globeflower, 143
Gooseberries, 79–80
Grafting, 14
Grape hyacinth. *See* Hyacinth
Grapefruit spray, 33
Grapeholly, Oregon, 155–56
Grapes, 80–85
    cane training, 83, *84*
    making trellises for, 81–82
    spur training, 82–83, *83*
    Thompson Seedless, 80
Grass(es), 11
    clippings, 126
    ornamental, 147–49
Gray mold. *See* Molds
Gray water, 24–25
Green manure. *See* Manure, green
Green peas. *See* Peas
Ground covers:
    annuals as, 118
    bunchberry, 166
    juniper varieties for, 154
    pachysandra as, 156
    vine English ivy as, 156
Grubs, 7, *32*
Gypsophila. *See* Baby's-breath,
    annual
Gypsum, to help lower soil pH, 5
Gypsy moths, 191–93, *192*

Hackberry trees, 182, 191, 195
Hanging baskets. *See* Container
    gardens
Hawthorn trees, 165, 186
Head rot. *See* Rots
Heather, Scotch, 155
Heliotrope, 129
Hemlock trees, 185
    dwarf varieties of, 152
    pests of, 159, 191
    as windbreaks, 153
Herbaceous plants, 3, 128
Herbicides, 17, 178–79
    see also Fungicides; Pesticides;
      Preemergent weed controls
Herbs, 37
    see also individual names
Hickory trees, 191

Holly, 155, 160–63
    American, 11, 185
    berries not turning red, 162–63
    Japanese, 155, 161–62
    leaves turning yellow, 162
    yellow-berried varieties, 162
Holly-berry midge, 162–63
Holly leaf miner. *See* Leaf miners
Holly-tone fertilizer, 157
Hollyhock (*Althaea rosea*), 119
Honeybee, *35*
Horseradish, 55–56
Hosta, 131–32, 140, 146
Hummingbirds, attracting, 142, 172
Humus, 2–3
Hyacinth, 129, 140
    grape, 138, 140, 146
Hydroponic gardening, 1

Impatiens, 111, 115, 117, 123
Indoor plants, annuals as, 123–24
Insect pests, controlling:
    with chemicals, 7, 35
    with companion planting, 23
    with crop rotation, 23
    on fruit trees, 93–94, 105–106
    with nonchemical methods,
      7, 28–33, 94
    on perennials, 146, 147
    see also Insects; individual names
      of insects
Insecticidal soap, 33
Insecticides. *See* Pesticides
Insects, 2
    beneficial, 33, *34, 35, 36*
    life stages of, 26–28
    pests, 26–28, *29–32*
    see also Insect pests, controlling;
      individual names
Invasive perennials, 144–45
Iris borer. *See* Borers
Irises, 11, *13*, 140, 143
    bearded, 129, 136–37
    propagating, 13
    reticulate, 138, 140
    Siberian, 138
Ivy, Boston, 172
Ivy, English, 163
    vine, 156

Jack-in-the-pulpit, 145, 147

Japanese beetles. *See* Beetles
Jonquils, 136
Junipers, 154–55

Kale, 40
    flowering, 118
Katsura trees, 185
Kentucky bluegrass, 13
Kiwi fruit, 84–86
Kochia, 117–18

Lace bugs, *29,* 158–59
Lacewings, 33, *34*
Ladybugs, 33, *34*
Lady's slipper, 145
Lamb's-ears, 143
Larch trees, 191
Larkspur, 147
Laurel. *See* Mountain laurel
Lavender, 129, 143
Layering, propagating by, 14
Leaf hoppers, 147, 171
    life stages of, 28
Leaf miners, 53, 147
    arborvitae, 154
    birch, 188
    holly, 162
    spinach, 45–46
Leaf spot, 109, 137, 146
Leaves:
    as mulch, 26
    propagating with, 13–14
Leeks, 40
Lettuce, 37, 40, 61
Leucothoi, 155
Lilacs, 129, 167
Lilies:
    canna, 13, 123, 126
    day, 13, 139–40, 142, 144, 146
    for fragrance, 129
    torch, 143, 144
    trout, 138, 145
Lily-of-the-valley, 13, 129, 132,
        143, 147
Lima beans, 10, 41
Lime, to help correct low soil pH, 5
Liriope, 132, 146
Littleleaf linden trees, 181
Loam, 2
Lobelia, 115, 121, 124, 147

Location, garden, 15–16
Locust trees:
    black, 183, 191
    thornless honey, 182
Loganberries. *See* Blackberries
Long-day plants, 9
Loosestrife, 142, 144
    purple, 143, 145
    yellow, 145
Lupine, 142, 147

Maggots, 7
    cabbage, 54
Magnolia trees:
    Southern, 183
    star, 183
Malathion, 35
Manure, 2, 3, 5
    green, 3, 81
Maple trees, 26, 191, 194, 195
    Japanese, varieties of, 184
    Norway, 180
    red, 179, 180, 185
    silver, 179
    sugar, 184–85
Marigolds, 112, 113, 116, 124
    for pest control, 23
May apple, 147
Mealybugs, *29,* 147
Melons. *See* Cantaloupe;
        Watermelons
Mildew, 84–85, 146, 171
    downy, 47, 58
    powdery, 58, 126, 142
Millipede, *36*
Mimosa trees, 179
Miners. *See* Leaf miners
Minor bulbs. *See* Bulbs
Mint, 145
Miracle-Gro, 114, 170
Mites, 147
    spider, 50, 71
Mock orange, 129, 167–68
Molds, 146
    gray 71, 126, 142
Moles, *37*
Molybdenum, 5
Monarda. *See* Bee balm
Money plant, 143
Monkey flower, 111

Monkshood, 144
Monocots, 11, *12*
Moonflower, 122
Morning glory, 121–22
Morton, Julius Sterling, 173
Mosaic virus, 75
Moss rose. *See* Portulaca
Mothballs, 60, 95, 105, 147
Mountain bluet, 140
Mountain laurel, 155, 158, 159
Mulberry, 191
Mulch, 25–26
    tanbark as, 115
Mums. *See* Chrysanthemums

Narcissus, 136
Nasturtiums, 112, 115, 117, 129
    for pest control, 23
Nectarine trees, 102, 104–106
    see also Peach trees
Nematodes, 7, 33
Nicotiana, 111, 116
Nutrients, 5–7

Oak trees, 191, 194, 195
    pin, 180
    pruning wound dressing for,
        177, 178
    red, 180, 185
Oil spray for pest control, 33
Onions, 10, 11, 13, 16, 37, 40, 54–55
    as a companion plant, 23
Organic matter. *See* Humus
Oriental fruit moth, 105

Pachysandra, 156, 163
Pansies, 115, 121
Parsnips, 41
Peach borer, flat-headed. *See* Borers
Peach-leaf curl, 105
Peach trees, 102–104, 105–106
    chill hours required for, 92, 102
    dwarf, 103
    fruit with best flavor, 103
    pollination, 92, 104
Peanuts, 11
Pear psylla, 107
Pear trees, 106–107
    callery, 'Bradford', 181, 185
    callery, 'Redspire', 181

pests of, 165, 191
pollination of, 92
Pearly everlasting, 143
Peas, 10, 12, 37, 40, 47–48, 61
Peat moss, 2
Peat soils, amount of humus in, 2–3
Peonies, 129, 138–39, 142, 146
    tree, 139
Peppers, 10, 16, 19, 38, 41, 51
Perennials. *See* individual names
Periwinkle, Madagascar, 118
Pesticides, 35
    on fruit trees, 105–106
    pyrethrum, 33
    rotenone, 33
    spraying of, 93–94
    see also Fungicides; Herbicides
Peter's Root 'N Bloom, 114
Petunias, 111–13, 115, 117, 121
pH scale, 4
Phlox, 144
Phlox, annual, 118
Photoperiods, 9
Phytophthora dieback, 160
Pieris, Japanese, 155, 158
Pillbugs, *32*, 126
Pinching:
    annuals, 113
    chrysanthemums, 141
Pine trees, 14, 191
    Bhutan, 184
    dwarf varieties of, 152
    Korean, 184
    needles, *153*
    white, 79, 153, 186
    white, Japanese, 184
    white, weeping, 184
Plum curculio, 109
Plum trees, 105, 107–109, 183
    Japanese, 107–108
    pollination of, 92
    prune (European), 107, 108
Poinsettia, summer. *See* Amaranthus
Poisonous plants, 147–48
Pollination, 12, 91–92
Pome fruits, 95
Poplar trees, 14, 179
    tulip, 185, 191
Portulaca, 111, 115, 117, 118
Potato beetles, Colorado. *See* Beetles

Potatoes, *13*, 41, 56–57
  percentage of water in, 8
  propagating, 13
  supermarket, 56
  yellow-fleshed varieties, 56
  see also Sweet potatoes
Powdery mildew. *See* Mildew
Praying mantises, 33, *34*
Preemergent weed controls, 26
Propagation, 12–14
Pruning:
  cane, 83, *84*
  flowering shrubs, 168, 169
  fruit trees, *93*
  shade trees, 176–77
  spur, 82–83, *83*
  trees at planting time, 176
  see also Pinching
Pruning wounds, 177
Pumpkins, 58–59
Pyracantha. *See* Firethorn
Pyrethrum, 33

Quince, flowering, 168

Radishes, 10, 16, 40
Raspberries, 71–75
  black, 72
  red, 72
  wild, 75
Raspberry fruitworm, 74
Red pepper spray, 33
Redbud, eastern, 182
Rednecked cane borer. *See* Borers
Rhizomes, *13*
Rhododendron borer. *See* Borers
Rhododendrons, 14, 155, 156–57,
    158–60
Rhubarb, 13, 40, 43–44
Rhubarb curculio, 44
Rodents, 91, 135
  see also Voles
Root rot. *See* Rots
Root weevils, 71
  black vine, *30*, 159
Roots:
  propagating with, 13–14
  tuberous, 13, *14*
  see also Bulbs; Corms; Rhizomes;
    Tubers
Rose-tone, 170
Rosemary, for pest control, 23

Roses, 14, 131, 168–71
  Christmas, 147
  miniature, 171
  shrub, 171
Rotenone, 33
Rots, 146
  belly, 59
  black, 47, 84
  blossom-end, 50, 51
  botrytis neck, 55
  brown, 105
  head, 47
  root, 47–48
  wet, 59
  white, 47
Rusts, 126, 146
  asparagus, 44–45
  cedar-apple, 97
  white-pine blister, 79
Rutabagas, 10, 41, 53–54
Rye, winter, 3, 81

Sage, 140, 143
  for pest control, 23
Salt:
  for controlling slugs, 71, 126,
    131, 147
  for controlling weeds in asparagus
    beds, 44
Salvia, 116, 117, 121
  red, 142
Scab, 58–59, 164–65
Scale, *31*, 147
  euonymus, 163–64
Scilla, 140
Sea holly, 143
Sea lavender, 143
Seaweed, 6
Sedum, 144
Seed starting:
  annuals, 111–12
  vegetables, 19–22
Seedlings:
  hardening off, 22
  sowing, 41–42
  spacing, 41–42
  transplanting, 22
Seeds, 11
  and how plants form, 10
  saving, 113
Serviceberry, 182–83
Sevin, 35

Shady areas:
  annuals for, 116–17
  fern varieties for, 134
  perennials for, 131–32
Short-day plants, 9
Shrubs:
  and adequate space for, 10
  conifer species of, 151
  juniper varieties of, 154
  see also individual names
Silktree. *See* Mimosa trees
Slugs, *32,* 33, 71, 126, 131, 147
Snails, *32,* 33, 147
Snapdragons, 111, 112, 116, 124, 142
Snow peas. *See* Peas
Snowbell, Japanese, 183
Snowdrop, 132, 138, 146
Soil, 1–3
  and nutrients in, 5–7
  and organisms in, 7
Soil mixes, sterilizing, 38
Soil pH, 4–5
Soil testing, 4–5
Soilless mixtures, 1
Solomon's seal, 145
Sourwood trees, 182, 183, 185
Sowbugs. *See* Pillbugs
Soybeans, 22
Spanish moss, 1
Spider mites. *See* Mites
Spiders, *30, 34*
Spiderwort, 140
Spinach, 10, 16, 40, 45–46
Spinach leaf miner. *See* Leaf miners
Spirea, 168
Spittle bugs, 71
Spring beauty, 145
Spruce trees, 191
  Colorado blue, 184, 185, 189–90
  dwarf varieties of, 152
  Englemann, 189
  needles, *153*
  Norway, 185, 186, 190
  Norway, weeping, 184
  Serbian, weeping, 184
  white, 186, 189
Squash, 16, 41
  acorn, 60–61
  diseases of, 58–59
  pests of, 59–60
  summer, 60
  winter, 60–61

Squash bugs, 26, 30, 60
Squash vine borer. *See* Borers
Squill, 138
Squirrel corn, 147
Staking trees, 176
Starflowers, 123
Statice, 120, 122
Stems, propagating with, 13–14
Strawberries, 66–71
  planting, 67, *68*
  propagating by runners, 13,
    68–69, *69*
  protecting from birds, 70–71
  renovating the beds, 69–70
  varieties, 70
Strawberry root weevil. *See* Root
    weevils
Strawflowers, 111, 112, 116, 122–23
Succession planting, 23
Sugar snap peas. *See* Peas
Sumac, 191
Sunflowers, 119
Sunscald, 51
Sweet alyssum, 111, 115, 117, 118, 129
Sweet gum, 181, 191
  American, 181, 185
Sweet peas, 112, 129
  climbing varieties, 122
Sweet potatoes, 13, 38, 41
Sweet William, 118
Sycamore trees, 182, 191

Tanbark, 115, 178
Tansy, 147
  common, 145
Tar spot, 162
Temperature, 9–10
Tent caterpillars, Eastern.
    See Caterpillars
Theophrastus, 173
Thistle, globe, 140, 143
Thrip, 147, 171
Thyme, for pest control, 23
Tilling, 17–18
Tomato hornworm, 26, *31,* 50–51
Tomatoes, 9, 10, 14, 16, 19, 38, 40,
    41, 49–51, 56
  amount of water needed, 8
  cherry, 37
  rotating, 23
  water-stressed, 24

Topsoil, 2
Torch lilies. *See* Lilies
Torenia, 117
Toxins. *See* Pesticides
Transplants. *See* Seedlings
Tree cricket, 74
Tree peonies. *See* Peonies
Trees. *See* Christmas trees; Fruit
 trees; individual names
Trellises, 81–82
Trillium, 132, 145
Trout lilies. *See* Lilies
Trumpet vine, 142, 172
Tubers, *13*, 125–26
Tulip trees. *See* Poplar trees
Tulips, 11, 13, *14*, 134–36
Turnips, 16, 40, 46
 see also Rutabagas

Vegetables:
 arranging in garden, 22
 for container gardens, 37–38
 cool-season, 40–41
 definition of, 40
 for fall harvest, 61
 for large gardens, 16
 proper spacing of, 10
 for small gardens, 16
 starting from seed, 19
 transplanting seedlings, 22
 varieties, 61, 64–65
 warm-season, 41
 see also individual names
Verbena, 115, 118
Verticillium wilt. *See* Wilts
VFN, 49
Viburnum, 168
 burkwood, 155
 evergreen varieties, 164
 flowering varieties, 165–66
 fragrant, 131
 leatherleaf, 155
Vines, hardy, 171–72
Vining annuals, 121–22
Violets, 144, 145
Virginia bluebells, 132, 140
 wild, 145
Virginia creeper, 172
Voles, 36, *37*, 135, 159

Wall o' Water, 18–19, *19*
Walnut trees, 160
Warm-season crops, 10, 41
Wasps, 33, *35*
Watering, 8, 23–24
 using gray water for, 24–25
Watermelons, 16, 40, 41
 diseases of, 58–59
 percentage of water in, 8
 seedless, 61
Wax begonias. *See* Begonias
Weed control:
 with chemical preemergent, 26
 with cultivation, 18
 see also Herbicides
Weevils. *See* Root weevils
Weigela, 167
Wet rot. *See* Rots
Wheat, winter, 3
White-pine blister rust. *See* Rusts
White rot. *See* Rots
Whiteflies, 26, *30*, 33, 50, 71,
 127, 147
Wild indigo, 140
Wildflowers, 145
Willow trees, weeping, 182
Wilt-Pruf, 156, 160
Wilts, 36, 71
 bacterial, 59
 fusarium, 48, 49, 51, 59
 verticillium, 49, 51, 52
Windbreaks, 153
Windflower, 140
Winter care:
 for corm plants, 124–25
 for tuber plants, 125–26
Wireworms, 7, 26, 57
Wishbone flower. *See* Torenia
Wisteria, 171–72
Wood ash, to help correct low
 soil pH, 5

Yarrow, 143, 144
Yellowwood trees, American,
 182, 183
Yews, 14, 159

Zelkova, 181, 185
Zinnias, 112, 116, 117, 124
Zucchini, 60